FORTRESS
FALKLANDS

Dedication

*For the Bound and al-Khudairy families
in the Falklands and in the UK*

Other books by Graham Bound

Falkland Islanders at War
Pen & Sword, 2002

Invasion 1982: The Falkland Islanders' Story
Pen & Sword, 2007

FORTRESS FALKLANDS

Life Under Siege in Britain's Last Outpost

Graham Bound

Pen & Sword
MILITARY

First published in Great Britain in 2012
By Pen and Sword Military
an imprint of
Pen and Sword Books Ltd
47 Church Street
Barnsley
South Yorkshire S70 2AS

ISBN 978 1 84884 745 3

A CIP record for this book is available from the British Library.

Printed and bound in England by
CPI Group (UK) Ltd, Croydon, CR0 4YY

Typeset in Times New Roman by
Chic Media Ltd

Pen & Sword Books Ltd incorporates the imprints of
Pen & Sword Aviation, Pen & Sword Family History, Pen & Sword Maritime,
Pen & Sword Military, Pen & Sword Discovery, Wharncliffe Local History,
Wharncliffe True Crime, Wharncliffe Transport, Pen & Sword Select,
Pen & Sword Military Classics, Leo Cooper, Remember When,
The Praetorian Press, Seaforth Publishing and Frontline Publishing

For a complete list of Pen and Sword titles please contact
Pen and Sword Books Limited
47 Church Street, Barnsley, South Yorkshire, S70 2AS, England
E-mail: enquiries@pen-and-sword.co.uk
Website: www.pen-and-sword.co.uk

Contents

Acknowledgements and Thanks

I have many friends and family members in the Falklands. Seeing them again when I returned home was such a pleasure. I was picked up, dropped off, fed, entertained, housed and made to feel welcome by everyone.

Most of the information that I have used here was gleaned from helpful conversations and more formal interviews. Some of my interviewees had not met me before but they readily agreed to talk, often very candidly.

These people are listed below, along with those who gave me useful background information, allowed me to use their photographs or helped me in other ways. I am very grateful to them. I regret there are probably a few people whose contributions I have overlooked. If so, I apologize to them.

Joan Bound
Peter and Rosemary King
Robert King
Alison Howe
Anna King
Gordon Moulds
Trudi McPhee
Neil and Glenda Watson
Lisa Watson
John Fowler
Nigel Haywood
Rick Nye
Andrew Rosindell MP
Daniel Kawczynski MP
Phyl Rendell
Richard Cockwell

Ben Cockwell
Roddy Cordeiro
Raymond Davis
Keith Padgett
Peter Biggs
James Fenton
David Jenkins
Ian Strange
Stuart and Lillian Wallace
Lewis Clifton
Neil McKay
Neil Rowlands
Cheryl Roberts
Paul Trowell
Carlos Escudé
Klaus Dodds
Lara Manovil

Sam Moody
Ken Humphrey
Jamie Fotheringham
Jan Cheek MLA
Dick Sawle MLA
Gavin Short MLA
Bernard Jones
Gustavo Meikle
Tim Miller
Osvaldo Radicci
Roberto Maggio
Jara Americo
Raúl Agustin Vasquez
Nicolas Urbieta
Oscar Alberto Recalde
Teddy and Sybella Summers

Staff at Pen and Sword Books have been very patient and encouraging. I am particularly grateful to Jonathan Wright, Linne Matthews, Laura Wilkinson, Matt Jones and Jon Wilkinson.

In writing this book, I have relied heavily on interviews. My own knowledge and impressions have also been important. I have not referred to any other author (except, briefly, Mark Twain and Oscar Wilde), but I have used guide books to the armed forces published by the Ministry of Defence and sourced some material from reputable Internet sources. The most useful of these sites were: MercoPress, the CIA World Fact Book, the UK Ministry of Defence, iCD Research, Defencetalk.com, Nationmaster.com, Globalfirepower.com, and the Falkland Islands Government.

Finally, I want to thank my wonderfully supportive wife, Nadia. She was remarkably patient as I researched and wrote this book to a very tight schedule, while neglecting many other responsibilities. I'm not at all sure I would have been as tolerant.

Graham Bound
January 2012

Author's Note

I may need to defend myself against charges of hyperbole in the title of this book, and I am happy to do so.

Is this territory a fortress? In the broadest sense of the word, it is. The credible military deterrent is a defining feature of the Islands, and if it did not exist, then another flag would be flying over the Falklands in very short order.

Are the Islands under siege? In a very real sense, yes. Their economy is being squeezed by a blockade. There is a sustained effort to build an alliance against them and break their communications links with mainland South America. The community's viability can only be guaranteed through a long, tenuous and expensive lifeline to Britain.

There are other British Overseas Territories, of course, so one could debate whether the Falklands are Britain's last outpost. But no other British territory is so coveted, threatened and vulnerable. The Falklands perfectly match most people's idea of a remote territorial outpost.

This book was researched and written in late 2011 and early 2012. Even as it went to press, relations between Britain and Argentina were becoming more fractious, and the situation in the far South Atlantic was becoming more tense. This is by no means the end of the story, but I hope that my portrait of the Islands and their people will help to explain whatever is to come.

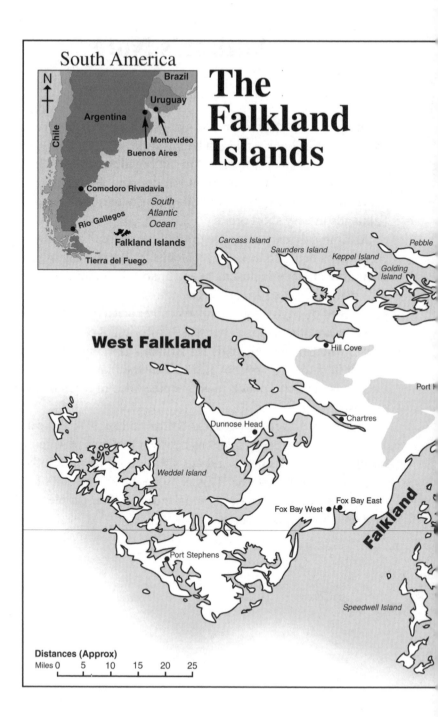

South America

N

Brazil

Uruguay

Argentina

Chile

Montevideo

Buenos Aires

Comodoro Rivadavia

South
Atlantic
Ocean

Rio Gallegos

Falkland Islands

Tierra del Fuego

The Falkland Islands

West Falkland

Carcass Island

Saunders Island

Keppel Island

Pebble

Golding
Island

Hill Cove

Port H

Chartres

Dunnose Head

Weddel Island

Fox Bay East

Fox Bay West

Falkland

Port Stephens

Speedwell Island

Distances (Approx)

Miles 0   5   10   15   20   25

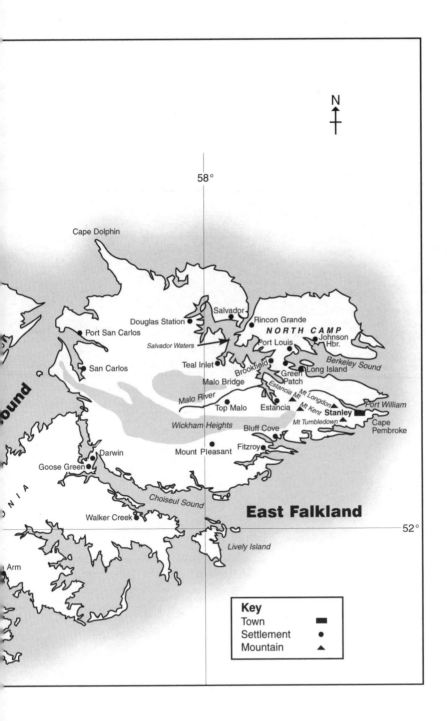

N

58°

Cape Dolphin

Douglas Station
Port San Carlos
Salvador
Rincon Grande
NORTH CAMP
Port Louis
Johnson Hbr.
Salvador Waters
San Carlos
Teal Inlet
Brookfield
Green Patch
Long Island
Berkeley Sound
Malo Bridge
Malo River
Estancia Mt
Mt Longdon
Top Malo
Estancia
Mt Kent
Stanley
Port William
Wickham Heights
Mt Tumbledown
Cape Pembroke
Bluff Cove
Darwin
Mount Pleasant
Fitzroy
Goose Green
N I A
Choiseul Sound
Walker Creek
Lively Island

East Falkland

52°

Arm

Key
Town   ▬
Settlement   ●
Mountain   ▲

CHAPTER 1

Blockade Busting

Twenty-nine years ago, I flew from Ascension Island to the Falklands perched atop a pile of mailbags in the cavernous cargo hold of a RAF C130 Hercules. The aircraft's four stubby propellers dragged the Herc's bulk along painfully slowly, but it was designed to get military freight or emergency aid into battle zones, even if it took days. This is work that C130s have been doing supremely well since the late 1950s, but the designers at Lockheed apparently gave no thought at all to passenger comfort.

The journey was a dreadfully uncomfortable, deafeningly noisy, seemingly endless and even frightening endurance test.

The then prime minister, Margaret Thatcher, had made the same journey just a few months before and emerged at the end of the fourteen-hour flight looking fresh, her blue frock hardly rumpled and without a blonde hair out of place. She, however, had spent the journey in a soundproofed and opulently furnished Portakabin, which had been installed in the cargo hold just for her.

But Margaret Thatcher (still plain Mrs then) was the PM and I was just the editor of the Falklands newspaper, a Roneoed collection of roughly assembled news and iconoclastic comment that hit the streets of Stanley at no particular frequency, made a few ripples and ended up, like a newspaper should, as wrapping paper for soldiers' suppers at the recently-opened fish and chip shop. I had wandered rather far from home, and it crossed my mind that someone was now punishing me for not knowing that my place, as a Falkland Islander, was back in the South Atlantic.

I had travelled to Britain in search of investment and new equipment so that *Penguin News* could develop and exploit the post-Falklands War influx of troops, government advisors, entrepreneurs, carpet baggers and builders, who were rehabilitating the shelled and strafed infrastructure.

The mission was a failure. Bizarre as it now seems, publishing mogul Robert Maxwell had initially offered generous assistance ('on the condition that the paper never supports the bloody Argentines; they had their chance and fucked it up,' he said). But this was withdrawn when news of his plans to help a little local paper was portrayed as a megalomaniacal plan to monopolize the Falklands media industry. He had long wanted to do just that in the UK, apparently, so wasn't it rather amusing that Maxwell had settled for the tiny Falklands, said Henry Porter in the *Sunday Times'* Atticus column.

Not for me, it wasn't. Captain Bob, as *Private Eye* loved to call him, cut me off. He failed to return my calls, apparently thinking I had blown the gaff on our little deal. Eventually I stopped calling 'Maxwell House', and I went back alone to continue cranking the handle of the duplicator for another few years. But perhaps I had a lucky escape. A year or so later the mogul was exposed for raiding his own employees' pension funds, and he died mysteriously at sea.

So there I was, hitching a ride north to south down the Atlantic with a pleasant if boisterous RAF crew who were still operating with a wartime approach to health, safety and other formalities. I knew from a friend who had also flown with the Herc pilots that the preferred refreshment in the cockpit were Harvey Wallbangers, and sure enough, I did see a few bottles of fluorescent yellow Galliano entering the aircraft.

Being a reporter, I was, initially at least, happy to suffer if it meant a front row seat during the mid-air refuelling operation, which was necessary if our aircraft was not to make a very big splash somewhere off Brazil. So I made the best of my nest in the mailbags, and filled my ears with cotton wool to block out the roar of those turboprops. Some seven hours out over the ocean we met the tanker aircraft. The loadmaster beckoned me up the ladder into the cockpit to view our rendezvous with probably the only other friendly aircraft within 1,000 miles. We flew through a dark grey sky and above an even darker grey ocean. I thought that as in-flight entertainment went, this was going to be novel, and it was sure to make a good story. Instead, I soon found it was nerve jangling.

We flew alongside the second Hercules, as its crew laboured furiously to unwind and trail the hose that our crew would mate with, and from which our plane would suck in thousands of gallons of kerosene. But it did not work. The tanker repeatedly forced out its hose by a few tens of metres, rather like a defecating goldfish, then withdrew it. Each time there seemed to be less hose dragging in the slipstream.

I stood forgotten behind the pilots and next to the navigator, who was busy with dividers, parallel rulers and a calculator the size of a cobblestone. The pilots were looking increasingly stressed as each attempt to mate our probe with the shuttlecock-like dispenser at the end of the hose failed. We just did not have enough room to manoeuvre. The crews of the two planes were clearly talking to each other by radio. I could not hear their words, but they certainly were not sharing tips about making the perfect Harvey Wallbanger.

I deliberately did not look over the pilot's shoulders at the fuel gauges, which I feared might be spinning towards a red section that probably said, 'fumes only'. After about twenty minutes, the captain decided enough was enough. The fuselage of the tanker had almost filled the windscreen, but now it pulled ahead and rose out of sight. We turned 180 degrees and began the flight back to Ascension. The Herc had enough fuel – although probably only just – to get us back.

Seven hours later, fourteen hours after we had left the island, I stumbled down the cargo ramp and onto the concrete of Ascension's Wideawake Airfield. Through my buzzing ears came the shouted advice that we could rest for a few hours before embarking again for a second attempt to reach RAF Stanley. I collapsed on a thin rubber mattress in a tent and slept.

On our second attempt, we rendezvoused with the tanker successfully. Again I was in the cockpit to see the refuelling operation, and I held my breath as this time the shuttlecock at the end of the refuelling hose seemed to be totally unconstrained. We entered a turbulent pocket of air and the shuttlecock smashed into our windscreen, spewing fuel over it. But eventually we mated, and this time I did look at the gauges. The needles were creeping, very satisfyingly, in the right direction. To cut another fourteen-hour story short, we reached the Falklands. My father was at the airport, which in those days was still littered with sandbagged temporary hangars and Rapier anti-missile emplacements. The air was full of the screaming sound signatures of Harrier interceptors.

'Good flight?' said my father, as we walked towards his Land Rover (which still bore the deep scars of the battering it received when it was taken from him by Argentine forces and then captured by British Paras). I grumpily ignored the platitude and reached for a door, which had no window and no handle.

As I wrote about my post-1982 war adventure for the first time almost three decades later, I was repeating that journey. This time, however, I was reclined comfortably in a Boeing 767 airliner. I looked frequently at the ever-changing map on the video screens that showed the aircraft's direction and position in relation to the nearest land mass. I never feel comfortable with these devices, because I have always assumed that if an aircraft was being thrown around the sky by forces greater than its engines, its wild movement would be etched out horribly on the screen. Ignorance would then be a blessing. But I could hardly take my eyes off the screen as we approached Mount Pleasant, the airport/airbase that had replaced Stanley Airport in 1986. We seemed to be flying into a vulnerable dot in the ocean that almost nestled in the curving tip of South America. Or was that a beckoning and grasping tip?

In casual conversation with one of the flight attendants, I had established that under no circumstances would our aircraft get any closer to that beckoning finger of land. 'Where do we go if the weather is too bad for us to land?' I asked a woman called Betty (her badge suggested she had no surname), as she served me coffee.

'Back to Ascension. We're not allowed to divert to Chile, Uruguay or Brazil because they might not let us land. That wouldn't be very good. Sugar?'

I nodded, took the sachet, and smiled gratefully but incomprehensibly at her. In at least one way, the air link still seemed a tad shaky.

I decided that when I arrived I would explore all aspects of the Islands' economy, industries, people and politics, all of which I felt sure would have to be portrayed against a backdrop of the dispute with Argentina. I would start with defence, and if this proved as interesting and complex as I thought possible, then it might dominate my work. That was logical too because one end of the airbridge is the grim tri-service base known, without a hint of irony, as Mount Pleasant.

I had been living in Britain for almost two decades. I had returned home briefly every now and again to see my mother and friends, but now I had come back with a job to do: to learn more about the state of the Islands, the attitudes of their people, the nature of the Argentine threat and the capability of the British defenders.

Before the Falklands War, the territory had been a decaying colony, abandoned by London to face apparently inevitable decline and death. However, everything I had learned during earlier visits home and from occasional online scans of *Penguin News* (which still thrives some thirty-two years after I started it) suggested strongly that the place had been transformed into a modern and wealthy community, with a considerable degree of independence from the old country.

This, I believed, was the right time to take an in-depth look at the Falklands. At no time since 1982 had the Argentine-British-Falklands cold war been so chilled, and yet so capable of become dangerously hot.

Tension had been building for several years, and the approaching thirtieth anniversary of Argentina's invasion and ultimately its humiliating defeat was fast approaching. Aggressive rhetoric was being pumped out of Buenos Aires at a volume that increased almost daily, and normal diplomacy had ceased. Britain and Argentina were not talking to each other, and Argentina had even removed its ambassador to the United Kingdom. Argentine lawmakers had passed a bill making it 'illegal' for any ship to go to the Islands without first obtaining permission from Buenos Aires. And it had explicitly warned that companies doing business with the Falklands would not be able to do so within Argentina.

While Buenos Aires and London were just staring daggers at each other, Argentines were having enthusiastic, if sometimes somewhat haranguing, conversations with their neighbours, Uruguay, Chile and Brazil. As a result, these countries were supporting, at least to some extent, the effort to cut the Falklands off and ruin their economy.

With Falkland Islanders digging in to survive what they openly described as a blockade, with oil exploration showing real signs of success, and with the British Government seemingly rattled, it looked very much as if the thirtieth anniversary year would be very troubled.

Despite Buenos Aires' insistence that the Islands will again come under the Argentine flag only through peaceful means, many people were not so sure. They asked themselves if Mrs Kirchner, the Argentine President, was whipping up passions to a dangerous level. Could events take on a momentum of their own? Could the blockade that Argentina seemed determined to enforce lead to renewed conflict? I wanted to find out.

CHAPTER 2

Welcome to Mount Pleasant

The door of the Boeing 767 slid open and a late spring breeze relieved the stale atmosphere. I had once been on an aircraft that landed here in such strong winds that the doors could not be opened because they might be torn from their hinges. Only when the airliner had been towed into a hangar was it safe to disembark. But today, the wind was gentle, and it was also laden with the scent of November: the smoky aroma of the local bracken, called diddle-dee, and the sweeter smell of the glorious yellow gorse. It is a time of particular beauty, when the dun-coloured moorland produces blossoms and penguins, seals and albatrosses return from their ocean wandering to breed and nurture their young.

Two of my best friends, Peter and Rosemary King, were waiting outside the rough-and-ready military terminal at RAF Mount Pleasant, and I had a smile on my face as I pushed my way through the crowd of servicemen and women who had arrived with me. Many of them were looking distinctly dejected and underwhelmed by the reality of the life they would face for the next four months on the 'Death Star', as the base is sometimes known, or on the naval ships that patrol the coasts.

'You see what we laid on for you?' said Rosie, gesturing at a sky that was blue and a sun that was wonderfully warm for a Falklands late spring day. It was indeed a lovely day.

Peter and Rosie had also collected her brother, David, who was the UK representative of Byron Marine Ltd, a Falklands company that owned and operated a fisheries patrol ship and supported the oil rig that was drilling off the north of the Islands. I made a mental note that I would have to learn more about this local initiative.

We chatted about old times, caught up on some gossip, and laughed at the same old stories we had shared a dozen times. It would take us an hour to motor just 35 miles to Port Stanley, driving on an unmetalled, narrow and inherently dangerous road. Handling a Land Rover on this surface is like driving on marbles, and normal cars simply cannot manage it. We had all lost friends on that road.

We came over the shoulder of Sapper Hill and saw before us the multi-coloured corrugated metal roofs of Stanley; beyond it the harbour, and on the other side of that, the old naval depot for which British and German warships fought horribly in 1914.

'What are you doing for dinner tonight, Gray?' said Rosie.

'Well, let me consult my diary … ah, precisely nothing. So thanks, I'll be there.'

'Good,' Peter added. 'Jack's coming too.'

'Jack who?'

'Daniels.' Drinking with Peter was not always the safest of pursuits, but I was in the mood for it.

They left me at my mother's little house near the Post Office on Stanley's seafront to settle in. She was in Britain being treated for the multiple complaints that make life as an octogenarian challenging. Broadly, Mum was not in bad shape, but it would be some weeks before she came home, so I had her house to myself, and I was grateful for that.

The big question in my mind was defence: just how committed was the British Government to deterring another Argentine attack, and would they be able to cope if the cold war became hot as a result of increasingly aggressive attitude 'across the water' (to use a common Falklands euphemism). I knew that to get reasonable access to the defence establishment, to interview key people and understand their doctrine, I would need to have advance approval, and the Ministry of Defence (MOD) could be cagey.

I had first approached the Ministry of Defence's Directorate of

Media and Communications in Whitehall five months earlier, and initially received an encouraging response. The brigadier in charge of operational communications suggested that it might be possible to be officially 'embedded', the kind of status regularly accorded to approved writers, photographers and film-makers visiting UK forces on operations. I met with his staff, filled in forms and settled down to wait for a decision. I believed it would be little more than a formality.

Three months later, I was still waiting and I again approached the Ministry of Defence. There had been staffing difficulties, I was told, but my bid would be properly considered soon. Two months later, I could delay the trip no longer, so, after a third bid for assistance received no response, I booked a passage and left for the Islands. Now I was here, but without the pass I needed to access the Army, Navy and RAF camps, ships and outstations.

I thumbed through my mother's telephone book and found a number for 'Media Ops' at Mount Pleasant. The phone rang for a leisurely thirty seconds or so and was eventually answered by a pleasant sounding woman. She was bright and friendly and as I introduced myself I felt optimistic that I might have been able to outflank the Ministry of Defence officials back in London and gain access to the Falklands military community this way.

My ray of military light turned out to be SO3 J9 Captain Christine Wilson (which is not her real surname). I did not catch her name the first time around, and asked her to repeat it. 'Christine. As in Stephen King's book,' she said. I did not get the reference.

'Erm, I'm not too familiar with his books, I'm afraid. Are you named after one of his characters?'

'Yes,' she giggled, 'the murderous car, Christine.'

Within a minute, our conversation had taken on a surreal character. And it did not feel quite right. 'Oh,' I said. 'Well, I'm visiting the Falklands to learn about the defence of the Islands, among other things, and I would be really grateful if you can arrange for me to visit Mount Pleasant and learn about your equipment and capability. To start with, do you think I could interview the Commander British Forces?'

'I'm afraid not.'

'You mean not possible to visit the camp, or not possible to interview the Brigadier?'

'Both, really. We have orders from MOD in London that no "one-star" – that's the Brigadier – can speak to the media without ministerial approval. And we need approval from the Directorate of Media and Communications for you to visit us at all.' I could hear Christine smiling in the friendliest fashion. But she was stonewalling me entirely.

'Well, I've come all this way, so is there anything we can do?'

We had moved imperceptibly on to first name terms now. 'The thing is, Graham, there really isn't much we can do without the OK from London.'

'Could you contact them, please, Christine? Maybe you can get the green light.'

'No. Sorry.'

'Well, Christine, how would it be if I contact the Brigadier in London to see if he can send you the authorization you need?'

'Yes, that would be OK, but we'll still need our brigadier's agreement.'

'You rather implied, Christine, that the only thing holding back your full co-operation was the lack of authority from London to do so.'

'Well, Graham, the Brigadier's very busy. But please do what you can and then get back to us.'

'Thank you, Christine.'

'Goodbye, Graham.'

This was a strange outcome. I had just agreed to go off and obtain permission for her to give me permission. I had the feeling that an iron curtain was descending at some point along that road from Stanley to Mount Pleasant. Perhaps, with hindsight, I should have appealed to Peter, Rosemary and Dave's sense of adventure. Before leaving Mount Pleasant, we could have explored the vast Army and RAF base for ourselves. But one of the rumours I had already picked up was the military police were far more alert than they used to be, and that anyone found on the camp without a pass was being hauled into the MP's HQ for a polite but firm talking-to; as the military would say, a chat without coffee.

I had rather liked the media spokesperson for Fortress Falklands, as pleasantly, almost flirtatiously, she gave me absolutely no help whatsoever. I felt sure that she was, at that very moment, congratulating herself on resolving another enquiry to the military's satisfaction. But I was intrigued. Why did 'Media Ops' at Mount Pleasant have such an unhelpful attitude? Why did they not want visitors? During previous visits I had looked around the camp, sometimes with journalists who did not have my local credentials, and doors were thrown open. I even recall touring the operations centre, which was a bunker carved into the side of a hill. The only precaution my hosts had taken then was to throw some sheets over a few maps, which I assume showed their ability to monitor Argentine movements on their coast.

The view was beginning to form in my mind that the sense of normality around the Islands, at least on the military side, might be false. Were the comfortable airliners and the friendly Christines just veneers hiding the fact that all was not normal in the Falklands?

I sat down at my laptop to compose an email to the brigadier who had originally said he could help. It was a mystery, as he had been so pleasant, positive and encouraging.

Good afternoon Brigadier
You may not be surprised to hear that I am back in the Falklands and am busy lining up interviews for my writing project. I really had to go, as the deadline I face for my book is tight. As you may know, before I left, I had not received confirmation that the military authorities here have London's permission to help me. I am told that Commander British Forces will not even be able to grant me an interview without authority from Directorate of Media and Communications.

I was under the impression that consideration of my request was moving ahead. I did write to you before I left the UK, again pointing out the urgency, and ensuring that my personal email is known. But so far I have heard nothing.

The assistance that I need should now cost MOD virtually

11

nothing. I have my own accommodation and transport here, and all I need is the chance to talk to key personnel and learn about capability and equipment. I will abide by whatever constraints of security are required.

I am now becoming rather desperate. Is there anything that you can do to move this along, please? I started requesting assistance in the Islands about five months ago, and while I know there have been some real reasons for the delay, it has been a very long-drawn-out process. If I can't write about the defences of the Falklands then I am soon going to be in a very difficult position.

Anything you can do to help me progress my current project will be hugely appreciated. Thanks for your help.

The Brigadier replied promptly:

Graham, I am glad you have arrived safely.

I am sorry that the book process is taking so long. There are ongoing discussions with the policy people but we will get back to you soon. There are sensitivities, of which I am sure you are aware, with the Argentinians and others.

So there it was in black and white. The help I needed to describe the military machine in the Falkland Islands was in doubt because of the relationship with the Argentine Government, and because policy officials were grappling with the issue.

Undoubtedly, the Brigadier was behaving prudently by liaising with policy desks both at the Ministry of Defence and at the Foreign and Commonwealth Office. It was quite likely that he would have liked to be on the forward foot over the media challenge of the coming anniversary. But ministers in both departments would be increasingly interested in such plans, and they were probably nervous about the increased volume and intensity of Argentine words and deeds.

It would be interesting to gauge the attitude at Government House in Stanley, where the Governor, Nigel Haywood represented the

Foreign and Commonwealth Office and the Queen, and held a highly influential position, although few executive powers.

I had a personal reason for calling Government House. In London, back in the early 1990s, I had got to know Rick Nye, a then fairly junior civil servant on the Falklands desk at the Foreign Office. Our meetings had always been enjoyable, and I always felt that Rick shared my low level of tolerance for government timidity and secrecy. It seemed right to call Rick first, and let him know that I was keen to meet him for a drink and a chat about old times, regardless of how the official face of the British Government regarded me. Rick had done well: he would occasionally assume the title of Acting Governor.

I called him at Government House. 'Hello Rick. Or should I call you "Your Excellency"?'

From the rambling brick, timber and corrugated iron, Rick was as friendly as ever, and apparently happy to hear my voice. 'Graham! I heard you were back. Welcome home! I've been meaning to contact you for a long time.'

Rick told me about his life over the intervening nineteen years. He'd left the Foreign Office for a while ('good move,' I suggested), but then rejoined for the chance to travel the world again. He had barely been back to the dusty Victorian splendour of the Foreign Office building in Whitehall since, and was now using his early Falklands experience to work in Stanley.

We agreed to meet the following week for lunch at Stanley's only hotel, the Malvina House, which I anticipated pleasantly, not just for the good food, but also for Rick's company. I asked him about meeting his boss for a brief about the political and diplomatic situation. Understanding this, I explained, would enable me to understand everything else that was going on in the Islands. Rick understood, and said the Governor's secretary, Vicki, was out at the moment, but he would leave a note for her. We signed off looking forward to the meal at the Malvina the next week.

I waited several hours for Vicki to call, but the phone did not ring. Offices close early in Stanley, so just before 4.30 pm, I called Government House again and asked to speak to her. She was there, but told me she had not been able to arrange an appointment, and of course, the Governor was very busy. She took my email address and promised to contact me before going home. This seemed fair enough, and I assumed that she would scan the Governor's diary, find a slot in the next few days and email the details to me.

Instead, I received this email within a few minutes.

Dear Graham
Further to your call this morning requesting an interview with the Governor, I'd be grateful if you could let me have further information about your visit (research about your book and dates of travel etc) and background information on yourself if you don't mind.
With thanks in advance, Vicki

Here it was again; not quite stonewalling, but caution, tinged with a hint of suspicion. I rattled off a reply, which read, in part:

I will be writing about most aspects of the Falklands economy and society, as well as defence, diplomacy and relations with Argentina. It is likely to be written in a fairly informal way, and it will clearly be through my eyes, but making extensive references to people here – including, I hope, the Governor.

In particular I would like to ask him about his personal impressions of the Islands and the Islanders; the social, economic and other challenges they may face; the economy; the relationship with Argentina; defence of the Islands; the relationship with Britain and how that might develop; and the oil industry.

Vicki responded quickly, advising me that the Governor would see me in the only slot he had available, which was a week away. So much for an early briefing, but at least he would speak to me.

I brewed a contemplative cup of tea and, seeing my mother's kitchen radio, tuned into the British Forces Broadcasting Service

(BFBS). It entertains the troops and the locals with a diet of pop music, inconsequential chat and domestic British news. Usually the rest of the world matters little to BFBS, but even they could not ignore the gravity of the Greek economic implosion and possibly that of the entire European Union. This was top of the news agenda, but the third or fourth item was about one of John Lennon's teeth. An American dentist had just parted with around $30,000 to buy the yellow molar at auction, and he now intended to display it reverentially in his surgery.

It seemed to me that I might spend the next few weeks pulling metaphorical teeth. Indications so far were that senior officials regarded me and my like with the kind of dread that John Lennon must have felt as he saw that pair of dental pliers approaching his open jaws. I wondered if I would ever extract any nice big molars of information and then put them on display.

The jet lag was kicking in, though, and I was hungry. I looked at my watch and was pleased to see it was only 7.00 pm, more or less time for my date with Rosie, Peter and Jack.

CHAPTER 3

Dark Clouds to the West

Almost as I arrived back in Port Stanley, notebook and tape recorder in hand, Barack Obama was meeting Cristina Kirchner in France. The presidents of the United States and Argentina met in the fringes of the G20 meeting of industrialized and developing economies in Cannes. The confidential discussions were, the Argentines claimed, held at President Obama's request.

At this time the G20 had events of almost cataclysmic potential to consider. Greece was confronting bankruptcy, and the rest of Europe was squabbling about what it should do to help its profligate partner. China was relishing Brussels' humiliating request to pump money into Europe, and Italy was struggling to fight off the Greek 'contagion'. The global economy was on the verge of returning to deep and dark recession, perhaps even worse.

This did not appear to be a Malvinas moment. And yet, Mrs Kirchner, who had been re-elected in a landslide victory just weeks before, wanted to discuss that very subject with President Obama. The meeting was virtually private, with just four officials supporting each head of state. Fortunately perhaps, even the unsubtle Mrs Kirchner's sense of occasion was enough to stop her from giving reporters chapter and verse about her conversation with the American President. But her agenda had been clear. Barack Obama pointedly told the press afterwards that Mrs Kirchner was a firm friend of the United States and that her very un-European achievement in leading the Argentine economy to growth was something to be admired and emulated. These were more than platitudes; Obama appeared to admire Kirchner.

From that meeting in Cannes came a strong hint that Britain – never having been the natural recipient of Obama's warmth – might soon be told to stop clinging to the residue of empire and talk to this South American economic paragon. In fact, Mr Obama's Secretary of State, Hillary Clinton, had already implied disapproval of Britain's refusal to talk, by offering to mediate between the two countries. That had delighted Buenos Aires.

This energetic and aggressive Malvinas policy was not new, although it had entered a reinvigorated stage following Mrs Kirchner's re-election. Over the previous eight years, the governments of first Néstor Kirchner and then his wife had ripped up the important pragmatic agreements reached between London and Buenos Aires, and endorsed by Port Stanley, in 1999.

These had been landmark achievements. Under Carlos Menem and his imaginative Foreign Minister, Guido di Tella, Britain and Argentine had agreed to co-operate over the search for oil in areas that straddled their disputed frontiers and to co-operate in the conservation of fish stocks that were important to both the Falklands and Argentina. The air link between the southern Chilean town of Punta Arenas and Mount Pleasant, which had ceased during a disagreement between London and Santiago over the arrest in Britain of the former dictator Augusto Pinochet, was to be reinstated with full Argentine co-operation. In return, Falkland Islanders would drop their ban on visits by Argentine citizens. It was good news, and Islanders believed they could now go full-throttle towards further development of tourism, fishing and hydrocarbons.

They had not reckoned on the visceral hostility of the power couple who arrived at the Pink House in May 2003 in the wake of a period of terrible economic chaos. They had an entirely different Malvinas agenda. Coming from Santa Cruz, in the south of Patagonia, and the point in the country closest to the Falklands, the Kirchners probably had more reason than most politicians to be bitter about the 1982 conflict. Many of the intense air attacks were conducted from their constituency. Had they wanted to do so, they could probably have counted the Argentine Skyhawks and Mirages out from the nearby airbases, and counted far fewer of them coming back (to borrow an iconic phrase). In any case, when Néstor was elected, he immediately put the brakes on the policy of reconciliation. Oil and fishing agreements were ripped up.

As planned, Néstor's wife Cristina ran for election in 2007. She succeeded and took over the presidency from her husband in October. He became a congressional deputy and, it was assumed, remained the power behind the throne. The two would probably have continued to alternate in the top job for as long as possible. But in October 2010, Néstor died of a heart attack. Any hope that his passing might have meant a relaxing of hostility was not borne out. His widow was equally aggressive; possibly more so.

In February of that year, while Néstor was still alive and apparently in response to the imminent arrival in the Falklands of an ocean drilling platform, Team Kirchner pushed through a decree requiring any ships bound for the Islands to first obtain permission from Buenos Aires. Neighbouring countries were also asked to refuse their port facilities to Falklands-bound ships. Drilling and support companies had already been told that if they worked in the Falklands, they could forget any ambitions they may have in Argentina.

Oil prospecting went ahead anyway, but the shipping restrictions had an immediate effect. Many owners were reluctant to expose themselves to Argentine ire (although, notably, the growing number of cruise liners operating in the area ignored the issue). The scheduled freight-shipping link between Stanley and South America ceased when its vessel found trouble berthing, first in Punta Arenas, then Montevideo and finally, Rio Grande in Brazil.

The air link with Chile was not cut, but requests for a second weekly flight and for ad hoc charters to pass through Argentine airspace were turned down. The weekly flight had survived simply because severing it would be an escalation that Argentina was not prepared for – yet. By 2010, however, Islanders did not doubt that they were under economic siege and they were openly speaking of a blockade. Britain did not appear to be doing much to oppose it, although the new coalition government had said that it placed importance on improving diplomatic and trading relations with South America, an area they said had been ignored by the previous Labour government.

It was hoped in late 2011 that Buenos Aires had revved-up its Malvinas fundamentalism just to help Mrs Kirchner bag a second election, and that the temperature would be reduced when she felt secure and was preoccupied with bigger issues. That was a mistaken view. If anything, the rhetoric became more shrill, and more aggressive action that was soon to follow proved that the Malvinas was an obsession. De-facto endorsement of Mrs Kirchner's statesmanship by President Obama and Hillary Clinton would only have convinced her that the policy was not unreasonable or without a fair chance of success.

The governments in the Falklands and the UK were only too aware of the thirtieth anniversary of the Falklands War coming up in 2012, and it was depressingly obvious that Mrs Kirchner would not let the anniversary months pass without exploiting them noisily and, if at all possible, to Argentina's benefit. Most likely, British celebrations would be portrayed as neo-colonial triumphalism, insulting to Argentines and their allies. This must have been deeply depressing to officials in the British Ministry of Defence, the Foreign and Commonwealth Office, and the Falklands Government, although none were going to admit it.

At more or less the same time as Cristina Kirchner and Barack Obama were chatting earnestly in Cannes, a much more mundane meeting was going on in my little corner of Stanley. One day into my visit, I had not succeeded in securing an appointment to meet the Commander British Forces. I was a little down, and felt the need for a good cup of tea and the food that I most identify with the Falklands: the humble homemade mutton sausage roll. I assumed I could get such comfort food at Stanley's main supermarket, the West Store, which was a five-minute walk east down Ross Road, past children playing around the nineteenth-century cannons on Victory Green.

The staff, mainly from the Falklands' South Atlantic neighbour, the island of St Helena, were busying themselves stacking shelves. The tills were eerily quiet, but what would otherwise be an almost funereal atmosphere was warmed by formulaic country and western music blaring from speakers concealed somewhere in the tinned fish section.

This was no Tesco or Waitrose (although they did stock goods from the latter). A hand-written sign pointed out that although the labelling on some products suggested shelf lives might have been exceeded, customers should not worry. Shelf life and best-before dates do not, apparently, indicate that food is dangerously out of date. Falkland Islanders had always ignored such warnings anyway; if they had not, they would have endured some hungry winters. But newcomers, such as the oil explorers, were rather more squeamish.

A friendly St Helenian girl was pleased to direct me to the shelves that held the locally processed delicacies, long-life milk imported from Britain and teabags. There, weighing up the comparative qualities of Typhoo versus Lipton was an old friend, Richard Cockwell, whom I had come to know well when he managed a large sheep farm at Fox Bay on West Falkland. He looked at me blankly for a second and then smiled a welcome. 'Good heavens, Graham! Where did you come from?'

I explained that I was back for just a few weeks, and that I wanted to talk to as many people as possible about the Falklands today. It occurred to me that Richard would be, in some ways, every bit as good as a governor or a brigadier. He had been an elected member of the Legislative Assembly until recently but was now unfettered by official responsibilities, media strategies and such. Furthermore, I knew that Richard always had his finger on the pulse. This suddenly seemed like a fortuitous meeting.

The electorate had rather rudely dumped Richard in 2010. Perhaps he should have taken a leaf from Mrs Kirchner's book and ranted on about some populist issue like, well … like the sovereignty dispute. But he told me life outside council was just fine for him, and he invited me home to try the quality of the West Store tea.

We drove to Richard's bungalow to the west of Stanley. In his early seventies and free of work and politics, he was clearly a happier man. The big window of his lounge presented a stunning view of Stanley

Harbour and the beached wreck of the sailing ship *Jhelum*. She was a big bluff-bowed nineteenth-century windjammer that had once belonged to the East India Company, but had fallen foul of Cape Horn and limped back to this final resting place.

Richard dedicates most of his time now to painting bucolic watercolour land- and seascapes, and the wreck of the *Jhelum* is a frequent theme in his work. His paintings are good, and they command prices of a few hundred pounds.

He was as ebullient and hospitable as ever. But I had the feeling that, like the wreck outside his window, Richard had fallen foul of the spiky bottom end of South America. As an Assembly member, he had expended much energy travelling the world, attending any forum that would host Islanders and listen to their views, including the United Nations, where he stood face to face with Argentine diplomats who did not acknowledge his right to speak. He seemed relaxed and relieved to be out of that world.

I steered our conversation to the toxic relationship with Argentina. He heaved a sigh. 'You know, the Falklands would be a fantastic place if it wasn't for them.' This was a deceptively simple but poignant little statement, which went right to the heart of the matter. How different it could be! Co-operation over shared fish stocks to ensure the survival of a resource. Co-operation over the search for oil would benefit the Argentine petroleum support industry as well as both exchequers. If things were different, there would be freight and passenger shipping links with the ports of the River Plate and with Chile. Cruise ships would use the Falklands as a base, transferring their passengers on scheduled or charter aircraft flying from the continent. None of this would benefit the Falklands alone; it would be good for the region. But it seemed development, wealth, and even peace had to be sacrificed for the sake of nineteenth-century nationalism.

'They say they're not going to use force,' continued Richard. 'But I'm sure that if they felt it would work, they would do it. They say they're not going to use force only because they know it wouldn't succeed.'

The current Argentine Government's inflammatory rhetoric and their blockade bothered him (by now, I was calling it that, too). He looked back on less hostile Argentine governments with something verging on nostalgia. He mentioned President Menem's eccentric and anglophile Foreign Minister, Guido Di Tella, who had served until the turn of the century. 'In Di Tella's time we really had quite a good relationship. We avoided sovereignty and agreed to differ so we could sort out things of mutual interest. We had a fisheries agreement and an oil agreement, and other things. That all seems remarkable now.'

Di Tella, who died on New Year's Eve 2001, had a sophisticated mind and achieved the virtually impossible by becoming liked in the Falklands. This was down to his conviction that Islanders had to be involved in any discussions about their future; that and his charming habit of sending Christmas cards and gifts to Islanders. 'Dear old Guido', as I once heard an Islander call him.

Di Tella had a memorable turn of phrase, too. 'At last we have become a boring country,' he said once. By boring, he meant sensible and mature. I met Dr Di Tella on several occasions, and even had dinner at his house in Buenos Aires. He was self-effacing, possessed an impish sense of humour and was far from boring. When the country's Condor ballistic missile programme was abandoned on grounds of cost and, probably, inconsistency with the peaceful image the country was cultivating, he obtained the carcase of a test missile and strung it up across the ground floor of his modernist concrete home in Buenos Aires. The Condor burst through partitions and its nose cone hung over the Di Tella family dining table.

I felt that, in truth, he did not care that much whether the Argentine flag would again fly over Stanley, and defusing the situation would be a humane outcome and a sign of Argentine maturity.

Any sense of pragmatism that had been established among Islanders during the Di Tella years had long since gone. Even if Buenos Aires changed tack and suggest co-operation in some minor areas of mutual concern, they would be wasting their time. 'There is no way that any council could now go back and talk to them about agreeing on anything,' said Richard. 'They've ruined any good relations that had built up in the nineties. Totally ruined them.'

This was about as close as Richard and, I was later to find, any Islander was likely to get to an outburst. Emotional and passionate rhetoric is for Argentine politicians. He learned a little about Argentine emotions and how to handle them in 1982, when he was locked up under armed guard with other Islanders thought to be a threat.

He recalled dealing with his guards: 'If you got angry, they coped fine. But if you were just terribly firm and British, they couldn't understand it. They really can't fathom people who don't have a Latin temperament. That's one of our saving graces: stoicism. They've never actually been able to do anything that has really upset us. I think Cristina thinks that we will collapse under pressure. But we won't.'

I think we both felt a little despondent, but we moved on from tea to wine and our conversation moved on too. Part of the Falklands character is that you don't dwell on those problems that cannot be resolved. Move on. Stiffen the sinew and don't give up on the simple desire to live your life as you want to. We talked for a while about painting and the landscapes that he tried, with some success, to capture.

I had a date at the Malvina House Hotel in an hour or so with a group of visiting British Members of Parliament. The MPs were touring the Islands as guests of the Falklands Government, and they were holding a press conference. I was sure they would share some wonderful platitudes, but I felt a duty to attend. So I said goodbye to Richard and walked down Ross Road in the gathering gloom of a wet evening.

The politicians, two each from the Tory Party and the opposition Labour Party, were too canny to allow Stanley Radio, Falkland Islands TV, *Penguin News*, and me – a rather suspicious scribbler with an unknown purpose – to trap them into saying things that would rock boats in both London and Buenos Aires. But amid the pleasantries about weather ('much nicer than we thought'), the locals ('hospitable') and the wildlife ('spectacular'), there were some words indicating they understood what the Argentines were trying to do, and that they would see that colleagues back in Whitehall also got the message.

I was, for the time being at least, persona non grata at Mount Pleasant base, but the MPs had toured it, had coffee with the Commander British Forces, and – best of all – been given a grandstand viewing position as two RAF pilots pushed forward the throttles of their super-modern Eurofighter Typhoon interceptors and ripped into the sky. As a demonstration of the capability of the military to defend the Islands, it was, by their account, very impressive.

After that, they had spent several hours inspecting the equipment and soldiers of the Falkland Islands Defence Force (FIDF), the company-strength force of local men and a few women who turned out on Thursday evenings, come rain or shine, to hone their martial skills with Steyr automatic rifles, general purpose machine guns, sniper rifles, grenade launchers, .5-inch heavy machine guns, and even a 20mm automatic cannon.

The threat and what British troops and local people alike were prepared to do to deter it had got through to them. Conservative MP Philip Dunne did not shy away from calling the Argentine action a 'blockade'. It was stronger stuff than I had expected.

'The Islanders are a very resilient people,' said the other Conservative MP, Mark Francois. 'They will determine their own future without any interference from a third party. The Islanders clearly feel proud to be linked to Britain, and we all see that continuing very long into the future.'

They noted that the blockade and the consequent need to import supplies over a huge distance was causing inflation and a rising cost of living. No doubt this would be music to Mrs Kirchner's ears when she or her foreign affairs staff read it in *Penguin News* online, but it was not in her interest that the MPs had noted it. They would, they said, be reporting back to their ministers, and they would be urging the Foreign Office to send a minister to the Falklands urgently.

It was pointed out that British Ministry of Defence minister Gerald Howarth had visited Brazil earlier that week, and the issue of allowing ships access to Brazilian ports en route to and from the Falklands was 'very firmly on his agenda'. That in particular would be of interest to Buenos Aires, and one could be sure that a senior official in Buenos

Aires would be ringing the Brazilian foreign minister's office within a day or two.

Labour MP Ian Murray said that the diplomatic channels with Argentina would remain open, but at the same time the government would look at other options for the Islands' air and sea links. Support for this would, he said, extend across both ruling and opposition parties in Parliament.

I was still a little irked by the show of military power that the MPs had enjoyed. I would contact the cheery but unhelpful SO1 J3 Captain Christine Wilson at Mount Pleasant again soon, but in the meantime, I would see about a visit to the family regiment, the Falkland Islands Defence Force. My father and his friends had kept guard on a mountaintop, armed with a formidable 6-inch gun for much of the Second World War, and I had done a little inglorious time as a private in the FIDF twenty-five years or so ago, which made me a member of the FIDF Association. Furthermore, the CO was Major Peter Biggs, a friend of many years. The FIDF had nothing to match a Typhoon for sheer punching power, but stripped-down Land Rovers bristling with machine guns would do for the time being.

Among the local journalists at the MPs' presser was Lisa Watson, the recently appointed editor of *Penguin News*. She had asked some probing questions of the MPs, before dashing back to her office to meet a horribly close printer's deadline. But not before she had suggested I come over for a chat. The following afternoon would be good, said Lisa. By that time the last of the pages would have gone to the printer and she and her three colleagues would be opening a bottle of wine.

I happily accepted the invitation, and pondered three major things that had changed since my days on the paper. We never had more than two members of staff, and back then I wound the handle of a duplicator, rather than contracted a printer. The other major development was that *Penguin News* was online. I felt vaguely, and quite unreasonably, jealous.

CHAPTER 4

Return to *Penguin News*

O ne thing was reassuringly familiar about *Penguin News*. It was still housed within the General Employees' Union headquarters, a single-story weatherboard building on the seafront. The paper originally had a noticeable left-wing slant to its editorials, and back then the union had recognized an ally and offered us a room. The paper had moved premises a few times since then, but had eventually returned to the union, this time taking over almost all of the building. The paper no longer showed any particular ideological bias, left or right. The union had declined in membership and power, and presumably needed the rental income. A rather sad handwritten sign at the entrance to the building said that the union no longer had a full-time representative, but meetings could be arranged by calling her at home.

I was a little early, and Lisa was still correcting proofs in her alcove, but in the general office it was already time for a wine, and I sat down to chat to the deputy editor, John Fowler, advertising sales manager and old school friend, Fran Biggs, and the cub reporter, Teslyn Barkman. Fran took her job seriously, and had done much to make the newspaper profitable – far more so than it was in my time. Without her efforts none of the staff would be paid. Nevertheless, she grumbled a little about a dedicated Facebook 'Falklands Bring and Buy' that had taken away many of her small ads. Social networking was becoming as important here as it was in the rest of the world. 'Better get used to it,' I suggested to Fran. *Penguin News* did not have its own Facebook page yet and it would be wise to start one.

Lisa breezed in, grabbed a glass and helped herself to some white Chilean wine. Relief at having hit the weekly deadline was written across her face. I knew how she felt. If anything had been done wrongly, then it was too late to fix it now. Petite and intensely pretty, with shining blue eyes, Lisa had been among the first generation of Falklands children for whom a university education was a routine possibility. She had seized it after studying at sixth-form college in England (a cost-free opportunity open to all Falklands children with aptitude and ambition). She then studied English. Incredibly, she was now in her early forties, but she looked about fifteen years younger and radiated a sense of energy.

Lisa worked hard on the paper all week, and often spent her weekends on her parents' small sheep farm at Long Island, where she rode horses and revelled in the camp (a term derived from the gaucho word 'campo' and local vernacular for the sheep farming land outside Stanley). I was also friendly with her parents, Glenda and Neil, and I hoped to visit them before I left. Lisa had just published a small book about her experiences as a child during the 1982 conflict, and I had noticed it in several shops around town.

It was a jovial setting and we chatted briefly about the old days of the newspaper. But here, as I noticed elsewhere, there was what I considered to be a healthy tendency to enjoy today and look ahead to tomorrow, rather than dwell on the past. From what I was seeing, the past really is a foreign country. I asked about the paper's financial health and circulation. Distribution of hard copies, it emerged, had not changed a great deal in three decades. We distributed just over 1,000 copies then and Lisa and her team delivered about 1,400 to the shops every week now. But hundreds more overseas readers paid to receive a PDF version of the paper over the Internet, an innovation that, of course, we did not even dream of in my time. And in the past six months a regularly updated *Penguin News* website was breaking news that occurred between print issues and feeding teasers for stories coming up in the next edition.

The local broadband network was strangled by a tenuous satellite link, and eye-wateringly expensive charges from the monopoly service provider, Cable and Wireless, meaning that visitors like me who were accustomed to lightning-fast Internet services hardly had the patience to use it. But if you have never had anything better, then it must be wonderful, and Islanders had taken to the web with gusto. I had been told that there is no community in the world in which a greater percentage of its citizens have access to the Internet. I could not confirm this. But there had recently been criticism of those people – apparently quite a number – who spend up to four hours a day on Facebook. That could well be considered a time-waster, but eBay and Amazon were also popular, so I had been told, and their bargain shopping services made a lot of sense in an isolated little community, especially when the neighbours were trying to block the sea lanes. Online shopping was playing a part in keeping the Falklands going.

'We've had up to 2,500 hits on one story,' said Lisa. Her eyes lit up even more and I thought they could not possibly get any brighter. 'At about 9.00 am Monday to Friday, the viewing figures shoot up. We think that the first thing people do when they go into work is look at *PN* online to see what's happening. I try to put on one story a day, but it might be a teaser for what's going to be in the paper later that week. But recently a story about a revision of the constitution broke between issues, so that was published first online.'

In my day, and those of some subsequent editors, *Penguin News* had been iconoclastic, satirical and fond of rocking the boat. It sometimes got us into trouble from Government House, councillors and even the court (I was threatened with contempt on two occasions because of my reporting). I wondered if the little *Penguin* was still pugnacious. Lisa nodded enthusiastically. 'We'll look for ways to take a pop at the government and the establishment, to be perfectly honest. We haven't got any political parties here, so we keep an eye on what the Members of the Legislative Assembly (MLAs) are up to and criticize them when necessary. We sort of shout from the back, booing and hissing, and trying to embarrass them occasionally.

'One councillor did once try to influence what we were going to report, but we wrote about his attempt in the editorial, so he never tried that again. You can never win, though, as MLAs will say we are picking on them for the sake of it and you'll get readers saying we are not being confrontational enough.'

Tempting though it may be to publish sensational stories, moderation was sometimes necessary, John said. 'We tend to be self-censoring simply because of the size and the sensibilities of the community. It's not as if you are putting something out for an audience of millions, none of whom will recognize you when you're shopping in the West Store.'

Lisa agreed, perhaps for more practical reasons: 'We don't want to be horribly offending against people who we want to buy the paper.'

If you want to check the vital signs of a community, especially a small one, have a chat with the local journos. They have an instinctive feeling for the mood, obtained from the letters page, interviews, the ebb and flow of sales and a dozen other subtle indicators. *Penguin News* definitely had its fingers on the pulse. A recent effort to pull the paper from an operating loss into profit revealed some interesting data. The first move was to raise the cover price from £1.00 to £1.50. Lisa recalled: 'Sales dropped off for a week or so, but came back when they realized that this was the same price as a tot of whisky in the Victory Bar.'

But the initial reluctance to spend even a paltry additional fifty pence a week suggested that Islanders were tightening their belts in response to aggressive Argentine moves that might soon hit them in the pocket. In fact, that did happen, when it had become impossible to import cheaper foodstuffs and other essentials from Chile, and shops had to revert to the 8,000 mile supply line to Britain.

'Prices shot up and people got terribly worried,' said Lisa. 'They were terrified that that was the end; that the economy was just going to come screeching to a halt. But it didn't, and because people are now optimistic about oil, there is a greater feeling of optimism. You can feel the mood. Although oil makes Argentina an angrier country to deal with, it makes people here more confident and optimistic.'

The oil industry, she said, had made a big impact on the economy, even though the companies were only exploring, and were at least five years away from commercial exploitation. A large number of people had been employed on shore in support of the rig, which was drilling 100 miles or so to the north. They were working in the locally-owned support depot, on the dock and providing security and fuel supply services for the rig's helicopters.

That up-beat mood appeared to reflect in *Penguin News*'s ringing cash till. The paper is now covering its considerable costs, and even display ads – at £195 per page in colour – are selling well.

Lisa had been leaning back in her chair nursing her large glass of wine. Then she remembered something. In the rush to meet the deadline, she and the team had forgotten that they had promised *The Sun* in London a short piece on local reaction to the news that Prince William would be posted to the Falklands early in 2012, where he would fly Sea King search and rescue helicopters. Teslyn had been working on the story, and it just needed to be attached to an email and sent off. Lisa saw to it, and while she was gone, I asked John what he thought the Royal presence would mean. He said Buenos Aires had reacted with fake outrage, claiming that it was the latest evidence of British imperialism and aggression. And it was typical of London to appease them by stating that the future king would not be involved in any official Royal activity.

Everyone knew that had it not been for the Argentines, William would certainly have been meeting Stanley's movers and shakers at Government House, cutting ribbons to open church bazaars, and taking the salute at parades. Of course it is quite normal for younger members of the Royal Family serving in military units to carry out Royal duties. But there was going to be none of it in the Falklands, lest it upset the Argentines even further.

John shrugged his shoulders. He is semi-retired and works only half of each year at *Penguin News*, exchanging the deputy editor's green visor with his job-share colleague at the end of each southern summer. He'd seen a lot of life and he was not about to get worked up about the Royals. During the 1982 war his house in Stanley was accidently hit by a shell fired by a Royal Navy ship and three friends whom he and his wife were sheltering died. If anyone deserved a quiet life and happy retirement, John did.

'They've started objecting to everything,' said John, with a shrug. 'Missile firing, the next warship coming down … you name it; they're activities that have been going on for thirty years.'

Lisa had returned to the room, having satisfied *The Sun*'s appetite for a Royal story. She introduced a new element to the discussion; the Argentine 'lunatic fringe', the easily influenced nationalistic types whom she thought lapped up Cristina Kirchner's inflammatory words and might, just might, be provoked into independent action.

Of course, I had been unable to find out how the threat of protests or even terrorism by Argentine citizens figured in the military thinking, but I felt sure that staff officers at Mount Pleasant would have contingency plans in place. A year or so earlier, activists in Tierra del Fuego had attempted to form a protest flotilla of small boats to cross the few hundred miles of sea and enter Stanley waving blue and white flags, and swamping the customs and immigration authorities. It was the stuff of jokes here. 'You never know,' said John, 'the idiots from Tierra del Fuego might launch an armada of jet ski things.'

Lisa chipped in: 'Yeah, but last time there was a bit of bad weather and they changed their mind. Nothing happened and they didn't get that many recruits to the cause anyway.'

John was more concerned that, as he put it, 'the Argentines have got the stage to themselves.' Even fellow members of the British Commonwealth, who ought to be natural Falklands allies, were vulnerable to Argentine lobbying. And there was room for doubt that Britain was doing enough to counter this. 'The Argentines seem to pop up in any arena you can think of,' said John, and he claimed they were targeting the Caribbean Commonwealth states.

This kind of activity has, he suggested, given Buenos Aires the confidence to continue 'tightening the screws', and their latest, serious, initiative was to target Spanish fishing companies active in the Falklands, harassing their ships as they travelled to and from the Islands. He thought they might get short shrift from a Spain that valued relations with its EU partners more than with its old colonial territories, but no one could be sure.

I asked the people of the *Penguin* if they had faith in the British

Government, particularly the Foreign Office. 'No,' said Lisa. 'We don't feel complete confidence, but I think they probably are doing more than they've done before. They are always desperate to drag me and John off into corners and say: "You know, every time an Argentine minister is going to another country, we send our man to see their host first so that they know our views before they meet the Argentines." The British Government is being very verbal in support of the Falklands. It's better than nothing.'

Lisa has a son, Jake, in his late teens, and she had observed that youngsters like him were following the Argentine issue closely and intelligently. 'They talk about it a lot among themselves,' she said. 'They can discuss it quite factually. I would say that the younger generation are quite hard line on the issue.'

It is not just among the younger people that opinions are hardening. According to John, there is a sizeable proportion of the community that was so sick of the Argentines that they would like nothing better than to be cut off from South America. 'If the Lan Chile flight is threatened – and Mrs Kirchner has threatened it – there are people who would say "good". That is not a very well thought out attitude, but it exists.'

I mentioned Richard Cockwell's view, formed from listening to the Kirchner rhetoric that the Argentines would invade almost immediately if there was no Falklands garrison to stop them. Neither Lisa nor John agreed. 'You don't get the feeling from their politics that that is so,' said Lisa.

John added: 'The Kirchners always spoke about the need to avoid force. As Argentina's economy improves, they are keen to be players on the world stage, so they are going to have to abide a bit by the rules of the game.'

Lisa took a swig of wine and pondered for a moment. 'Yes, but just being present on the world stage doesn't mean that you won't do bad things.'

We all agreed that activity would reach some kind of climax around the thirtieth anniversary of the war; the period from 2 April to 14 June 2012. Little was known about official events being planned for the anniversary, except that British veterans of the war would be visiting. 'It'll be one of these things that *The Sun* and *Daily Mail* will write their rubbish about,' said John. 'There'll be a load of verbal aggression from Argentina, great excitement. We'll be getting phone calls from the UK papers, and we'll just say, well ... we're just carrying on with work.'

And that was undoubtedly true. While the high-octane rhetoric continued from across the water and was high-octane material is extracted from the seabed to the north, ordinary Falkland Islanders just got on with work and with life.

'You'd go insane if you let it take over your life,' said Lisa. 'When I was a kid Argentina was like the big bogey man. It's still there, but you have to find a way to deal with it. My way is to consider that things could be so much worse. I count my blessings. There are lots of good things in our lives. We can't be constantly crying like victims. I look at other countries and see people being killed and suffering, and think yes, it's bad here, but it's not that bad.'

The contented faces of the little group taking it easy in my old office confirmed Lisa's view. There were plenty of qualities here that I missed in London. The strangled broadband wasn't one of them. But then I realized that I had gone several days without logging on to Facebook or Twitter. I had not even developed a twitch. I was going cold turkey and something about being home was ensuring I did not miss my old addiction at all.

CHAPTER 5

Zen and the Art of Dealing with Argentina

The Governor, Nigel Haywood, was, I felt sure, going to be very useful in exploring some of the issues raised by Richard Cockwell and by Lisa and John at *Penguin News*. It would be particularly good to have his take on the gravity of Mrs Kirchner's Malvinas policy and what Britain was doing to counter it. Since my email exchange with his cautious but pleasant secretary Vicki, he had agreed a time and date. In response to my request for photos, he had even sent me a picture of him cradling a very large sea trout that he had caught on the Malo River. That was good, because I was planning to do some fishing while I was here, and now it was clear that we had at least one thing in common.

Getting hold of him had certainly been much easier than reaching the Commander British Forces. The Foreign Office was normally every bit as jittery as the Ministry of Defence about talking to journalists, so there was obviously no cross-government ban on officials talking publicly about the Falklands in the run-up to the anniversary. In any case, I could not see why anyone needed to be concerned. The situation was already serious, and my conversations were not going to provoke Buenos Aires into cutting the Lan Chile air link or doing anything else rash.

As the office of governor was created some 200 years ago for the direct administration of the colonies, and, technically at least, there are no more colonies, I wondered what the job of governor actually was in 2011. The Falklands is a British Overseas Territory, and a fully elected local assembly runs the place. Governor Haywood's duties as a diplomat were quite clear; he keeps an eye on the quality of governance and on issues that could have British foreign affairs implications, feeding information on these areas back to London in the form of restricted 'e-grams'.

I knew what a governor's power and privileges used to be in the 1950s, 1960s and 1970s, and the further back one goes, the more autocratic they were. The Governor was once the instrument of direct rule from London, as well as the ceremonial incarnation of the monarch. His Excellency (calling him 'HE' was about as familiar as anyone could be until very recently) managed the civil service, was the chief executive, supervised government spending and chaired the law-making Legislative Council. They really were governors.

They would benefit from the advice of Executive Councillors (Exco), which formed something like a cabinet. But there was not much that was democratic about that. The Governor selected those members that did not have a seat on Exco by virtue of their civil service rank, and more often than not the chosen ones were deferential farm and business managers, who represented the British companies that dominated the economy.

As time went by, locally elected representatives replaced the appointed members of both Executive and Legislative Councils. Recently, the balance of power had shifted significantly. In 2011, the eight members of the Executive and Legislative Assemblies were nearly all locally born and included a teacher, a union leader and the manager of the power generating plant. Each had de-facto ministerial portfolios. The Governor no longer presided over Legislative Council – he had been replaced by a local speaker – but he did still chair Executive Council. Theoretically, he could overrule the decisions of Exco members, but in practice he could not do so without huge implications. If any governor exercised such old-fashioned authority without copper-bottom justification, he would probably be leaving on the next aircraft heading north.

I was happy to be walking up the drive to Government House, past two nineteenth-century bronze cannon and an incongruous harpoon gun from an old whale hunter. Forcing the door open against the strong westerly wind, I wondered if there were still signs of the ferocious three-hour battle that had taken place here on 2 April 1982. The wooden west wing had been riddled with bullet holes and Argentine soldiers lay dead and wounded in the courtyard. But there were no obvious signs: it appeared the bullet holes had all been patched and painted over.

I signed the visitors' book in the foyer. Legend had it that if you did this, you would, sooner or later, receive an invitation for drinks, coffee, lunch or dinner with Her Majesty's representative. I had not even brought a sports jacket and tie to the Falklands, so I rather hoped I would not be drinking Foreign Office gins-and-tonic, but I thought the ritual was an interesting experiment.

I looked into an office near the entrance and said hello to my friend Rick Nye. Then Vicki, who was one of just four staff posted here from London, ushered me into the Governor's office. It was smaller than I remembered it, but my last visit had been about two decades earlier, and perhaps I was rather smaller then. Or perhaps I was then in greater awe of the man in the office.

It is a comfortable, warm and dignified room, with burnished old wooden furniture clustered around a coffee table at one end, and antique maps of the Islands on the wall. It was said that General Menendez, the Argentine Governor in 1982, so liked the office that he did not rearrange the furniture or even take the Queen's portrait off the wall. The French-polished desk was the one behind which Governor Sir Rex Hunt had sheltered at the height of the battle, while nursing a 9mm Browning pistol and preparing to take a few invaders with him. (Fortunately, it never came to that, and Rex was able to emerge alive, dignified and embodying the British spirit of defiance. He will always be remembered fondly here for that.)

Nigel Haywood unravelled a lean and fiftyish pinstripe-clad body from behind the desk and strode over to meet me. He smiled, extended a hand, and gestured for me to take a seat in one of the armchairs. Vicki came back into the room with a tray of tea and coffee. The Governor invited me to help myself, and I poured some excellently aromatic tea into a china cup. It was the kind of tea one would expect in a setting so reminiscent of colonialism. I suspected that both of us would have preferred mugs, but some things must be done the correct way.

We chatted for a bit about fishing and the other leisure interests that seemed to make him suited to such a remote and wild place. A sense of wilderness could be enjoyed within a ten-minute drive of Government House, and the Governor probably found this some consolation for being apart from his wife. She, the Governor explained, spent much of her time back home in Cornwall, looking after children and an elderly mother. She was there now.

He had enjoyed terrific sport with the almost legendary Falklands sea trout. His exploits with a fly rod on the river Malo seemed to be more successful than mine had ever been. He had recently completed a master's degree in conservations science, and he had been developing a fairly grand plan to establish an international scientific research institute in the Islands. His plan was to welcome academics, scientists and conservationists from around the world who would study such diverse topics as fisheries, seaweed, meteorology, flora and fauna, peat fields and wind power. (If there is one thing that the Islands have in abundance, it is wind, and an impressive wind farm on the outskirts of the town generates much of Stanley's electricity.)

The British Antarctic Survey, which operates its ships and aircraft out of the Falklands during the southern summer, had agreed to produce a business plan (I was to learn that most things in the Falklands these days require a business plan, whether they are about business or not). The eight Members of the Legislative Assembly had already given the idea thought, and might be persuaded to come up with the money.

Meanwhile, the Governor had been working on his own research topic: butterflies. He had found an important breeding ground for the Falklands fritillary, a beautiful red butterfly that is locally known as the Queen of the Falklands, and he planned to learn more about them during his time here. I played with a PG Wodehousian image of the Governor in plus fours running across the moorlands waving a voluminous butterfly net. I could almost feel him reading my thoughts, and so abandoned them.

From what I already knew, it seemed to me that Nigel Haywood's role was approaching that of a British ambassador to a minor or medium sized country. With a population of less than 3,000 (not counting some 1,200 men and women at Mount Pleasant), the Falklands are tiny, but the complexity of their affairs and their possible effect on British trade, diplomacy and defence are much greater than many other territories and some countries. He would be spending much time observing, analysing and advising his colleagues in the UK and schmoozing with the locals to enhance their opinion of the British Government.

It was not long before the scowling spectre of the Argentine President was stalking our conversation. Interestingly, the Governor called Mrs Kirchner by her first name, as is the tendency in Argentina. But that did not betray any warmth towards her. Indeed, feelings towards Cristina had become even chillier over recent weeks, mainly because her gaze had now settled on the vulnerable weekly scheduled Lan Chile air link. I suggested to him that they could cut it, as the Chilean Boeing 737s must pass through Argentine air space. But would that not turn down the thermostat dangerously low?

The Governor rubbed his chin thoughtfully. 'When Cristina said at the United Nations "We can stop the air link," I wasn't sure what she meant. I assumed she meant stopping it from going through Rio Gallegos. Because how can I imagine that a country that sees itself as a major power and a member of the G20 – a responsible and mature group of nations – can actually be threatening to stop an air link between two other countries?'

Once a month, the Falklands-Chile flights touch down in the southern Argentine town of Rio Gallegos, which happens to be Mrs Kirchner's hometown. It was a mainly symbolic gesture agreed during negotiations in 1999. The transit stop in Argentina was a concession granted to secure the resumption of the flights through Argentine air space.

I thought he was being generous to Cristina, perhaps giving her a little useful wriggle room. It seemed clear to me that she had been talking about stopping the entire service, and judging by past form, there was little reason to think she would not move against the air link.

I repeated my suggestion that if she did this, it would represent a major escalation in the South Atlantic cold war. 'I think it would,' said the Governor. He pointed out that, apart from anything else, there is a sizeable community of Chileans in the Falklands, and they would be denied ease of access to their own country. Furthermore, he said, trade between the Magallanes region of Chile and the Falklands, thought to be worth about £8 million to the Chileans, would be reduced to zero with one swipe.

'Would Chile be happy about [Argentina] cutting off that service? I don't know, but these are the sorts of questions that I'm hoping countries in Latin America are beginning to ask. Is this [Argentine attitude] now getting to a stage where their pressure or rhetoric is just disproportionate?'

He did not mention the likely consequences of isolation on the Islands' medical services. Seriously ill or injured Islanders are routinely evacuated to Chile, where they receive care that simply cannot be available in Stanley's tiny hospital. Perhaps this consequence was too painful to consider.

The Governor was getting into his stride. 'You can see that [Argentine Foreign Minister] Héctor Timerman, [Ambassador to the US] Jorge Arguello and the rest are popping up everywhere and making statements. Argentina simply makes up things and presents them as fact, which is quite extraordinary.

'There is a constant thread of activity at any international meeting: they will always raise the Falklands issue. There has, for example, just been a conference on albatrosses and petrels, attended by both Falklands and Argentine experts. During that conference there were something like forty Argentine interventions stating that our people could not say anything independently because they are part of Argentina.'

I agreed that this activity had been reaching ridiculous proportions. A few weeks earlier, Argentina had appealed to the international committee that controls national Internet codes, claiming that the Islands' .fk suffix was illegal as the Islands were Argentine and should therefore share that country's code. The organization politely but firmly told the Argentines to pipe down. Then legislators in Buenos Aires tried to push through a bill that would require the Argentine team to the 2012 Olympic Games in London to wear shirts emblazoned with the slogan '*Las Malvinas son Argentinas*'. It remained to be seen whether the Olympic organization would tolerate that.

The Governor's disdain for this strategy was clear, but so was his frustration. 'If your only foreign policy appears to be "let's bang on about the Falklands," then that's quite difficult to handle,' he said.

Argentine Ambassador to the US, Jorge Arguello, had taken the campaign to the Twittersphere, and his followers were being told such massive fibs as, 'The British military are occupying the Islands against the Islanders' wishes,' and 'The Falklands economy would not survive if it was not for subsidies from the British Government.' No, he said. He did not. But he was aware of the Argentine 'facts' circulating on the Internet.

The blockade – the term was ubiquitous in conversation – was the most tangible evidence of Argentine hostility. The Falklands' few ships that had occasional need to travel through or near Argentine territorial waters were often hailed by Argentine coastguard ships and ordered to stop. The captains typically responded by stating that they were pursuing their internationally recognized right of passage between two ports, neither of which was Argentine. The coastguard and navy had not – so far, at least – enforced their demands. The Governor suggested the Argentines had shot their bolt in this particular initiative. 'What are they going to do?' he said. 'Fire across the bows? That would be a massive escalation.'

Indeed it would be, but they have done it in the past. In 1976, during a previous spike in tension, an Argentine warship, the ARA *Almirante Storni*, intercepted the Royal Research Ship *Shackleton*, en route for Stanley, and the warship did fire across the *Shackleton's* bows. The captain bravely refused to stop, and made it safely to the Falklands. There were furious diplomatic exchanges but it went no further.

Just as it was in 1976, the Foreign Office was almost certainly desperate to avoid escalating the dispute. So what was the British Government doing to counter the Argentine offensive today? As if on cue, there was a roar of jet engines overhead. The Governor looked out the window, but the Eurofighter Typhoon from Mount Pleasant had gone long before its sound waves reached the ground. The military deterrent was one British measure, and probably the vital one. Each of these aircraft could take on half a dozen or more Argentine Skyhawks and old Mirages at once. They may not be able to stop a sudden coup de main full-scale attack, but even that would be at huge expense to Argentina.

UK counter-diplomacy is, however, more difficult to get to grips with. Nigel Haywood conceded this with a little sigh. 'It's quite easy for the Argentines to go to, say, Thailand, and say, "those Brits are occupying our Islands." But it's very difficult to counter that. It would be like having a demonstration and saying, "what do we want? The status quo! When do we want it? Well, we've got it already." You have to get your head around the rather Zen concept of what success looks like. It looks like nothing is happening.

'What we do essentially is respond, even if we are responding first. [Our ambassador may say to a foreign government] we know this [Argentine] person is coming to see you, so let's give you the background. But that natural, careful diplomacy produces quite invisible results. If Cristina has had a bilateral with a world leader, and the Falklands do not emerge as part of the communiqué or as part of what she says afterwards, then nothing has happened. But that might have taken quite a lot of preparation by quite a lot of people.'

I thought this was a difficult, almost existential, explanation that he must have gone through numerous times with other interviewers. Many Islanders would have considered it suspiciously, especially because the Foreign Office had form. In the past their agendas had not always dovetailed with those of Islanders. Quite behind-the-scenes diplomacy made Islanders twitchy.

The Governor reverted to what sounded like the official script. 'We have a very robust policy in support of Falkland Islanders and their

41

right of self-determination. There is an absolutely strong British government and institutional view that says, if the Falkland Islanders want to remain British, then we'll do everything possible to support that.'

Kirchner, Timerman, Arguello and the rest are going to become even more vocal and busy during the thirtieth anniversary year, I suggested. He agreed. 'We are trying to do several things over the next year. One very obvious one is correcting misconceptions that the Argentines are planting in people's minds about the history and about their claim, most of which simply do not stand up to analysis. There is a great deal of work going on to brief countries about the facts.'

I assumed that priority target countries would be those that border Argentina, and which Buenos Aires is courting for support over the Malvinas. The politicians and the people of those countries generally have no fondness for Argentina, and have always had good relations with the UK. There had even been fears of armed conflict between Uruguay and Argentina in 2009 and 2010 over plans to site massive wood pulp mills on the Uruguayan side of the River Plate. Chile quietly makes it clear whenever possible that it is embarrassed by the need to publicly endorse Argentine ambitions, while Brazil probably teeters between supporting its regional colleague or its old European trading partner. And yet all three neighbours feel they must give ritual support to Buenos Aires, and the future of the alliance is the biggest threat to the Falklands.

The Foreign Office had been sponsoring journalists from the three countries to visit the Falklands and take an objective view of whether the people are really living under a military occupation and economically reliant on British subsidies. The resulting TV and press reports have indeed contradicted the Argentine version of reality, but whether they have any deep or lasting effect is arguable.

The Governor places great importance on the ability of Falkland Islanders themselves to get out and plead their case internationally. Their claim to self-determination is powerful when it comes from their own lips, and their lack of diplomatic lustre gives them credibility. 'It's really down to the Islanders to sell themselves,' said the Governor.

'We have to get our message across about the importance of self-determination.'

As we sat in Government House drinking tea, two members of the Legislative Assembly were attending an international conference on the Caribbean islands of St Kitts and Nevis. A few months earlier, others had made the annual trip to the UN, where they countered the Argentines' demands for negotiations. The votes here never went their way, and there was no binding requirement to do the bidding of the UN anyway, but it would look much worse if Islanders could not be bothered to defend their case.

Neither the Governor nor anyone else I had met in the preceding days seemed confident that any amount of diplomacy would do much more than take some of the sting out of the current Argentine offensive. Buenos Aires had religion over the Malvinas. It was not surprising, therefore, that the Governor articulated a degree of fatalism. He said the Argentines had made a 'miscalculation', and the more aggressive the Argentines became, the more Islanders and Britain would stand firm and fast. 'There is a point – and I think this [Argentine] government might have reached it – when the Islanders will just say, "to hell with you. There are enough ways of connecting up the dots without involving you. We want to have links with the rest of South America, but if you're going to make it difficult, we don't care, we'll go and do something else."'

The Argentines have been cutting off their nose to spite their face, he said, citing the broken 1999 agreements. 'They have said "no, we don't want to become rich if it means you becoming rich." But the oil companies have worked out that they can fly people directly here, and should they start to extract oil it will involve ships coming straight to the Falklands and going away again. Short of piracy, no one can stop that.'

But getting back to that vulnerable air link; what if Mrs Kirchner did what some felt was almost inevitable? Fatalism again, this time with some steely determination: 'Once it's happened then the only card they had to play has been played. Then you get on with answering it. There has been a lot of contingency planning around that, both locally and in the UK. We could still shift things around on ships. There is a tourism strategy for an independent air link to somewhere. Miami would be a good idea. And there is nothing to stop us looking for a link to South Africa.

'The greatest fear that we can have is of fear itself, and Argentine success is rather built on the idea that people will just shy away because they are afraid of what might happen. They seem to be calculating that they can turn up the pressure, and then turn up the pressure again, until eventually they will force the British Government to the negotiating table. This is mistaken on so many levels. It's not how the British character reacts to pressure, never mind the Falkland Islanders, who are even more robust. Give us more pressure? That's just going to make us stronger. It's like pressing carbon – you end up with diamonds.'

The Governor poured some more tea, and we sipped it delicately. We had started off talking dull and coded diplomatic language, but then some real emotion had emerged. It crossed my mind that Nigel Haywood just might have the potential to 'go native', a criticism that Governor Sir Rex Hunt's colleagues had applied to him in the lead up to the invasion of 1982, and for which Islanders had grown to love him. I quietly hoped that much more fly-fishing success and many more sightings of beautiful butterflies would cement this governor's relationship with the Islands.

CHAPTER 6

Invasion of the Oilies

The news that Prince William, the Duke of Cambridge, would be visiting the Falklands to fly with the Air Force had an immediate effect on everyone I knew. Even the republicans – and there are a few even in the Falklands – were pleased. After all, just a few months earlier, the man who will be king had been the centre of delighted global attention as he tied the knot with Kate. He embodied new hope for the British Royal Family, offered a brief fillip for Brits who were reeling under spending cuts, and cheered Europe as it looked into the abyss of a financial crisis. His bride was gorgeous and he seemed modest. And now he was coming to the Falklands.

Some of the Islanders I spoke to were, however, unhappy that he would not be carrying out any official functions, meaning they would see little of him and there would certainly be no opportunities to shake his hand. 'Oh, they're just saying that to keep the Argentines happy,' said one female friend. 'I'm sure that when he gets here he'll want to do something that we can all enjoy.'

This was the main topic of conversation when I joined my old friend Robert King for a few drinks at Malvina House Hotel. He agreed with me that the most common emotion was relief that, even though everyone knew the Argentines would become wound up over it, the Ministry of Defence had still decided to post him here. That was a subtle but meaningful message.

Robert has a senior post in the Falklands Government, running the Customs and Immigration Department, so he knew a thing or two about the ebb and flow of the population here, and the group of predominantly men whom we saw here tonight definitely represented a flow. Since the Falkland Islands Company had, rather foolishly, closed the Upland Goose, the oldest hotel in Stanley and an iconic institution, Malvina House was the only hotel. And it was doing a roaring trade. The forty-three-room establishment was charging upwards of £100 per night and men and women involved with the great offshore search for petroleum had booked it up for months.

The scene around us was boisterous. The hotel had laid on a curry buffet and men were just back from the rig and expecting to fly back to the UK the following day on their company's chartered airliner. 'The Oilies are letting their hair down a bit tonight,' observed Robert.

'Oilies'. I liked the name. It didn't seem to be derogatory and I thought I could use it, but wondered if this still relatively small community of drillers and technicians might have a negative impact on the Falklands. I had seen resentment building up in the past around small cliquish groups with money aplenty. I thought, though I could not be sure, that there were a few more local girls circulating here than might normally have been the case in genteel Malvina, and that might cause some friction.

'I suppose they're pleased to be heading home, and I bet their pockets are well lined,' I said.

Robert smiled a little wryly. 'Yeah, but not as well lined as all that. They have to pay tax here, and we've done pretty well out of that.' He explained that the Falklands Government had benefited from a £19.5 million windfall in the last economic year, and much of that was due to taxation on the Oilies or on the companies that supported them onshore. This sounded good. I recalled that years ago the government had said that even if no oil or gas were found, the period when merely exploratory drills were biting into the seabed would generate considerable revenue. It looked as if they were right.

'It's more than that, though,' said Robert. 'They've just had another strike.' I sipped my excellent malt whisky (at just £2.00 for a generous shot, fine drinking is cheap across the Falklands and especially in the Malvina). He had my attention and told me more.

Rockhopper Exploration, which had just announced its second

strike, was one of a wave of companies, including Desire, Falklands Oil and Gas and Argos, that had been formed specially to explore off the Falklands. They had chartered a floating rig, the *Ocean Guardian*, and began sinking holes in the seabed to the north of the Falklands in early 2010. So far, Rockhopper had been the only company to find the black stuff, and they had done so twice. By industry standards, that was rather like being dealt a royal flush in two consecutive hands.

These small companies were not the first to drill off the Falklands. Some fourteen years earlier, the Falkland Islands Government granted several large companies – the likes of Shell and Amerada Hess – rights to explore. They spent vast sums of money on seismic surveys to narrow down the areas that were most likely to yield petroleum, then brought in a rig called *Borgney Dolphin*, and drilled. And drilled. But, while traces of oil and gas were found, it was not enough to become excited about. To make matters worse, oil prices had crashed to just $10 a barrel and in that economic environment, it would have taken an underground ocean of perfect quality oil to justify further investment. And so the big boys surrendered their licences, passed on the useful data they had acquired about their drilling zones, and left. There was a hiatus while oil prices increased to around $100 a barrel, and the zone became interesting again. At this point, several bold small companies entered the fray. They had been set up to search beneath Falklands waters.

There had been many ups and downs during the latest exploratory phase. The share prices of Desire, Falklands Oil and Gas and Rockhopper Exploration had soared and dived many times over about twenty months as newspapers speculated wildly about this curious and distant enterprise. And of course they never failed to link it to the territorial dispute. Seismic data looked good, but holes were drilled that yielded nothing. Once, notoriously, a Desire well was said to have yielded oil one day, and then water the next. There was much sniggering and, for a while, the mood was gloomy. But then Rockhopper, operating over a block of relatively shallow seabed codenamed Sealion, almost directly due north of the centre of the Islands, announced it had hit something big. The oil that came to the surface was viscous, about the consistency of Marmite, and therefore difficult to pump, but was of good quality and appeared to be plentiful.

The markets reacted predictably, and suddenly everyone in the industry, and many people who were not, but fancied a flutter, was talking about vast riches that were about to be unleashed in the South Atlantic. The Falklands Government celebrated too, but they knew that if this was the only find, then no riches were guaranteed, and they might yet have to go back to living off the sales of fishing licences, cruise ship landing fees and even the sale of postage stamps.

But then, in the last day or so, Rockhopper had done it again. This time, the well was near the Sea Lion oil field, but the reservoir was believed to be separate. Much analysis of underground pressure, oil quality, viscosity and many other arcane things understood only by the oil industry had yet to be made, and there was no great hurry to do the work, but coming on top of the news about Prince William's visit, Falkland Islanders felt as if they were having an early Christmas, and a very nice one at that. The Oilies in the Malvina and their local friends certainly had something to celebrate.

Robert and I walked home talking about other things, including the fishing trip that we planned over the coming days. We had both spent some of the best days of our youth fishing for the big sea trout that had also charmed the Governor. It was one of those nights, typical of the Falklands, where there is almost no light pollution, when the stars appeared so bright and close that one might almost reach up and touch them. The Milky Way formed a banner across the south, and the longer one looked at it, the more densely packed with stars it became. It was, I hoped, a portent of good fishing weather. I imagined that the Oilies on the rig about 150 miles away were also enjoying the night.

The next morning, intrigued by our conversation in the Malvina, I decided to find out more about oil from the Islander who is tasked to licence and control the nascent industry. I rang Phyl Rendell to ask if I could see her that morning. She said her diary was not very full, so I should come along to her office.

Phyl is a skilled and clever civil servant of some twenty-five years' service, who had been trained as a teacher and previously ran the

Department of Education. When the British Government approved the legislation that made oil exploration possible, Phyl embarked on a crash course in the new industry and took on the new post of Director of Mineral Resources.

She is an attractive woman with a ready smile, and she is a fluent talker. That was probably why the government had been keen to send her to oil conferences and exhibitions around the world, wherever the Falklands profile needed to be raised. She gave me a fulsome welcome in her office. To call the single-story, timber-framed building a government 'department' seems a little grandiose. There are just three other civil servants here: Diana Aldridge, the receptionist and Phyl's secretary; and Roddy Cordeiro and Sam Cockwell, both Islanders in their twenties, and recent graduates from British universities. Sam is a geologist and Roddy a linguist.

The discoveries have been made just in time for Phyl. She was due to retire within a few months and then planned to spend much of her time with her husband on Bleaker Island, about 100 miles to the southeast of Stanley. The island is home to a spectacular range of penguins, seals and other wildlife, as well as her family's sheep and beef cattle. They have built several tourist cabins on the island, and Phyl was now about to say goodbye to oil. It would, I suggested, have been a shame had she done so before there had been a strike. As it was, this now seemed like a good time to be moving on. She would be handing over to another Islander who had studied geology in Britain.

Phyl was full of admiration for the little companies that had come from nothing more than a vibrant spirit of adventure to explore here. 'All of our companies are driven by entrepreneurs,' she said. It needs people like that, who believe in the place. It was unusual to have the likes of Shell and Amerada Hess coming into a frontier as they did back in 1996, and it's much more normal to have smaller companies who can do things on a lower budget. They then look to selling the asset on and let other companies develop their finds.'

The current drilling programme, using a rig shared between three companies, was costing approximately $1 million a day (rather a lot, I thought, for 'little' companies), with the vast bulk of that being paid by whichever company was using the rig. I always knew that the oil industry spent vast amounts of money, but these figures were still staggering. Never before had so much money been spent on any commercial enterprise associated with the Islands. But, as Phyl explained, expenditure was about much more than just renting a rig to drill holes. The companies had to run two large helicopters, both for resupply and to ensure rapid evacuation of crew if there was an accident. They operated a chartered Boeing 747 air link directly with Britain, flying fortnightly, and funded two large rig support ships. Furthermore – and this was great for the local economy – they were employing a significant number of locals on terra firma to maintain the supply depot and support air operations. The government's £19.5 million windfall suddenly seemed like very small beer.

Rockhopper, said Phyl, is moving ahead on the basis of their finds. They are looking for investors to buy into the company, and working out how the oil may be extracted. 'They have said it will cost about $2 billion dollars to develop their field, and they believe that it can be done using an offshore floating production and storage vessel, the same system that's used off Shetland, so there would be very low impact on the Falklands.'

Things would, she said, become much more complicated if any of the explorers find large quantities of natural gas. This is much more difficult to process, and the companies concerned would almost certainly need to build a plant onshore connected to the field by pipelines. That would mean massive planning and expenditure, and it would threaten the government's principal of exploiting hydrocarbons for maximum profit and minimum impact. But the global demand for the clean energy that gas provides means that it might justify the investment and the compromised principle.

The area of seabed to the north of the Falklands has already demonstrated its potential, and the next explorers will move their attention to tranches south and east of the Falklands, which lies in water as deep as 2,000 feet. There is less knowledge of the geology of that area, although some seismic exploration has been carried out. The third rig to drill off the Falklands was scheduled to arrive in early 2012.

Two other companies, Borders and Southern and Falklands Oil and Gas, would fund the work, which will be the kind of deep water campaign that became so controversial after BP's disastrous accident in the Gulf of Mexico.

The new rig, the *Leiv Eriksson*, is huge, and its Norwegian owners had, until recently, been using it to explore off Greenland. It was expected to drill just three wells before leaving again, after which the albatrosses and petrels of the South Atlantic would be able to soar on the west winds again without fear of running into a monstrous steel island. But it was possible to imagine that if any of those wells produced the desired goods, funds would be found to extend the programme.

'This is all great for the Falklands economy,' said Phyl. 'It's already got us through two winters when recession would otherwise have hit us, and the next round will take us through next winter. Money is turning over here. It's terrific.'

The explorers may continue with ship-borne seismic survey work, but otherwise will be snugly based in the UK studying their data, assessing their finds and raising money for a possible exploitation phase. They will need in the region of $2 billion. Those seabirds will have the frigid seas and skies to themselves for several years. But they will be back, insisted Phyl Rendell. 'It is not going to go away. I'm very optimistic, but it will take time.'

This degree of optimism was quite understandable, but might it not all be in vain if the market value of crude once again plunged to $10 a barrel? Phyl was frank. 'If that happens, forget it. If it went down to $50, forget it. But the prize for the Falklands is in the exploration activity. Never mind production at the end; it's highly profitable for our businesses.'

What businesses, precisely, I asked. Quite a few it seemed. Providing security to the support ships, helicopters and the chartered Boeing had become a money-spinner and at least one security company had been set up. The Malvina House Hotel was – as I had seen – chock-a-block. The local coach company had had to buy new vehicles to cope with demand and, most importantly, two prominent local entrepreneurs had to take on a massive contract to build and run an onshore logistics base for the machinery, drill pipes and other hardware for which oil rigs have insatiable appetites.

Phyl Rendell was one contented civil servant. She had seen her patience and dedication rewarded and could now go into retirement knowing that she had played a major role in something important. I wondered if life on a remote island with a trickle of tourists – albeit high-paying ones – a flock of sheep and a herd of cattle would sustain her interest. But Falkland Islanders generally enjoy isolation.

As a result of all this, and assuming all goes well industrially and politically, Islanders could, one day, be among the richest people in the world. There are fewer than 3,000 of them, and their per capita share in the income from a successful oil industry would be almost unimaginable. I broached the subject of filthy riches and what to do with them. Would the Falklands have a sovereign wealth fund developing a portfolio of assets in competition with the likes of Kuwait?

'It's possible,' said Phyl. 'The government had already been giving thought to this, and we think the Norwegian model is probably one of the best. We could have a lot to learn from them. What we do know about these funds is that you need to put the money away immediately rather than fritter it away. But we're not there yet. It's actually very important that we continue to plan for a future with no oil. We definitely need to keep our feet on the ground.'

Socio-economic impact of such a major industry had emerged as a major issue, Phyl said. The oil companies have to fund studies about likely impact, and she said that Rockhopper Exploration was currently working on one. She referred me to the company's local representative, Ken Humphrey, a helpful and very nice guy, she said. I said I would certainly call him.

I reminded Phyl of the recent Gulf of Mexico disaster. Could a similar event occur off the Falklands? And if it did, would they be able to handle it? 'You cannot say it wouldn't happen,' she replied. 'The next rig will be drilling in deep water, but it is not so much about water depth, it's about the type of structure that one is drilling into, and the pressure that there may be within that rock. We don't think that we have high pressure in this area, whereas the Gulf of Mexico is a very high-pressure area. Nevertheless, we are taking all precautions to prevent an incident, and we are making sure that the companies would know what to do if there was a disaster.'

And the Argentines (no need to say more)? 'They are not going to derail this. It will make it difficult for an industry if the supply lines cannot touch South America, but the industry will find a way around that. They will go ahead with this regardless of the politics if it makes commercial sense.'

But, there had been suggestions that Buenos Aires would penalize the very highly specialized petroleum support companies involved in a Falklands industry by banning them from employment in Argentina's considerable industry. That would be one way of sticking an oily spanner in the works. It was possible but not probable, said Phyl. 'These are massive companies, and the Argentines know that they need them as well. They can't afford to ban them.' One major specialist outfit was, she said, already involved in the Falklands and was, effectively, testing this theory.

Phyl walked me to the door, and as an aside gestured to a small Robertson's jam jar on a display shelf in the reception area. I said, 'That doesn't look like jam in there, although it could be Marmite. Is it what I think it is?'

She laughed. 'Yes, that's it; the first Falklands oil.' Sam Cockwell twisted the top off the jar and passed it to me. It smelt of kerosene and was far more solid than it was liquid. I dipped a finger in tentatively, and it quickly began to absorb the warmth from my skin and become less viscous. 'It's much warmer where it comes from,' explained Phyl. 'But by the time it gets to the surface it's very dense. The oil companies would have to install insulated pipes and pump hot water down to keep it thin, and that would cost something, but it can be done.'

I thanked her, carefully wiping that Falklands crude off my finger before I extend my hand. 'Don't forget to ring Ken Humphrey. He's got an interesting story to tell.' I said I would and stepped out of the mineral resources department into a brisk westerly wind that was blowing down Ross Road.

I searched for my mobile phone in my rucksack, found it and dialled the number that Phyl Rendell had given me. An extraordinarily cheerful voice answered. Ken Humphrey sounded as if he had been expecting me, which seemed unlikely, but Stanley is a very small town. Within ten seconds he had invited me to lunch. It would have been foolish to refuse. Where? I asked him. 'The Malvina in an hour? Is that OK with you?'

Of course it would be the Malvina. There is nowhere else to eat a civilized lunch in Stanley. I thanked him, said goodbye and began to look forward to a good meal at the expense of the oil industry.

CHAPTER 7

Local Heroes

In 1983, the film director Bill Forsyth directed a subtle and touching comedy-drama called *Local Hero*. Set in a town on a remote Scottish island near the North Sea oil fields, the plot revolves around an American oil mogul, played by Burt Lancaster, who has set his sights on it as the perfect location for a refinery. He sends his cheque book-toting men to the island, where they unexpectedly meet a cast of canny locals who are determined that, if they are to sacrifice aspects of their island's beauty and remoteness, it will be done on their terms. But, little by little, the oil executives are seduced by those very qualities of the island, and eventually even the Lancaster character decides this lonely place does not need and should not have oil. The Americans are redeemed by their realization that beauty transcends mere money. The islanders are disappointed, but they shrug their shoulders and resume their gentle, slow and rather special way of life.

I have watched the film many times. It always makes me think of the Falklands and how they might cope in such a situation. True to the plot of *Local Hero*, I felt we had been canny. People like Phyl Rendell were making sure that Islanders stood to gain – indeed, were already gaining, even before oil had been extracted – and I had been told about the local entrepreneurs who were setting up to provide sophisticated onshore support. But I was sure the soft and sensitive oilman was a myth. These guys had to be hard-boiled, and were not going to limit activity for fear of damaging the beautiful South Atlantic wilderness. Neither would they care if local people became rich, idle, fat and short-lived. But when I was introduced to Rockhopper Exploration, I had to question that assumption. The Falklands may indeed have spun a little of its remote islands magic, nurturing more sensitivity than I would have thought possible.

Ken Humphrey recognized me as I stepped into the bar of the Malvina for the second time in about eighteen hours, although I have no idea how. He beamed a smile at me, strode across the room and grabbed my hand with, I imagined, the kind of grip he had learned while heaving big lumps of metal around oil rigs. I had been able to hear him smiling when we spoke on the phone and he was a smiler in the flesh. The trouble was that I did not know if this was PR glad-handing, the kind of warmth that the American oil men flashed with their wallets when they flew into that mythical land of *Local Hero*, or the real thing.

The lunch was to be on him, Ken insisted, and he picked up our bar tab too. We talked small talk while the waitress wasted time and flirted a little with the barman. Ken had been in the industry for much of his working life, and had spent most of the last decade in Wellington, New Zealand. He had met his wife there and they were going to make a new home in Italy. The oil industry is truly global, he pointed out, and it did not matter where he hung his hat. But finding that perfect place in Italy would have to wait until the first phase of Rockhopper's Falklands project had been completed.

He explained that his job here had little to do with the actual drilling, or even with the onshore supply base – there were contractors for that. It was more about oiling relationships. 'I maintain the reputation of Rockhopper as a high safety orientated, responsible corporate citizen,' he said.

He was proud of the fact that the Falklands exchequer had already benefited from a windfall generated directly by drilling in the last financial year, and that another windfall was building up ready to land in their laps. He was proud too that money has been spread around the economy's small private sector. The guys running the logistics base (whom I was starting to think of as the Ewing boys) were probably taking the biggest slice of the cake, but far more than mere crumbs were being passed to coach drivers, security personnel, shipping agencies and, of course, the Malvina House Hotel.

'Our intent is to work with local people as much as we can,' said smiling Ken. 'The problem is that there is no unemployment here, and it seems like most people have about three jobs. But we spend money with all sorts of people across the private sector, and there are about sixty local people employed by us onshore. Working with people here is a great pleasure. They're wonderful. The comment from the base manager has been that you would never find a better bunch of guys to work with anywhere in the world. And I believe it.'

He was less complimentary about the Ministry of Defence, which had originally agreed to allow its privately owned chartered helicopters to be used to service the oil rig, and to allow Rockhopper and the other companies to rotate staff on its twice-weekly charter flight to and from the UK. 'That was a disaster. MOD's objectives are not commercial and ours are. There was a reliability problem because of that. We learned never to rely on the MOD. That's why we have our own charter air link and our own helicopters.'

I detected a slight end-of-term mood in Ken Humphrey. Rockhopper and the rig had been working hard down here for approaching two years, but soon the Ocean Guardian was to be hitched to a huge tug and head off beyond the horizon to oil deposits new. Fellow Falklands companies Desire and Argos Resources were hoping to raise enough money to enable them to drill a few more wells with the rig after Rockhopper had left, but it was more likely that they too would draw a line under exploration for the time being, leaving it to other companies and a new rig to take up the exploration cudgels in the new year in the much deeper waters to the south.

Many in the oil industry, certainly everyone in Rockhopper, and those on the periphery who stood to gain, were very happy with what had been found. And why would they not be? As Ken explained, 'The volumes of oil look to be commercial; we are working in reasonable water depth – about 500 metres, compared to about 200 metres in the North Sea, and the rock is pretty easy to drill into. Oh, and weather conditions are rather better than in the North Sea. Technically, it's not a problem.'

But could Rockhopper expect to come back and begin production alone? Probably not, but it still stood to make a vast profit. The company is a tiddler by industry standards, and billions of dollars would have to be raised for the next phase. It might be easier to raise that money by climbing into bed with one of the massive multi-national companies; the likes of Shell and BP. Rockhopper might even sell out to them entirely. The digits involved in a transaction of that kind would probably not fit onto a cheque.

But despite the smiles of pleasure at that which has been accomplished so far and the optimism about the future, the risks remain terrifying. Ken Humphrey was surprisingly frank about this. 'You are gambling with $25 million rolls of the dice. You have to find something of decent quality and size to justify that. When we think about risk, we think about the risk of not finding oil; the difficulty of making a find commercial; oil price fluctuations; exchange rate and interest rate changes. And behind those are things like sovereign, or political, risk.'

This latter risk was, I suggested, particularly pertinent in the Falklands. Ken agreed. 'Will the banks finance the development in the South Atlantic when you have Argentina, which is a little on the hostile side? From our point of view, the sovereign risk can be managed, as long as we and the financiers are convinced that the British Government will stand by the Falklands. As long as they do, we can manage the rest of it.'

So, short of a war or a remarkable diplomatic campaign that Argentina wins, the Argentines cannot stick that oily spanner in the works? Ken could hardly have been more bullish. 'I would be surprised if there is any area of activity through which the Argentines could cause a cessation of work here. We don't need the mainland. We can run these operations out of Houston, Aberdeen or somewhere in Africa. We can ship the oil to the US or Europe or Africa. We can fly our people in and out as we do today. That isn't to say that we wouldn't like to be working with service companies based in Argentina or Brazil, because the distances are less and it would be cheaper for us. But if we can't do it that way, we'll do it another way.'

I had not detected much, if any, concern in the Falklands about the possible environmental impact of an oil industry. Even the presumably powerful local organization Falklands Conservation seemed fairly sanguine. And there was no sign of militants like Greenpeace taking an interest. But ocean drilling easily evokes appalling images of the Macondo oil leak in the Gulf of Mexico, which took months to bring under control, and ruined whatever good PR the industry had laboriously built up over the preceding years. The Falklands oil companies have to think about such disasters and form contingency plans for the virtually unthinkable. But it does not appear to give them sleepless nights. I asked Ken about this.

'If a Macondo-like incident happened in our field, the oil would probably not flow very quickly, as the crude is very viscous and there is little pressure in the reservoir. The impact would not be as great and environmentally damaging. Most of the weather is westerly so it would probably take any oil out to sea rather than onto shore.

'But that's not how we think about it. We have to consider worst-case scenarios. We have to assume northerly prevailing weather [which would take the crude towards land] and we have to assume it would flow a bit more freely. We would have to get more equipment in to cope with that, but it's very specialist equipment, and that applies almost anywhere in the world.'

Rockhopper's frontman was rather less confident about the possible social impact of an industry on the Falkland Islanders' way of life. For a minute or two, as Ken completed his pasta Bolognese and moved on to coffee, I thought I saw the soft-centred oil man of *Local Hero*.

He sighed gently and gathered his thoughts. 'The soul of this country is in the camp, and it's a country of one-on-one relationships. And there is enormous self-pride; a real sense of survival. The Falkland Islanders are survivors. And if you make life too easy, that sense of survival, that rugged independence and initiative, self-belief, community values ....'

Ken ran out of words, but his theme was clear. This industry was something of a wild animal. Keep it under control or it will control you. He had another sip of coffee and sighed again. 'You've just got to be really careful.'

'How so?' I asked.

'It's the money,' he replied. 'Supposing you get £200 million a year coming into the government. What do you do with it? You might give some of it to the British Government to contribute to defence costs, you might invest some of it in a sovereign wealth fund for the future, and you could then use some of it to do more "stuff". But with a population of 3,000 how much do you want to spend? Calculated on a per capita basis, the Falklands could be the richest country on earth.'

Ken and his family lived for a while in Alaska, where there had been an oil boom and every man woman and child, whether born in the state or not, received a cheque every year; their very own dividend from the massive wealth fund. He had certainly appreciated this, but payouts from a Falklands wealth fund could be immense. 'What you don't want to do is make life so easy that no one will want to work any more, because then you would destroy the way of life here. And the key to this place is what I call the soul, the culture and the way of life. You have to be really careful with that.'

Rockhopper had just commissioned a socio-economic study looking at the effects that an oil industry might have on the Islands. The Falklands Government had done something similar in the late 1990s, at the time of the first, failed, attempt to find oil. But since then the government had been guided by mantra of 'maximum benefit for minimum impact', which was dangerous in its simplicity because the key terms 'benefit' and 'impact' were open to interpretation; one person's benefit could be another's impact.

And so Rockhopper grasped the nettle. The contracted consultants, Plexus, had already visited the Islands briefly, and would return in early 2012 to carry out in-depth research. Again there was a glimpse of *Local Hero*, when Ken said simply and, I was sure, sincerely, 'We want to leave it the way we found it.'

We finished our coffee in silence. Eventually, I asked Ken if he would be able to get me a seat on the helicopter next time it flew out to the oil rig. I would probably not learn anything I did not already know, but it would have been good to see so many words transformed into deeds. The answer was a brisk but polite negative. Space on helicopters was at a premium and he felt that the crew would not welcome the need to spend time talking to me. I did not doubt that the metal island was a very busy place and there was always the risk of getting stuck on it for a few days if the weather blew up, so perhaps that was for the best.

'You really need to talk to Byron Marine and Byron McKay,' Ken said by way of consolation. I thanked Ken and Rockhopper for lunch. He smilingly bid me farewell, and I sat there for a few more minutes. He was right; I did need to meet Lewis Clifton and Neil McKay, the JR and Bobby Ewing of Stanley. But nagging away at me was the feeling that I was becoming seduced by the optimism and the excitement about oil. A few years earlier I had written a piece for *Penguin News* in which I considered the threats that oil could bring to the tiny society and to the spectacularly beautiful but vulnerable natural flora and fauna.

Both Ken Humphrey and Phyl Rendell had, I felt, been perfectly up-front and honest about the former, but I had a sneaking suspicion that the risk to the Islands' natural habitat and the creatures that lived within them was being understated. In my conversations so far about oil, the issue had been addressed, but only at my instigation, and my interviewees were most definitely addressing the subject as people who did not want to see an oil industry at any cost, but accepting that the risks were manageable. The question was, were they? I could think of a few people to speak to about this, and I made a note to do so.

I thought I would follow advice that Phyl Rendell had given me, and try to obtain an interview with Sam Moody, Ken Humphrey's boss. The young and buccaneering chairman of Rockhopper Exploration was assuming almost heroic status around Stanley. With no background in the oil industry at all, he had raised hundreds of millions of pounds in the City of London and taken a punt on something that might not exist. He was known to be shy of the media and had so far granted just one interview, to the *Daily Telegraph*. Nevertheless, Sam Moody was said to be friendly, if you could get through to him. The

Rockhopper Exploration website revealed the number of his press advisor in London, and I gave him a call.

The response was almost immediate and it was positive. Sam Moody would speak to me, but he would only do so for my book. I was expressly forbidden to make a news story out of the interview. I agreed to that, and the hero of Falkland oil was soon on the other end of the telephone line.

Sometimes, and without obvious reason, one begins using a stranger's first name without invitation to do so. Perhaps it was because Moody was so youthful sounding – certainly more youthful than me – that I immediately began calling him Sam. He did not seem to mind and any thin layer of ice there may have been was immediately broken.

He was in an ebullient mood. Rockhopper had been drilling one final well before the rig lifted its anchors and this stab at the seabed had struck oil. The company's shares had spiked overnight and, from Sam Moody's point of view, it was a perfect note on which to close this phase of exploration. Who would not be ebullient?

'What next for you and your company?' I asked.

'We need to take a step back. We have to carry out the appraisal work now to establish how big that discovery and the others may be. And we need to decide where to go from here.'

I said that I assumed the way he wanted to go would be towards production, which everyone had been telling me was at least five years away. How optimistic was he that tankers would be filling up with that viscous crude by around 2016? 'We are as confident as it is humanly possible to be that this will be commercialized. It's important to understand that there are risks remaining, but we are as confident as we can be that this is a commercially viable discovery.'

Sam made it clear, though, that it may not be his company alone that takes production forward. Rockhopper may not even be involved. While his technicians were set to spend the coming months assessing the value of their finds, he would be considering how to raise the billions of pounds that would be needed to get the oil flowing. 'That means we could bring in another oil company as a partner; we could sell all or part of the asset, and Rockhopper could stay in existence; or we could sell the entire company. All of those are being considered at the moment. We could get a partner or be taken over very, very quickly indeed. It could happen next week.'

Raising money is something that Sam Moody is good at. He had started Rockhopper Exploration in 2004 with no experience of the oil industry, and went to the markets several times with a sales pitch that seemed insanely frank. He said he was looking for a resource that may not exist, in a politically disputed part of the world. Nevertheless, he raised between $450 million and $500 million, which had sustained the drilling programme throughout. But it would cost billions rather than millions of dollars to move on and make the finds commercial.

Sam Moody was not critical of anything about the Falklands. The Islanders' 'can-do' attitude had made them a joy to work with. The infrastructure had been more than adequate, and would probably still be good enough to sustain an offshore production terminal five or six years hence. He was indeed a happy man.

My last question was about the spectre of Argentina and Mrs Kirchner's policy to scupper oil exploration. I guessed that the Foreign Office and the Falklands Government had primed him on the best way to answer questions like that, which was, essentially, to say nothing. 'I'm not a political expert,' he said in an apologetic tone. 'You'll need to go the Foreign Office or the Falklands Government.'

I felt a little sorry for dampening Sam's enthusiasm with the wet rag of Argentina. But I knew the answer anyway. He was not going to be put off by threats and posturing in Buenos Aires. Mrs Kirchner would have to come up with some very much more serious threats, and probably some action, if she wanted the oil explorers to stop and think. Of course it was possible that she might do that.

CHAPTER 8

The Conservation Conundrum

To understand the Falklands' importance in the world, you have to accept one truth. Globally, almost no one cares about the people and the real estate. Well, no one other than Falkland Islanders and Argentines. But even Argentine passion for the Malvinas is something of a myth. When you ask ordinary Argentines to rate the importance of 'recovering' the Islands against issues such as the economy, education, medical care and the state of the national football team, the Falklands always comes out towards the bottom of the list. No, the cruel truth is that, as far as most of the world is concerned, events in the Central African Republic are a great deal more important.

However, among conservationists, birdwatchers, trout fishermen and lovers of lichens, the Falklands are near the top of the list of the world's most important places. For these special groups, the Falklands have a global importance far beyond their strategic location and potential for wealth. These Islands are among the two or three most important havens for flora and fauna in the southern hemisphere.

This is Planet Penguin, Seal Central and Killer Whale Corner. The spectacular species that live here, at least in the summer months, do so because a cold ocean, rich in fish, surrounds them. The lichens? They don't eat fish, but they do thrive in the pollution-free atmosphere.

Four species of penguins call the Falklands home, and two-thirds of the world's population of black-browed albatross return here from the ocean every summer to renew their vows with lifetime partners, then mate and raise their babies. These huge birds nest happily among squabbling rockhopper penguins and king cormorants to form pungent-smelling black and white colonies that may extend a mile or more along the rocky western shores of the archipelago.

These are the famous stars of the show, but there are impressive support acts as well. The Islands host what is thought to be the rarest raptor in the world, an absurdly bold bird called the johnny rook. These beefy birds are charming in an Artful Dodgerish kind of way. They will happily swagger into the middle of your picnic, separate the fish paste sandwiches from the Marmite ones and consume the former, before unwrapping a Kit-Kat and then retreating a few metres for a post-prandial snooze. They are partial to newly-born lambs also, which is why the johnny rook population is now down to fewer than 1,000 breeding pairs. They would probably be extinct, however, had they not been beaten back from the lambing grounds and found some safety from shotguns on the more outlying islands.

My Aunt Agnes, who died a few years ago, lived for many years on the very remote New Island. One very hot day while riding alone far from the farmhouse, she stripped off and went for a quick swim. Aunt Agnes had, however, been under observation by marauding johnny rooks, and while she was frolicking in the waves they stole her clothes.

These days, johnny rooks and most other creatures are protected by law. Local people are realizing that their wildlife is extremely attractive to an increasing number of tourists, who visit the Islands by cruise ship. The conservation movement is building in strength.

The government itself has a reasonable record for looking after wildlife. Seal hunting was regulated and controlled in the early part of the last century, and hunting was eventually banned outright. The government, which until the 1980s administered South Georgia and other sub-Antarctic islands, brought whaling under similar controls. Legislation creating nature reserves and nature sanctuaries appeared on the statute book in the 1960s, and more recently, national park legislation has been introduced (although I had heard concerns expressed that such status might be little more than a tourism marketing device).

But I saw little evidence that the principles of conservation had ever taken absolute precedence over commerce. True, controls over whaling many years ago had slowed the depletion of stocks so that the industry could continue for longer than it might have done otherwise, but the last whaling station in South Georgia only closed in 1966 because stocks of the blue, fin, sperm and other leviathans had become so low that the industry was no longer viable.

Sheep farming had continued in nature conservation areas, even though the animals chew vegetation to soil level, including the natural tussock grass that is a habitat for small birds. Johnny rooks are protected by law but their cousins, the beautiful but rather dimmer caranchos, can still be shot if a local concentration is considered a menace to sheep.

So it seemed to me that conservation policy might look a little better than it really was, and I worried that claims that an eventual oil industry would pose only a minimal risk amounted to spin. Such was the enthusiasm for oil that I doubted that the interests of wildlife and habitat would be allowed to stop its development.

I needed the opinion – perhaps not an entirely objective one – of the Falklands' longest serving and by far best-known conservationist, Ian Strange. This Englishman came to the Falklands in the 1950s, rather ironically considering his love of wild creatures, to establish a mink farm. I recall visiting the farm as a little boy with my father and being fascinated and rather saddened by these furry little creatures who were soon to be killed and exported to the furriers of Italy and France; this despite the fact that one mink had a serious attempt at biting my finger off.

Happily, the mink farm failed, but Ian remained, and became an early champion of conservation. With Roddy Napier, who was similarly keen on conservation, Ian went on to buy New Island off my Uncle Jack and Aunt Agnes. Eventually Roddy left the project but Ian created a foundation to promote academic study of the island and to protect it in perpetuity. I admired him for his stewardship of the island

and for being – almost literally – a voice in the wilderness for so long.

I rang his house in Stanley, which is a modernist glass-fronted wooden structure overlooking Stanley Harbour that he had built himself. I spoke to Maria, his charming Argentine wife. She told me that Ian was on New Island. No doubt I would have been welcomed there if I had chosen to visit, and I would have loved to do so. But the island is almost 100 miles from Stanley, an hour's flight in the light aircraft of the little local air taxi service, FIGAS. And in any case, the airstrip there is very short and rough. New Island has form in bending aircraft, so pilots had stopped going there except in cases of extreme need, such as medical evacuations. I might be able to get a free flight aboard a military helicopter, but considering that I seemed to be in bad odour at Mount Pleasant, this line of begging did not seem to be worth pursuing. So I rang Ian at New Island.

An apparently startled voice answered the phone. 'Hello?' It sounded as if he was responding to a voice coming from his washing machine. I imagined him detached and deeply engrossed in his latest writing or his meticulously detailed bird paintings.

Ian is actually one of the most intelligent, practical and – in the right circumstances – gregarious people I know, but he sometimes projects an image of dottiness. We had known each other for many years. I respected his work, both artistic and scientific.

I told him what I was doing and that I wanted his opinion about the oil industry. 'I'd be happy to talk to you about that, Graham. But I don't know if I'll be reflecting the official line.'

I assured him that was fine. Ian is generally seen as a lone operator, though by no means an outcast, but he speaks with authority. He can hit his chosen targets hard with bitingly critical comments if necessary. I gently tried to establish how old he was these days, but got nowhere. Ian sighed and emitted a low ironic chuckle. 'Well, Graham, that's somewhere I never go. I don't understand the meaning of the word retirement.'

And yet, he had acknowledged the need to slow down a little and share his workload. He is now in creative partnership with his daughter, Georgina, a trained and very accomplished wildlife photographer. They write, illustrate and publish their own books about the flora and fauna of the Islands, and Georgina is gradually taking over Ian's management role on the island.

Ian had been listening to the talk about oil and keeping an eye on the occasional developments, which led to the first drilling in the late 1990s. He even took himself off to Newfoundland to attend an oil management course, hoping to learn more about the risks the industry presented and what might be done to minimize them. The Eastern Canadian industry had clear parallels with what was being planned for the Falklands; it had a small, thinly distributed rural population, significant wildlife and natural habitat, and offshore drilling.

He shared his knowledge of risk with the Falklands Government for many years, but now seemed disillusioned with such work. He had left the official Environmental Advisory Board two years earlier, wondering what practical use such bodies had. 'I was finding that there was so much concentration on paperwork, and the practical side of conservation did not come into it,' he said. 'We have a new breed of very enthusiastic conservationists, which is good, but really they are about no more than putting things on paper that have no substance, and which, if we really had a problem, would be pretty worthless.

'I don't have a feeling of foreboding about a major catastrophe,' he stressed. But he believed that an event like the Gulf of Mexico disaster was at least possible. And if such a terrible thing did happen, no one could be sure that the industry and the Falklands Government were correct in their assessment that a spill to the north of the Falklands, where Rockhopper had struck oil, would, most probably, be driven away from land by the northerly currents and dispersed by the strong westerly winds. He did not know if Falklands sea birds routinely hunted for food in the area, but that was likely, and if so, they could be devastated.

Ian was more worried about the risks posed by drilling in the potential oil fields south and south-east of the Islands, where exploration was about to begin. From there, currents might carry spilled oil to the southern coasts of the Falklands, and possibly to his beloved New Island. It would probably be necessary to deploy dispersal spraying aircraft, containment booms and mopping up equipment in very short order. 'I understand that could be a very expensive operation,' said Ian. 'And there is nothing in place in the Falklands with which to clean up a mess.'

I said that Rockhopper Exploration's Ken Humphrey had told me that if anything went so disastrously wrong, then equipment to deal with the incident would be shipped immediately from Scotland and the south coast of England.

'Hmm,' said Ian. 'I just wonder if we are not a little more isolated than the average oil production field.'

The doyen of South Atlantic conservation does not believe that the threat of oil comes only from the companies who wish to extract it. 'I think the industry generally has improved dramatically, but you are going to need a very very strong government here to say "no" to certain things that the oil people might come up with.'

So did he think the authorities had a stiff enough backbone? 'We have some good people, like Phyl Rendell,' said Ian. 'But of course, she answers to the council and a higher administration.' He would not be drawn much further, but the implied message was that greed could overcome caution.

The New Island Conservation Trust is not the only such organization in the Islands. Falklands Conservation is a much bigger body, and has a much closer relationship with the Falklands Government. Ian even suggested, rather ominously, that this was an unhealthily close one, and he doubted if it would act as a useful check or balance. 'They do some good work,' he said. 'The kind of things that we wouldn't want to do. But they get a huge amount of money from the government – some £65,000 annually – to keep them going. I think an organization that is seen to be helping the government politically is likely to get more support than we do.'

If Ian Strange was right, then the conservation lobby was not going to put much of a break on an oil rush. His own New Island Conservation Trust was effective in the limited work that it chose to do, but it was not big enough to influence either the government or the oil industry. Furthermore, it did not seem likely that the two groups would join forces, regardless of how well meaning they may both be.

I thanked Ian for his candid observations, and told him that I would much rather be interviewing him in person overlooking the spectacular black-browed albatross colonies of New Island. I meant it too. I had visited Uncle Jack and Aunt Agnes's island as a child and as a young man. I have travelled much of the world since, but have rarely seen a place to equal its beauty.

The little expedition cruise ship MS *Lindblad Explorer* now lies at the bottom of the sea somewhere off the Antarctic Peninsula. She emitted little if any pollution as she went down, and all of the passengers were rescued from their open boats. Her owners said that it seemed appropriate that she would now create a permanent home for creatures of the sea. That spirit of respect for nature and conservation was the driving force behind the highly specialist tourism operation of Lars Eric Lindblad, the Swedish-American travel pioneer who had the ship built to his personal specifications and took it where few, if any, tourist vessels had gone before.

It was almost inevitable that the spirited little ship that put both the Falklands and the Antarctic on the cruising map would one day have a disastrous encounter with ice. By the time a gap was torn in her side and the pumps failed, she was old and in poor shape. But in her youth the *Explorer* had been a temporary floating home to both ordinary (if wealthy) tourists and famous people from the worlds of high latitude and high altitude exploration and nature conservation. I remember visiting the ship in Stanley and meeting Norgay Tensing, the man who, with Sir Edmund Hillary, was first to the summit of Everest. Heroes like Tensing thrilled their fellow passengers with stories of their glory days.

One evening in 1979, a small group of tourists and adventurers was gathered in the *Explorer's* cosy lounge, no doubt attended by the young Swedish stewardesses who never failed to turn heads. Among them was Sir Peter Scott, the son of Britain's great Antarctic hero, Robert Falcon Scott, and an eminent conservationist, wildlife painter and sailor in his own right. Sir Peter had already founded the Wildfowl Trust at Slimbridge on the Severn Estuary. Now, inspired, by the wildlife and habitat he had seen in the Falklands, he suggested that a similar body should be created to care for the wildlife here. The constitution was roughed up that very evening, and Sir Peter even drew the tiny vulnerable-looking rockhopper penguin that was to become the logo of the new organization.

Thirty-one years on, Falklands Conservation was thriving, albeit in a rather odd multi-purpose form, that its Chief Executive Officer, James Fenton, describes thus: 'We are a government agency, we are a non-governmental organization and we do research.' In the UK, where there are universities, trusts and government agencies, each of these functions would be addressed by different organizations; ones that are better tailored to the tasks. But, as James pointed out when he met me in his office, everyone in the Falklands must multi-task, even conservation organizations.

Falklands Conservation is, nominally at least, based in one of Stanley's most notable buildings, the terrace of typical British Victorian houses known as the Jubilee Villas. I say 'nominally' because most of the organization's membership is in the UK, and its board of trustees is mainly there.

James took some time off from what appeared to be tedious budget planning to talk to me. He has a relaxed manner and an easy laugh that appealed to me. Bearded and wiry of frame (as I felt a classic conservationist should be), this botanist had first come to the Falklands in the early 1970s, en route for a spell in the ice with the British Antarctic Survey. Since then, he had lived much of his life in Scotland.

I put to James Ian Strange's fear that Falklands Conservation's principles could be compromised by its proximity to the Falkland Islands Government. Would the organization not think twice or thrice before opposing economic and industrial plans, if they could endanger the £65,000 subsidy (which James described as a 'subvention')? A cheeky johnny rook might get away with biting the hand that fed it, but would 'Conservation' (as Falkland Islanders tended to call the body) be able to do so?

He thought for a few seconds, then said: 'No, it isn't in that position. But Falklands Conservation has to live in the community. If we just come out and say we are opposed to oil exploration I think we would not get any sympathy, have any credibility or be very effective.'

I asked him if, nevertheless, he worried about the oil industry's possible impact. 'I suppose I'm pragmatic. In the best of all possible worlds you would leave it in the ground. But oil is a commodity that's necessary. My fears are of a major oil spill. But it wouldn't be so disastrous, as the oil would be offshore, and if you look at it objectively and scientifically, then the risks are low. You can be emotional about it and say there will be a huge disaster and we will lose thousands of albatrosses and penguins, but that is statistically very unlikely because of where the oil is being drilled.'

Pragmatism appeared to mean that Conservation is on friendly terms with the industry. 'It's not as if the oil companies want to kill penguins,' explained James. He was undoubtedly right, both in terms of costly clean-ups and in terms of public relations. In any case, short of David Attenborough, I could hardly think of a less likely penguin murderer than Ken Humphrey, who was, as it happened, active in Conservation's youth education programme.

James repeated Ian's contention that north of the Falklands, prevailing tides and winds would tend to take any spilled crude north and east into the wide-open ocean, and the frequently rough seas would break it down quickly. This did not, however, answer Ian's point about the different and more worrying risks that would be posed by exploitation to the south and south-east of the Islands, where weather and currents would be more likely to carry oil towards the Falklands coast.

James' main concern was about the increased shipping traffic, especially tankers, that would have to navigate around the Islands. If one of them ran aground and spilled its load, especially during the summer seabird breeding season, then the disaster could be very serious indeed. That risk, it appeared to him, was only too real, and I was glad he had raised it. I wondered if the grounded-ship scenario was being eclipsed in popular conversation by the highly emotive, and yet relatively easily dismissed, imagery of Gulf of Mexico-type oil spills.

Falklands Conservation is, James insisted, consulted by the government regularly and offers its advice. That is how it earns its 'subvention'. The amount of time that he and his colleagues spent examining government papers, impact assessments, strategies and draft legislation was burdensome, but involvement was worthwhile, as it enabled them to influence government decisions.

Not for the first time, I heard someone comparing the Falklands with the North Sea. James pointed out that exploitation in that area had been going on for some fifty years with few environmental consequences. Yes, he admitted, there had been the notorious Piper Alpha incident, but that had been mainly a human rather than environmental disaster. And a tanker had been driven up on the Shetlands in the 1990s, resulting in a major spill. There had been a lesser incident recently. But in historical and, particularly, geological terms, these periods of intense industrial activity were brief. 'Fifty years, and it will be gone,' said James. 'That's a small blip in the great scheme of things.'

His daughter, a diver on her way south to work with the British Antarctic Survey, just as James had done some four decades earlier, was arriving on the airbridge that day, and he was looking forward to taking a few days off to enjoy with her. I thanked James, and wished him a happy break.

As I left, I wondered what a third generation of the Fenton family might find if he or she came to the Falklands forty years from now. Would it still be a wilderness home to a panoply of thriving and remarkable wildlife? Or would it have changed for the worse, still bearing the scars of a disaster that had overtaken it in the 2020s or 2030s? It seemed to me that a lot could happen in that mere 'blip' in Earth-time. I wanted to share James Fenton's optimism but was not convinced that I could.

CHAPTER 9

Dallas in the South Atlantic

S ummer holidays seemed almost endless when I was a child living in Stanley. Such days are supposed to be the happiest of one's life, and, in my case, they were. Even the notoriously volatile Falklands climate seemed to be predominantly warm, dry and little more than breezy in those days between December and March. Now, when I return home to the Islands after a long time abroad, I prepare for temperatures ranging from zero to 23 degrees centigrade, for horizontal rain and for winds that can – and do – rip the doors off Land Rovers. And that is just the summer.

Such trifles as the weather did not worry us as children. Outdoors was the place to be, fishing, and tramping across the white-grass countryside, or beach combing. The most halcyon times of all – although I feel sure that my memory exaggerates the number of occasions that we actually did this – were trips in my Uncle Jack Sollis's boat, the *Silver Spray*. We would load the boat full of food and fishing equipment and the throbbing diesel would then motor us out of Stanley Harbour and up the river Murrell.

Ostensibly, we were targeting mullet and trout, but I didn't care in the slightest whether we caught any. Life could not be any better than it was then, in the company of Uncle Jack, my father, his best friend Joe King, my brother Michael, and Joe's sons Peter and Robert.

We would take it in turns at the controls of the former Thames police launch, and Jack would keep a weather eye on what we were doing, stretching a sailor's tattooed arm over our shoulder every now and again to adjust the wheel a degree or two. Jack's day job was skippering the inter-island cargo steamer *Forrest*, and he knew these waters intimately. Unfortunately, our *Silver Spray* adventures ended after a few summers after we ran the boat aground. In all probability one of us lads was at the controls. In any case, Auntie Maud, from whom Jack received his orders, suddenly found many more jobs around the house and garden for Jack to do, and our trips became rarer before petering out altogether.

The next best thing was beach combing and conquering the hills around Stanley. For a couple of summers, my constant companion was Lewis Clifton. As 10- and 11-year-olds respectively, we enjoyed long Huck Finn-like days, leaving home early in the morning, probably dropping by Fred Coleman's little grocery store to buy cans of beans and some pop, then heading east down the length of the harbour to investigate the wrecks of the old sealing patrol vessel *Afterglow*, the rusting tugboats *Samson* and *Plym*, or the majestic hulk of the windjammer *Lady Elizabeth*, which had limped back to the Falklands sometime in the 1930s after a crippling encounter with Cape Horn.

En route, we would often have a poke around the municipal rubbish dump, checking out the old cars and sometimes digging in the ashes from a thousand peat-fired kitchen ranges to find nineteenth-century round-bottomed bottles and salt-glazed storage jars. Canvas baseball boots were fashionable among little boys at the time, and I recall being told off (very lightly) by my mother after one day out because battery acid from a wrecked car that we had been exploring had eaten through my shoes and left the rubber soles flapping loosely. The legs of my jeans had also developed myriad holes.

At that time, my most treasured possession was a Mamod steam engine. It was a beautifully engineered model, a birthday present that my parents had ordered from the UK. It was a static device, which, nevertheless, fascinated both Lewis and me. We went through gallons of purple methylated spirits fuelling the external combustion engine. The water in the boiler would slowly heat up, until one of us gave the hot little piston a gentle shove, and it burst into frantic, pounding life, shaking its way across the workbench in the garden shed. When I went off to school in Uruguay, and Lewis stayed in Stanley, he took the precious machine into care, and when I returned he gave it back to me. The steel base, once scorched by the spirits, was painted, and the brass boiler shone with polish. As I write, I am looking at the same little steam engine. It resides on the windowsill above my desk. The solder around the piston has broken, and it needs more care than it receives. But it still evokes those happy memories of a carefree and adventurous childhood.

Our lives went in different directions, but Lewis and I still met from time to time. When I was seriously ill in Britain, he rang me from the Falklands. The simple act of picking up the phone said a lot to me. Lewis had done amazingly well for himself. After running the Falklands Philatelic Bureau, which marketed revenue-earning stamps around the world, he established and ran the Falkland Islands Government office – a de facto high commission – in London. He then spent years as an elected member of the Legislative and Executive Councils, was awarded an OBE, and then left government service to launch one of the Islands' most successful companies, Byron Marine Ltd. Initially the company owned and ran a small ship that carried freight and a few passengers around the Islands, and ran monthly between Stanley and Chile. These were happier days, when Argentina allowed interaction with South America.

In due course, Byron also acquired two fisheries patrol ships and operated them on contracts to the government. The shipping business had taken a hit recently, thanks to increasing competition, but Byron Marine still owned one ocean-going vessel, the *Pharos*, which was patrolling around South Georgia, some 800 miles south-east of Stanley.

Along with a few other local entrepreneurs, Lewis had taken some major risks, most of which had succeeded, and he was now undoubtedly wealthy, at least in terms of assets. With other business people, he had usurped the monopolies of the Falkland Islands Company and a few other British corporations that had operated, largely unopposed, for generations. Their corrosive business model had been to extract all profits to the UK for the benefit of shareholders who rarely or never visited the Falklands, and seldom or never reinvested in the Islands. Now money generally remained in the Falklands.

The advent of oil exploration had presented my old friend and his partners with a new opportunity, one that had the potential to expand their business exponentially. Drilling operations offshore required an extensive and reliable logistical base on shore and servicing facilities for the specialist support ships. Seeing this need on the horizon, Lewis joined forces with another local entrepreneur, Neil McKay (who was also a friend, but less well known to me as a child), to form Byron McKay Ltd. They pursued the opportunity with daring and total commitment.

Byron Marine and Neil McKay shared stock in the joint venture fifty-fifty. Byron would fund and provide the laydown area, the warehouses, offices, security and other services, while Neil would provide the cranes, trucks, forklifts and the men and women to do the work.

Neil was another unique individual. As a teenager in the late 1970s, he had learned to drive bulldozers, scrapers, graders and cranes used to build Stanley Airport. He also learned to maintain the equipment, and when the airport contract was complete, he bought many of the machines to begin his own construction and plant rental outfit. He then gained the contract to run Stanley's floating port, a supposedly temporary facility that had been put in place by the Ministry of Defence in the immediate aftermath of the 1982 conflict. By rights it should have been towed out to sea and sunk years earlier, to be replaced by a permanent deep-water port, but the dock was still providing sterling service in 2011.

Only a decade or two earlier, it would have been preposterous to think that local businesses would be able to supply such a specialist and vastly expensive service. The Falkland Islands Company might have been a contender, but an international company would have been much more likely to secure the contract, bringing its manpower into the Falklands and benefiting the local economy very little. But here were local men thinking very big, raising and committing major amounts of money to build the laydown areas and the warehouses and recruit the work forces from the local community. It was nothing short of remarkable.

I had driven past the depot to the east of Stanley and marvelled at the extent of the yards, the warehouses, the 20 foot-high stacks of drilling pipes and the orange silos 100 feet or so high that contained the liquid mud and cement required for drilling. I had to see more and learn how on earth these guys had been able to do it. So I rang Lewis and he immediately invited me to talk and look over the yards with him.

Neil and Lewis looked about as happy as it was possible for businessmen to be. Probably happier. They had worked punishing hours with barely a break for two years, all the time knowing that they were pushing at the limits of what was possible for a Falklands business. And with the first round of successful drilling north of the Falklands about to end and another, south of the Islands, about to begin, this was no time to take it easy. It was, however, reasonable to be very chuffed about what they had done.

I said that I wanted to get a good photo of the depot, ideally with them in it, but was not sure how to set about it. The facility was vast. Neil's smile broadened further. 'How about an aerial shot?' I said that would be perfect, but as far as I knew they did not have a helicopter (yet). 'No problem. I'll give you a lift in that crane.' He gestured to an eight-wheeled monster, with a telescoped boom that I imagined might extend into the clouds. I have never been comfortable with heights, but he was right; if he could haul me aloft in the crane's bucket, the entire picture of Byron McKay's enterprise would be spread out beneath me.

I enjoyed an unlikely white-knuckle ride. The wind whistled around me and swayed the bucket backwards and forwards. I peered over the edge, ensuring that my camera was securely attached to my neck, and shouted at Neil to vacate the cab and join Lewis near one of the silos. I clicked the shutter several times, and then waved the thumb's-up sign. Neil shouted that they were off for a coffee and they would see me later. Lewis guffawed enormously, reminding me how his laugh would fill the Parish Hall cinema when we were kids, kicking off general hysteria at the antics of Norman Wisdom or Peter Sellers.

Ten minutes later we were all having coffee. Neil gulped his and rushed off. He was expecting some urgently needed spare parts for a large item of plant. I asked Lewis the obvious question: how much had all of this cost? His answer stunned me. 'I don't think it would be unreasonable to say that, between both companies, Byron and Neil McKay, there has been capital expenditure in the order of £8 million.'

It had to have cost a lot. But eight million pounds sterling? This was a remarkable figure. Stanley Airport had cost the British taxpayer only about £3 million in the late 1970s. In the early 1980s, the entire Falklands Government annual budget amount to about £8 million. Today, the entire profit from the wool industry, the product for which the Falklands were still most famous internationally, was probably worth less than £4 million. I asked how on earth they had raised this kind of money. Clearly, both Neil and Lewis were already highly successful and had money tucked away, but still ... eight million pounds!

Good businessmen and good journalists do not easily reveal their sources, and Lewis was good. He hesitated and smiled a little enigmatically. 'Come on, how did you get the money?' I insisted.

'Just by being fiscally prudent,' he replied. 'Having a little money in the bank and being able to make that work for us. We haven't had to go into big debt but each of us will be left with debt at the end of the current drilling campaign.'

Byron McKay surely had to be looking at a bottom line worth millions. But, if they were to be believed, and I had never doubted Lewis, they were planning long-term rather than going for a quick, very large, profit. 'No,' said Lewis. 'We are not going to make millions out of this. It is all about having a reasonable return so that we can make the investment into the facilities or into buying the plant to make it work. For example, buying a 100-ton crane means fronting up £600,000. And you need several of them.'

So did it all make sense – the investment, the stress, the gamble?

'Yes, it's made sense to this point, although it has been very risky, and I sit here most days with a bit of a twitch. And I probably twitch a bit in bed at night as well. But it has worked well.'

The risks had commenced well before the 2010/11 exploration round, when Byron McKay had to prime their initiative with real money and effort. At that point, they looked back on the 1999 exploration phase, which had offered local businesses very little, and they scoped the opportunities that would exist if the oil men came back. They travelled to the Gulf of Mexico to learn about the latest developments in the offshore oil industry and its onshore support needs. 'We felt that the moment was going to come, irrespective of all the political crap coming from Argentina, and even from the British Foreign Office, which was saying "calm down and take it easy"; all the nonsense that we've heard here for decades about anything that would prove of economic advantage to the Falklands.

'In September 2009, Desire announced they were going to drill in the North Falklands Basin, and we decided to take a chance on purchasing modular warehouses and offices. We bid for the support contract in late September 2009, and we got the nod on 9 November to start constructing a logistics base. We had to have that functional by the middle of January. It was a huge amount of work.'

If that tight deadline had not been enough to cause some twitching, the projected lifespan of the drilling campaign would. It was expected to be brief. Desire Petroleum and Rockhopper Exploration would each drill four wells, and each would be completed within twenty days. Allowing for preparation time, movement of the rig between sites and unforeseen delays, the rig would be in place for about four months. That could mean that Byron McKay Ltd would have invested a huge amount of cash for a business that would be gone very quickly indeed. But into this scenario, it was necessary to factor some justifiable optimism. Lewis explained: 'We pretty much all thought that someone had to find something there, because the data from seismic survey work was so much better than it had been during the first round in the late 1990s. We were taking a punt on the fact that if oil was found it would lead to more drilling. And, in fact, Rockhopper came in good, and the campaign has since spiralled into much more. We have now had eighteen months of activity in the northern basin and in February more drilling will start to the south.'

The anticipated next phase had required more building work and more investment. The depot now covers 17,200 square metres, including a new section that had to be functioning by the time the deep water rig *Leiv Eriksson* completed its long journey from Greenland.

Lewis insists that this local effort is about more than mere profit. A contractor from the UK, such as that which had supported the 1999 drilling campaign, would have imported its labour and returned its profits to Britain, save perhaps for a skimming of tax. 'We want funds to reticulate through the community,' Lewis said. (This was a new word to me, but later, when I had looked it up, I found that it was almost perfect. Reticulation is the process by which nutrients pass through the veins of a plant, nurturing and developing growth.)

There was another reason behind the drive. It was about national pride; about proving that Islanders had reached a point in their history at which they could play, and win, in the big world beyond their shores. 'If you don't do that, then nationhood and all that goes with it disappears,' said Lewis.

Lewis's brother Stephen, who is also a director of Byron, had been supervising local builders, electrical contractors and truckers, 'a whole range of folks', as Lewis put it. 'All labour has been sourced in the Falklands. We were keen to prove that there is capability within the private sector in the Falklands, and that it is hungry for capacity building.'

I appreciated the just principle of keeping money in the community, but still, I could not quite understand what had driven Lewis and his colleagues to jump into such deep industrial and financial waters. 'Well,' said Lewis, 'like you, I'm on the wrong side of fifty, and that opportunity might not have come by again. I didn't want us to be treated as local folks were when the fishing industry arrived here in the 1980s. I didn't want to be patronized and just be picking up the scraps, or for foreign companies to be using us just because they had to. You can be an agent for this or that for your entire life, but now there is the finance we need to take such big steps.'

So far, so good, I thought. The fledgling oil industry was going very much to plan, with amazing local involvement. But what about the 'Argentine political crap' that Lewis had mentioned? Drilling in the North Falkland Basin, and soon in the southern basin, could have been designed to provoke fury in Buenos Aires. It was probably the main reason why Mrs Kirchner's rhetoric and actions were being ratcheted up. Was the oil industry really not under threat from across the water?

So far during my time in the Falklands, I had heard defiant talk, sometimes almost inviting Argentina to do its worst. It did not always seem rational. The Milwall Football Club mantra, 'Everybody hates us, we don't care', seemed to find sympathy in the Falklands. Lewis was as determined as anyone here not to give in to the Argentine efforts to strangle the Falklands economy with a shipping blockade that involved Chile, Uruguay and Brazil. But he did not take the threat lightly. 'Yes, that has created some difficulty,' he said. 'We have been able to get around it, but quite how much longer we and others will be able to do so is ….'' He did not complete the sentence, but his meaning was obvious.

He would rather have seen Néstor and Cristina Kirchner honouring the pragmatic agreements their predecessors had reached with Britain over oil and fishing in 1999. He had been one of the councillors involved in negotiating those agreements and believed that the Kirchners had made a great mistake by ripping them up. The action was, Lewis said, 'Complete and utter nonsense, almost at the gutter level.'

Lewis agreed that it was a real, sustained and dangerous offensive. 'I think things are going to get a little tougher too,' he said. 'But on the other hand, how much tougher can they really get? We're seeing the true colours of Kirchnerism or Peronism, call it what you will. It's doing the Argentines no good in terms of the Falklands dispute. I can't see how, in my lifetime, they are going to make any kind of comeback from that.'

Buenos Aires undoubtedly saw oil exploration not just as a threat, but also as an opportunity. The government was threatening to penalize companies that were involved in both Argentina and the Falklands. 'I can't imagine any oil operators or contractors will find an easy ride in Argentina if they also have business in the Falklands,' said Lewis. 'So it makes sense for us to find those businesses that are not involved there, and get them in here pretty damn quick.'

Lewis was not sanguine. 'As the days creep on,' he said, 'Argentina seems to be cutting off its nose to spite its face. It doesn't seem to care. Argentine politics are very populist but they are not caring. So those difficulties will continue. We can work around them to a degree. But it is getting more difficult and complex to do proper business as you would anywhere else in the world.'

Like many other Islanders whom I interviewed, he referred to the relationship with Argentina as a cold war and valued the deterrent based 35 miles away at Mount Pleasant, and the diplomatic efforts of the British Foreign Office – although the former much more than the latter. 'The UK has said it will promote our interests in foreign affairs and defence,' he said. 'I feel reasonably comfortable with that.' He gestured in the approximate direction of Mount Pleasant. 'There is real commitment out there. A squadron of Typhoon fighters sends a very good signal. But I don't believe the British Government is able to counter the constant pumping of Argentine propaganda and untruths, and certainly the Falklands Government is not able to do much about it. I would not disagree that there is some quiet work going on behind the scenes, but I would always be slightly wary of relying on the Foreign Office.'

But then he brightened up. We were suddenly back from the gloomy crystal ball gazing of diplomacy and defence. Oil, said Lewis, may help the Islands other than just financially. 'It is there, and I wouldn't have got involved in the present round of exploration if I did not hold the view that oil will deliver long-term economic and political security for the Falklands. We don't yet know what proportion of revenue the British Government will wish to have, but it would be wise to let them have a good share, as this will secure their ongoing support for us.'

Lewis, it seemed to me, had a very good point. At a time when economists and politicians were predicting a decade of economic suffering, would London want to give away another North Sea, at least as long as there was oil to suck from it? Surely it would take remarkably stupid Foreign Office diplomacy to do such a thing.

I was proud of what these men, my friends and fellow Islanders, had achieved. I hope they knew that. I remembered Nicholas Ridley, a minister in Margaret Thatcher's government before 1982, who had visited the Falklands and managed to insult almost every Islander by saying they were 'supine'. Falkland Islanders could no longer be accused of that.

CHAPTER 10

Locals at the Controls

Nigel Haywood, the Governor, had expressed some admiration for the elected Member of the Legislative Assembly when I spoke to him over that very pleasant brew of tea in Government House. He seemed impressed by the workload and the diversity of the duties they accept, to which could be added rotating responsibilities on his own Executive Council. Like many people, he found it faintly amusing, but admirable, that the unpaid community leaders could, almost simultaneously, be considering the future of the public toilets on Stanley's main drag, and a strategy for a sovereign wealth fund that might one day vie with Kuwait to buy Harrods.

In fact, Members of the Legislative Assembly (MLAs, as they are more succinctly known) had not always concerned themselves with public plumbing and the like. Back in the 1960s, there had been a Stanley Town Council that looked after the itty-bitty things that made the town work – or, as it happened, increasingly not work, as the community became smaller, the economy shrank and Britain cared less about its colony. Eventually, the Town Council was wound up and its duties were assumed by the bigger Legislative and Executive Councils. Under their care, and recently under the new Legislative Assembly, the capital began to be tidied up, painted and fixed, becoming a more pleasant place in which to live or to visit.

This sprucing up of Stanley had struck me as significant. Along the mile or so of seafront and to a lesser extent on the roads two, three and four blocks behind the front road, the vista was undeniably pretty. The main street was clear of the potholes that had cursed it for years, and car parks had been built and were filled with expensive new, or newish, Japanese 4x4 vehicles and Land Rovers. Victory Green, with its canons and saluting guns facing north, was manicured and lush (although a tourist had, I was told, recently complained about the amount of upland goose droppings on the green).

The Harbour View, Capstan and Boat House gift shops, along with the Falkland Islands Company's West Store supermarket, were immaculate and inviting with their penguin souvenirs, penguin motif clothes, penguin mugs and ... well, penguin just about everything.

Giving the seafront some much-needed gravitas was Christ Church Cathedral, the Anglican centre of worship for the South Atlantic, which had also been given a facelift recently. It is a slightly stumpy construction, with a wriggly-tin roof, but its stained glass windows, oak doors and fine masonry walls are impressive. Within lie icons that are not so much religious as historical. A battle flag flown by British ships defeated off the Chilean coast at Coronel in 1914 is suspended from one wall, as are the colours of the 2nd Battalion the Parachute Regiment, which fought at Goose Green in 1982. And there are plaques honouring the dead of pioneering land-owning families, such as the Deans and the Pitalugas. The cathedral's clock had recently been restored and after many years of silence the bells were now echoing across the town on the hour, every hour.

The jewel in the town's commercial and tourism crown is the Jetty Visitor Centre, an information bureau, shop and exhibition area at the head of the wharf where the tenders from the cruise ships berth and passengers pass through security for half a day or so in Planet Penguin.

All of this was, I thought, an indicator of increasing prosperity and a sign that life continues normally in the Falklands in spite of the Argentine cloud that now hangs more ominously than usual over the place. Buenos Aires had not yet secured a stranglehold, and Islanders would exercise the make-do spirit that, as many had reminded me, was the Falklands way.

I received that message loud and clear when I sat down with two Members of the Legislative Assembly at their office in Gilbert House. It is a weatherboard single-story building that dates back to the nineteenth century, and had been given a degree of dignity through immaculate external and internal decoration, and by the presence of the territory's flag, which on the day I visited, extended ramrod-straight in 25 knots or so of westerly wind. Less salubrious metal sheds and workshops in what had now – for the benefit of tourism, I assumed – been labelled the 'Historic Dockyard' surrounded Gilbert House.

Jan Cheek and Dick Sawle had responded positively and immediately to my request for a meeting (no Ministry of Defence reticence here), and it soon became apparent that they really wanted to talk to me about plans for progress, not plans to man the ramparts and repel Argentines.

Each MLA holds several government portfolios. They are not quite ministers, and the civil servants' chain of command is not to them, but to so-called Super Heads, most of whom are experienced functionaries appointed – controversially and at great expense – from Britain. But the MLAs control strategic planning and budgeting, take a close interest in the functioning of departments and sectors of the economy, and receive regular briefings. There is no doubt that they have real power.

I had known Dick for almost thirty years, and Jan for longer. Jan had trained as a teacher and only left the profession when her husband John died and she was required to take his place on the board of Fortuna, the highly successful company that John had founded with my cousin Stuart Wallace (of which, more later). Recently, Jan had sold her share in the company to Stuart, reputedly for millions. She had then bought Johnson Harbour Farm, a medium sized establishment north of Stanley that included – and many people were envious of this – the remarkable wildlife sanctuary at Volunteer Point. This is the only location in the Falklands where the supremely beautiful king penguins reside in large numbers.

Dick's career had much in common with Jan's. He had come to the Falklands shortly after the 1982 conflict to teach Spanish. He left teaching in the late 1980s and then, at the height of the fisheries boom, joined a local company in joint venture with foreign outfits. He went on to run his own successful fishing company, Polar, and then recently sold out, reputedly also making a very useful profit. He then became a virtually full-time MLA.

By way of an icebreaker, I commented to Dick and Jan that Stanley had scrubbed up rather well since I had last visited. With its colourful roofs and walls, it had always had the potential and, according to my, no doubt flawed, childhood memories, the town was very pretty in the 1960s. But since then lack of funds and decay always seemed to be winning the battle.

They were both clearly pleased to hear me say it, and implied that I had seen nothing yet. Come back in a few years, and Stanley would – with a bit of luck – have a second hotel, a new museum, and that Historic Dockyard would be a gleaming tourism showpiece.

Jan enlarged up on that theme. 'I think we have barely scratched the surface of tourism,' she enthused. 'There is terrific potential for wilderness-based travel: lodges, hiking, fishing and so on. But we desperately need a new hotel. There are plans to expand the Malvina but I believe there should be another one. Even before this round of oil exploration started, it was very hard to get a room at the Malvina.'

I recalled the famous Upland Goose Hotel, which I was sorry to see had been closed. It was an iconic and very well-built stone building, and in 1982 many Stanley people had sheltered from the shelling within it. I had been one of them. The Upland Goose then became famous when Max Hastings, who told the story of the war better than almost anyone else, was said to have 'liberated' the building, being the first war correspondent to enjoy a gin and tonic in its bar.

Jan was scathing of the hotel's most recent owners. They had, she said, been terrible managers, ensuring that service was poor, cleanliness was lacking and the food was terrible. When customers, understandably, began to favour the Malvina House Hotel, the owners closed the Goose and transformed it into flats. They failed to sell these to Islanders, who traditionally enjoyed houses with a quarter of an acre or so of land, but the flats were subsequently rented to the oil men. At least the transformation from hotel to block of flats had been done sympathetically, and the old building still added to the beauty of the seafront. Nevertheless, said Jan, 'It was very sad and very incompetent of them. Now we need another hotel.'

I asked, rather sceptically, if there was room for another establishment of reasonable size and quality in the town. It seemed to me that the town centre was running out of space. Dick was quick to respond in the affirmative, lifting up a copy of the Tourism Development Strategy. A core element of this, he said, was the development of Stanley's entire seafront area, starting with the Historic Dockyard and extending east to the Falkland Islands Company's jetty, which was, quite literally, built upon the beached wrecks of windjammers from the heyday of Cape Horn. A hotel site could be made available within the dockyard, or Stanley House, a brick and slate-roofed mansion that had once competed in stature with Government House, could probably be made available. It was currently serving as a school hostel for the children of farmers, but there was no reason why the children had to occupy such prime real estate.

So if an international hotel operator, say the Hilton Group or the Holiday Inn, wanted to come along and take advantage of both the oil and tourism industries, they would be welcome? 'Yes,' said Dick. 'There are big opportunities for the private sector, whether it is locals in joint venture with companies elsewhere, or whether it is companies elsewhere wanting to invest in the Falklands alone. That's all up for grabs.'

I was a little reluctant to raise the issue, but it was obvious that if tourism is to be developed beyond the slim Lan Chile service, which can bring in 100 or so people a week at best, and the cruise ship industry, which brings in more than 50,000 people a summer, but only for very short stays, then better communications are needed. Ideally, the Lan Chile service would be expanded to two, three or more flights a week, but Argentina seemed to be preparing to sever the air link completely.

'This forms part of our tourism development strategy,' said Dick. 'The strategy relies very heavily on being able to tap into the North American market, although that is not the single string to our blow.

Cruise ships would be able to change their passengers through Stanley and that would have a good financial spin-off.'

He then revealed a plan of such boldness that I wondered for a few seconds if it was a joke. The Tourist Board, the Development Corporation and the Assembly members were seeking to establish a direct air link between Miami and the Falklands, and they were in talks with airlines that might operate it. The link, probably initially a charter service for cruise ship passenger exchanges, but with sufficient spare seats to cater for Islanders needing to travel, would follow a route that took it away from Argentine airspace and therefore from their ability to threaten it.

Logical it may have been, but surely this was too bold. After all, the route would be very long, perhaps a ten-hour flight, and aircraft would have to be large enough to handle this. There could be no assumption that Brazil or Uruguay, under pressure from Buenos Aires, would permit routine refuelling stops on their territory, although countries to the north of the Mercosur cluster might do so.

'We've done a lot of work on that,' said Dick. 'It is coming along well, but it is rather like putting a jigsaw puzzle together. There is no point in improving the link if we don't have the infrastructure on land. We need things like hotels and lodges.'

I broached the issue of oil. I had heard much about the geology and the industry itself, I said. The Rockhopper Petroleum rep himself, the very amiable Ken Humphrey, had expressed concern about the possible social impact of the immense wealth that might flow from it within a few years. If he could see it, and indeed was commissioning a study to quantify the social threat, what did the Assembly Members think? And what did they fear? Were they seeing adverse effects of wealth already?

Jan thought for a few second before answering. 'I think the doctors will tell you that there are more people sitting in their armchairs watching TV than there are digging their gardens, which is not healthy. But when people hark back to the "good old days", were they really that good? They had no leisure. They were paid peanuts. They spent all their time digging peat and digging their vegetable gardens. Life expectancy was quite significantly lower too. I wouldn't suggest returning to that.'

The point was, therefore, that it was possible to overstate the detrimental effects of such a major instrument of change as oil. Furthermore, said Jan, the Islands have some useful experience of wealth management to look back on. They had been here, albeit in a smaller way, and coped. 'We faced something similar when the fishing industry commenced [in the mid-1980s] and revenue increased ten-fold almost overnight. We managed that, I think, to the benefit of most Islanders. Back in 1982, people had similar worries about the possible social impact of thousands of troops being in the Islands, but we managed that well enough also. Most of the change we have experienced has been very much for the better.'

Most, but not all, I thought. Ken Humphrey was on to something when he spoke about the 'soul' of the Islands being a life that was rural and almost literally in touch with the earth of the Falklands and the elements. Yet there had been a huge migration away from the camp.

Jan herself had been very critical about the amount of time Islanders spend on social networking sites. And I had noticed – and would soon have my suspicions confirmed – that there was tendency towards obesity in the community, especially among younger people, which had come from a sedentary lifestyle and the wealth that made it possible to live largely on imported pizzas and processed foods.

But still, I was admiring of and sympathetic to this sense of historical context. The past was not that rosy. Jan and I are cousins, both members of the Biggs family, and descendants of an army pensioner who had come to the Falklands in the mid-1840s to help build Stanley after the capital's relocation from Port Louis. The family had lived in one of the tiny timber and tin pre-fabricated houses on Pioneer Row or Drury Street, most of which were still standing and still had des res status, both for their central location and basic soundness. The original Biggs had begun a lineage that had now reached nine generations on Jan's side. (My family had been slightly slower breeders and could only count eight.)

If one can see a family thread running back that far, and feel, as I believe both she and I did, that the past was still with us and influencing us, then one tends to feel a responsibility for the future also. For Jan in particular, the economic and social challenge is not simply a matter of enjoying the oil party while it lasts. It is equally important to consider how such sudden wealth might be harnessed for many decades to come, perhaps even in perpetuity. It seemed that these community leaders were thinking of investing money carefully in infrastructure that would last, and – more importantly – in a sovereign wealth fund that would generate wealth for future generations.

I had been joking about the Falklands vying with Kuwait to buy Harrods, next time it comes on the market, but perhaps it was not such a joke. Jan said the Islands were looking at the experiences of other countries that had sovereign wealth funds to see what might be learned from them.

The timescales involved in an oil economy are lengthy but measurable. Already there had been two exploration rounds in the Falklands, so there had been over a decade of activity. Assuming that oil prices did not plummet, and assuming that what the industry called the 'sovereign threat' from Argentina did not become a great deal worse, then the next phase, actual exploitation, might commence around 2016. The small exploration companies would need that much time to form strategic alliances with, or even sell out to, the huge companies that could supply the tens of billions of pounds they would need to drill further, establish floating offshore tanker terminals (there would be no terminals on land) and extract the petroleum. Exploitation might be under way, and that fabulous wealth might be flowing into the Falklands Exchequer, and into the pocket of local entrepreneurs like Lewis and Neil, by about 2020.

I asked Jan to describe the Falkland Islanders she expected to see in the early 2020s, by which time, I thought, she would probably be retired from local politics and spending most of her time on her farm, surrounded by those lovely king penguins.

'Many people will be earning their livings from the oil industry,' she said. Government will have bulked up to regulate the industry. And

I hope we'll see more people in the kind of professions that the oil industry needs.'

She suggested that a more educated population would be taking the reins of power. 'The great thing now is that we've got twenty-five years of investment in education really showing results. We have a very good body of well-educated people. We've had fourteen graduates this year, two with firsts and eight or nine with 2:1s. Already some are going on to postgraduate courses, aimed at getting them back to working in the Islands. But even if only half of them come back, that will be good.'

Would there be payments to Islanders so they could hold the direct benefits of the industry in their hands without doing much to earn it? The idea was no more ridiculous than local people setting up front companies for foreign fishing corporations in the 1980s, and taking considerable money just for procuring licences. And there are already countries in which citizens receive annual cheques of thousands of dollars. Ken Humphrey had told me about the system in Alaska, and it is common practice in some parts of the Middle East.

The idea of one-off cash payouts had already been raised in connection with windfall revenue, mainly from oil activity, that had just landed in the government's lap. *Penguin News* had reported one man calculating that the windfall would work out to £7,000 per Islander. He argued that after recent years, during which ordinary Islanders had tightened their belts, such a handout would only be fair.

Jan did not like the idea. 'Would you really want to see the sort of population that relied on handouts? The whole ethos of the Islands has been resilience, self-sufficiency and independence as far as we can get it. I would just hate to see us sitting around eating hamburgers. I would like to see a return to the holiday credit scheme, as that was hugely beneficial and has been sorely missed. But handouts generally, no.'

The holiday credit scheme had been a much-loved perk for all tax payers during the previous time of plenty. Each year, they would accrue a number of points, worth hard cash when paying for expensive flights out of the Islands. It meant that even poorer Islanders could afford a trip to South America or Europe every three or four years, which might cost up to £1,600 per person return. But the scheme was always portrayed as one that would exist only in the good economic times, and for a few years now, government revenue had been declining, so the holiday credit scheme ended.

I tried to turn the conversation to the bellicosity of Argentina. 'So, tell me what you make of things over there,' I said, waving vaguely in the direction of South America, which I had noticed was common physical shorthand here.

Dick responded first. 'Their efforts [to blockade us] are not having a great deal of effect economically, as we still have very large vessels that come in on a six-weekly basis from the UK, so we have no problems getting supplies in, and we export all our wool and meat on those ships.

'Argentina is, however, very threatening and threats have a value. In business terms, one of the hardest risks to manage is political risk. So if someone says they are going to cause trouble for you, you try to avoid it and do business differently. But that is not new. The fishing business here has been facing that challenge for years. And the Falklands' nature is to find ways around problems, which, in this case, I think we have done quite well.'

I asked whether the Argentine rhetoric was dangerous. Could it evolve into anything like a re-run of 1982? 'I'm probably not the right person to ask,' said Dick. I agreed, but as the military at Mount Pleasant, who presumably monitored such things very closely, were not talking to me, then I would value his opinion.

'OK,' he said. 'I think the deterrent is being carefully thought through and is being reconsidered regularly. The important thing to remember is that we have a very, very competent defence force here. We have RAF Typhoons, and a destroyer. We have a permanent inshore patrol vessel, HMS *Clyde*. We have troops on the ground. And there is the ability to reinforce from the UK with a well-established air route. We have a shipping link too, and any threat will not alter our physical links with the UK.

'Furthermore, I don't see that Argentina has the manpower, the firepower or the will to do anything militarily. They constantly state in public that they intend to retake the Islands, but only by peaceful means. I think it's highly unlikely that that would convert into some kind of military threat. Can I sleep easily in my bed? Yes, of course I can.'

I turned to Jan. 'I think the forces are an effective deterrent,' she said. 'And I think that deterrent is working. If it was not there I would be very concerned.'

She went on to surprise me with her explicit comments about Buenos Aires' diplomatic campaign, describing it as, 'sheer viciousness and falsehood'. She continued: 'They have said that we are under military rule and are hostages of the military. Internationally, they are annoying the hell out of people, because at every conference they attend, they drag up the Falklands. It's a case of shouting too much for too long. We don't respond every time they do this because it would be a full-time job for thirty people. But we are increasing our efforts to attend conferences overseas, making sure that the true story gets out.'

I reflected on the Governor's assurances that British diplomats were doing all they could to counter the Argentine actions. I had the feeling that the word of the Foreign Office was accepted but there was some doubt about the value of its work. 'We have evidence that they are doing what they say they are doing,' said Jan.

'Is it working, though?' I asked.

'Difficult to say. I've met William Hague, and when he speaks on our behalf, he is sincere.' This seemed rather less than fulsome praise for the Foreign Office, but it was to be expected. Bumbling British diplomacy had led the Falklands into war in 1982 and Islanders have long memories.

As far as I had been able to see, Dick had been speaking for many, perhaps most, Islanders when he said that he was still sleeping soundly at night. They believed that Argentine bellicosity was futile in the face of a considerable British force on the Islands, and that the British Government was at least saying the right things internationally. More importantly, though, I thought the Assembly members were reflecting a broad optimism for the future.

I thanked them both, and left Gilbert House. At my mother's house a few minutes later, I clicked onto the website of MercoPress, the Uruguayan news agency that is one of the few media outlets reporting Falklands issues prominently and objectively. The British Government had, I learned, just officially protested to the Argentine Government about its harassment of Falklands-flagged or licensed fishing vessels travelling to or from Montevideo, transiting shipping lanes that are shared by Argentina. A Foreign Office statement firmly rejected the Argentine senate's Decree 256, which authorized such action against Falklands shipping.

'We consider that it is not compliant with international law, including the United Nations Convention on the Law of the Sea (UNCLOS),' said the Foreign Office. 'UNCLOS provides for ships of all states to enjoy the right of innocent passage through territorial seas. The UK is clear that no vessel needs to comply with Argentine Decree 256 when transiting Argentine waters.'

The Argentines had told the Spanish Government that their vessels were committing the twin offence of 'illegally fishing' in Argentine waters and violating a 'legal' blockade of sea channels. The MercoPress report went on to say that a few days earlier, CELAC, a newly formed bloc of South American and Caribbean countries, had specifically backed Argentina's claim to the Islands and called for the UK and Argentina to talk about their sovereignty.

Britain, it seemed, was finding some diplomatic backbone, and I knew that this would be pleasing the occupants of Gilbert House. The dispute was also heating up, but that would be pleasing only the Argentines.

CHAPTER 11

The Argentine Veterans

T he ante appeared to be upping before my very eyes. No sooner had the Foreign Office at last made it clear that it was taking some robust diplomatic action against the imposition of the infamous decree that gave Buenos Aires a thin veil of faux legality over its aggressive blockade, than they also declared a vast maritime conservation area around South Georgia and the South Sandwich Islands. This had been done quietly and apparently without any consultation with Buenos Aires, but it was eminently sensible, as it would allow the South Georgia Government (essentially one Foreign Office official based at Government House in Stanley) to control fishing and other activities that could permanently damage the rich ecosystem.

Buenos Aires, of course, was outraged. They also claimed ownership of South Georgia and the South Sandwich Islands, although they had not bothered to create complex historical justification for these claims, as they had done for the Falklands. They just seemed to think they should have them. But neither group of islands could be disregarded in the context of the Falklands. In the years leading up to the 1982 conflict, the Argentines had set up an illegal base on Thule Island in the South Sandwich group (which the Foreign Office chose to ignore), and then there were the absurd activities of scrap metal collectors on South Georgia, which directly provoked the war.

The Argentine reaction was sadly predictable. Alfredo Atanasoff, a member of the Lower House of the Senate and President of the Malvinas Islands Parliamentary Observatory, described it as: 'A new abusive and illegitimate advance of the British Government, which is attempting to create a natural habitat for penguins, sea lions and whales in our islands. The initiative is another colonialist action from Britain and completely illegitimate, which requires the rejection of all sectors of the Argentine society and our Latin American partners.'

Whitehall responded dryly: 'Argentina, like the United Kingdom, is a signatory of the Commission for the Conservation of Antarctic Living Resources so we would like to think that common interest in conservation will carry more weight than the dispute over sovereignty.'

I could understand why many Islanders, not least the elected representatives whom I had met the day before, sometimes chose to ignore such things. Trying to rationalize these polemics was not good for the blood pressure, and most of the time it was better to accept the noise as part of the backbeat to life here. The important things, like making money from oil exploration, fishing for those fabulous Falklands trout or just exchanging the time of day with a neighbour over the garden fence, sometimes added more to the quality of life. No, not sometimes: always.

I wondered if Ordinary Argentines were similarly fed up with the whole business. Certainly my Argentine friends were. Perhaps even Alfredo Atanasoff was just ranting because his colleagues in the Malvinas Observatory – whatever that was – expected him to do so. Wouldn't Alfredo rather take a seat in the Café Tortoni, the finest café in Buenos Aires, and enjoy a Jockey Club cigarette and a stiff espresso?

Carlos Gardel once hummed *La Cumparsita* there, and Jorge Luis Borges contemplated his prose. Even Alfredo might for a few secret minutes push all that sovereignty stuff to one side in favour of finer things.

Sadly, Stanley has nothing to compare with the wonderful Café Tortoni. The Falkland Islands Company's recently opened café, which bore a pale likeness to a Starbucks establishment, was the best the town could do, and it was there, over a bitter cup of something that had been squirted from a digital machine, that I met Neil Rowlands. We went way back, and Neil had sought my advice about preserving his memories of working with the Army Medical Corps at their Teal Inlet field hospital during the 1982 war. It was a no-brainer to me: I advised him to write them down, if only for his children and grandchildren. They were valuable.

Neil was now in the tourism business – like so many others – using his small boat and 4x4 vehicle to take groups to the king penguin colony at Volunteer Point or to see the little jackass penguins at Gypsy Cove. We chatted over the coffee, and I gleaned the interesting information that there was a group of Argentine veterans in town. They had come to visit the places where they had fought in 1982 and to pay respects to their colleagues who did not go home.

Since 1999, when the Islands had relaxed the ban on Argentines travelling to the Falklands, there had been a trickle of such middle-aged former soldiers, sailors and airmen. I thought it would be interesting and helpful to talk to these veterans. Clearly, they would be seeing things from a very special point of view, and if I could talk to them, I might obtain a more human and less political picture of Argentines and their tragic obsession.

Neil thanked me for my advice and, in return, gave me the phone number of the Islander who was making arrangements for the group. I rang Neil's contact immediately and arranged to meet those veterans who wished to meet me at Lookout Lodge on the windy ridge above Stanley that evening. Lookout Lodge is very much at the cheaper end of the short list of accommodation in Stanley, but it is warm, clean and the food is generous.

A few hours later, I was sitting down in the Lodge with a group of six men, ranging in age from about fifty to sixty. All were from the southern Argentine sheep-farming town of Rio Gallegos, almost directly opposite the Falklands, and about 300 miles away. In 1982, Argentine attack aircraft had taken off from the town's windswept airport to sink several of Her Majesty's ships.

The veterans looked like typical working class Argentines; beefy, dark-skinned and with weather-beaten complexions. These were not well-educated men who made their livings seated at computers. They would have been of Spanish or Italian descent, but many generations back. They looked at me with curiosity rather than hostility, and may have been nervous about the attitude I might take. I may have seen some of them twenty-nine years earlier when they were among the cheerful invaders of 2 April and the filthy, demoralized and defeated enemy of 14 June.

I am sure that I felt more awkward than they did. None of them spoke any English, and my Spanish was not as good as it used to be. Nevertheless, I introduced myself to Osvaldo Enrique Radicci, Roberto Maggio, Jara Americo, Raúl Agustin Vasquez, Nicolas Urbieta and Oscar Alberto Recalde. Some of the men smiled and I felt they were all warming a little. On the other hand, perhaps they were amused by my bad Spanish accent. They began talking, and as they did so, they became increasingly animated and I found it impossible to note what each of the men was saying. So not all of the quotes that follow are attributed to individuals. I do not think they would mind.

I asked the men what they thought about the Falklands-Argentina situation today. They did not need reminding that Cristina Kirchner is from Santa Cruz, their region. 'She loves the Malvinas,' said Osvaldo Radicci, who had been a sub-official, a non-commissioned officer, in 1982. 'She is the one who has made most progress, and gone to the United Nations to ask for their support, because the United Kingdom does not want to have any type of relationship with us over the Malvinas. She has demanded this wherever she has gone.'

I asked if the other men agreed with the President's current policy and the way she was pursuing it. Raúl Vasquez, who had only ended his career as a NCO a few years ago, said he was 'apolitical', but said he felt what she was doing was better than conflict. 'If they can recover the Islands by political methods, and not by force, then that has to be good.'

This was a cue for most of the others to enter the conversation, nodding their heads in agreement, and to confirm that they too were against military measures at all costs. 'We've all had the experience,' said one man. 'You have to think what it is to be a soldier and kill another man. It is terrible; a thing of madness.'

'We are all against conflict,' said another. 'Nothing is gained through taking up arms; it only causes total destruction, and it is the poor people who suffer most.'

I suggested that Falkland Islanders still feel that there is a threat from Argentina. Now the six men vied to be heard. 'No, no, no! There is no threat. The Argentine armed forces are totally destroyed. They don't exist. Before there were military leaders who said we'll do this and that, but not any more. The armed forces are now totally inoperable because the people from within Argentina whom they were fighting in the 1970s and 1980s, those like the Montoneros [a left-wing guerrilla group linked to the Peronists who fought the Argentine military junta], are now in power.' That is probably arguable, but the broad point is correct: Argentine militarism is not popular in Kirchner's Peronist government.

'My wish,' said Osvaldo Radicci, 'is that Great Britain lowers its flag here and that it is replaced with ours, but at their initiative. It should not be lowered by us; rather by them. We can help Britain if necessary, but our flag must go up.'

'Can we – the Argentines and the Islanders – really live and work together while this dispute continues, and while there are so many strong feelings on both sides?' I asked.

Raúl Vasquez did not quite get my point (it may have been my Spanish). He seemed to think that Islanders were refusing to take advantage of what seemed obvious to him, the benefits of being Argentine. 'Argentina is a very open country,' he said. 'Our constitution says that anyone can come and live in the country. You don't have a visa? Go. No money? Go.'

I was starting to realize that these Argentines, all of whom seemed decent and likeable, were unable to imagine themselves in the position of Islanders. They saw integration as a perfectly logical and pragmatic step for all of us. There were no barriers, except those erected by the government in London. Why would anyone not want to take advantage of opportunities in their country? It was naïve of them, but nonetheless, almost touching.

I suggested that the Kirchner government was saying that there could be no co-operation between the Islands and Argentina unless we sat down to talk about the substantive issue of sovereignty, and that did not seem reasonable to people here.

'The problem is the United Kingdom because they are closing all the doors,' said a man who had not spoken until now. 'So what can Argentina do? It must close all avenues to the Islands. But it must do so diplomatically.' Six heads nodded in unison. 'If the British would commence a dialogue, then it could open the way to commerce and so on that could benefit you. All that we see in the shops here is brought in from Britain, a long way away. We are just 600kms away and it could come from there. All they have to do is begin a dialogue.'

I wondered how the Argentines saw Islanders. In their eyes were we the same as those in London who were being unreasonable by not talking? 'No, you're not English. You are Kelpers,' said one. 'You're not considered English. I can't be angry with a civilian Islander over what happened in 1982; that was all because of the military government.'

I was warming to these men, and I did so further when one asked me what Islanders – the Kelpers – thought of them. That was a hard one. I did not feel I could be totally honest. At least, I could not give them the full picture. Visits by Argentine veterans and the families of Argentines who are buried at Goose Green are now routine, but these victims of 1982 have been used as a political tool by both sides. At times the Argentine Government has wanted to conduct large-scale visits, during which their flag would fly over the cemetery. They have also wanted to construct a massive monument. A large proportion of local people opposed such demonstrations of nationalism outspokenly, and even today the Argentine cemetery is desolate, with no flag flying over it.

No Argentines at all were allowed to visit the Falklands for almost two decades. Islanders were prepared to admit them in return for Argentine concessions, such as the air link with Chile, and eventually they did so. But even today there were plenty of people who would rather the Argentine dead were repatriated, thus removing the need to allow next of kin and veterans to visit the graves.

On the other hand, many local people seemed to feel that allowing the visits was a simple humanitarian issue that should not be contaminated by politics. I would put myself in that group. 'People here feel no sense of hatred against you,' I said. 'But for political reasons very few people want to have any contact. They feel there is a threat; not a military threat, perhaps [although I was not so sure about that] but in other ways. They hear inflammatory talk from the politicians in Buenos Aires, say, and it scares them.'

I was surprised to find that I had their attention. A few of the men said '*claro*' ('of course'). So I went on. 'Look, a lot of Islanders – at least those who think seriously about it – would like to have contact with Argentina. They would like to see air and sea links, and trade, for example. But they think they will lose something ....'

'No, no! What could they lose?' interjected one man. I had been hoping to continue and point out that they feared they might lose something very important indeed: their freedom to live as they wish. But the men were still being influenced by the idea that it was Britain, and Britain alone, that was determining the Islands' isolation. It was London imposing its will on Islanders, convincing them that everything Argentine was bad. I felt these men actually felt sorry for Islanders.

'We have English schools in Argentina that teach children as well as they do in England,' said one. 'No one pays for education,' said another. 'They would give you somewhere to live. There are good salaries.' Just one of the men conceded there was a gulf of difference between the cultures, and that would be very hard to overcome.

I was aware that these six men were giving me their time and were being polite and increasingly friendly. I knew of no one in the Islands who would want to take up their offer of education, jobs and homes. But they were well meaning. And I was genuinely surprised that they felt no particular dislike for Islanders, whose intransigence (it could be argued) took them to war. I wanted to say something that might help them to close the book on 1982, even if it sounded a little sentimental. 'I don't know if this well help,' I said, 'but I have never spoken to anyone here who feels hatred for or who has said unkind things against the young men who were sent here from Argentina to fight. Everyone knows that it was not their fault. They feel very differently about the politicians and the heads of the armed forces who gave the orders, but they do not hate you.'

Osvaldo Radicci was the first to respond. 'We had to do what we were told. If we had said no, they would have shot us and killed us.'

I knew that to be true, and I said that I was pleased that, at long last, Argentine officers who had behaved appallingly during the 'Dirty War' and during the 1982 war were facing justice and being locked up. Heads nodded in approval.

'Those who sent us here are in prison,' said one man. 'They are old and they are in prison. They are in their seventies and they have none of the pleasures of those years that they might have earned. And that is right.'

I was pleased that my remarks had been well received, and that we had reached some common ground. People on all sides had been victims.

'Many boys died here,' said one man. 'They were only seventeen or eighteen years old. They died! I was older, but in my battalion we had what we called the "puppies", and they stayed here. They are dead.'

I asked if, now they had returned to the places like Mount William, Tumbledown and Two Sisters, where they had followed their orders and fought, they thought they might return again someday. There were mixed feelings. 'I love the Malvinas, I love my life, I love my country,' said Raúl Vasquez. 'What I saw here hurt me, and I will do all that I can to ensure that those who died here did not die in vain. But no, I have returned once, and that's enough for me.'

Two others thought they would return with their 19- and 20-year-old children. They were now the same age as their fathers were when they were ordered to come here to fight. The others agreed with Raúl Vasquez; they had done what they had to do, and that was enough.

I asked how ordinary Argentines, the privileged ones who had not had to fight, treated them. '*Eramos bichos raros*,' said one. 'We were strange creatures. Fifteen or sixteen years passed, during which they ignored us. They did it because we lost the Malvinas. Society marginalized us; we were the crazy guys from the war. You know, as many of the boys committed suicide afterwards as died here. But today it's better, and they treat us well.'

All seemed to be bothered by the absence of permanent memorials to the Argentines who died on the mountaintops. There was just the one big memorial in the Goose Green cemetery. They said they had seen plenty of crosses and memorial stones naming the British troops who had died on these windswept and lonely locations, but there were no such tributes to the Argentines.

They were right, and I did not have the heart to say that I knew other visiting Argentines had sometimes left engraved plaques in such locations, but these were always quietly removed when the Argentines had gone. That action seemed unnecessarily callous, and I did not agree with it. But it was fact.

My Spanish had served me fairly well, but it had been hard work. '*Gracias, señores, por su ayuda*,' I said. 'Thanks for your help. It's been very interesting talking to you.'

'*No, gracias a usted*,' came the reply. 'Thanks to you for listening to us.'

A day or so later, the Argentines were still kicking their heels in Stanley. They had done all that they intended to do in just a few days and now were ready to go home but could not do so because the Lan Chile Boeing flew just once a week. I was again in the West Store buying a few things when I felt a tap on my shoulder. It was one of the veterans. He had recognized me. He smiled broadly and explained that he was buying a few '*recuerdos*' to take home. He held up a bottle of malt whisky. *Recuerdos* are souvenirs, but the word also means memories. 'That's great,' I said. 'I wonder if you have been able to leave a few here, too.'

'Perhaps,' he said. 'Perhaps.' We shook hands, he smiled again, and left.

CHAPTER 12

Planet Penguin

I awoke later than planned one morning about ten days into my stay to the sound of a ship's horn. Judging by the number of decibels reverberating through my head, the vessel was bearing down on me from a point just east of my mother's garden shed. It was a macho blast that ensured it would never be mistaken for a harbour tug.

Drawing the blinds back to reveal a deep blue and sunny sky, and no sign of the *Titanic*, I remembered that my friends Alison Howe and Anna King had warned me that Stanley would be thronging with tourists that day, as one of the biggest cruise ships of the summer would be in port. Upwards of 1,500 Brits, Americans, South Americans and sundry other minority nationalities, would be thronging the town's seafront as they bought the inevitable penguin-themed souvenirs, and formed confused mobs by the coaches decorated with stylized penguin motifs that would take them to visit nearby farms and, yes, penguin colonies.

All going well, it would be a big day for the girls. They have two shops in Stanley, one, the Harbour View Gift Shop, perfectly sited to catch cruise ship tourists as they disembark from their ships' tenders. Alison and Anna, who are such close and old friends that I consider them surrogate sisters, were realistic, however. Cruise ship captains often turn away from the port if the wind is blowing strongly from the wrong direction, as, of course, it often does. When that happens, the Falklands lose a good deal of money. And it is not just the souvenir shops and coach operators who suffer. The Falklands Government can lose tens of thousands of pounds in landing fees and harbour dues, and the two shipping agencies say goodbye to most of their fees. Then there is the multitude of trained freelance guides, who are paid up to £25 an hour to lead groups on walking and coach tours: they lose their incomes.

But if everything goes well on a cruise ship day, then everyone is very happy. There are a great many people in Stanley who make good livings from the fifty or so cruise ships that visit every southern summer, and fortunately for them, neither the parlous state of the world economy or the Argentine blockade appears to be reducing the flow.

In fact, this was one way in which the Islanders were competing with the Argentines in a normal commercial fashion. The Port of Ushuaia in southern Argentine Patagonia was equally keen to host the cruise ships, but despite efforts to undercut Stanley, they had been unable to lure the operators away. The Falklands, with its combination of wildlife, proximity to the Antarctic and remarkable British culture, was a major attraction.

That day, fortunately for so many of my friends, the weather and sea conditions could hardly have been better. I knocked back a cup of tea and walked east down Ross Road towards the landing stage, where I could already see a crowd of big spenders waiting their turn to enter Alison and Anna's Harbour View Shop. The coaches and Land Rover taxis were at the head of the jetty, and the shipping agency's staff were marshalling red-anoraked tourists into coaches, among which was a wonderfully incongruous classic red Routemaster double-decker bus. Despite the sign above the driver's position that suggested it would be terminating in Ealing and getting there via Piccadilly, it would soon be trundling back and forth along the largely unsurfaced 3-mile route between Stanley and the Magellanic penguin colony at Gypsy Cove.

Islanders have traditionally protected their clapboard and corrugated iron buildings from the wind and the salty air with whatever oil-based paint they could find. Availability and price were more likely to dictate the colour schemes than any aesthetic consideration. If there were a few gallons of lime green gloss going cheaply, then slap it on the roof. Pink on the walls? Well, it was cheap, so why not? I like Stanley's haphazard colour scheme. But the riotous outbreak of colour at the jetty head was pushing the boundaries of taste, even for Stanley.

The almost fluorescently bright-red Routemaster was parked by The Pod, the little gift shop that probably has the best location of all Stanley's penguin-themed emporia. The Pod's bright yellow walls, blue-trimmed windows and pinkish-red roof, combined with the bus's London Transport red colour scheme was bilious, but this was what the visitors had seen in the brochures, and they were burning up their cameras' megapixels on the scene.

I wasn't sure who owned the little shop these days, but I stepped in to say hello. As it turned out, the new owners were Teddy and Sybella Summers, and very happy shopkeepers they were too. They greeted me warmly and proudly. Teddy in particular surprised me with his ebullience. The shop was neat and packed with the inevitable penguin produce, some of it made in the Falklands, but much imported from the UK. I had known both for a long time. I asked Teddy when he had left his job as a dockworker, unloading general cargo from the UK and then loading the ships again with wool.

'Oh, that was ages ago, *che*.' He was using the Anglo/Argentine for friend or mate; a word I like very much, which was imported from the River Plate area in the early colonial times. 'I started the tyre repair business, and then we bought The Pod.' He was beaming with pride at his accomplishment.

Sybella had worked for the Falkland Islands Company, running cash tills and stocking shelves at the West Store. She too was clearly proud. I pointed at Teddy: 'What's he like as a shopkeeper?' I asked.

'He's learning,' she joked, and we all laughed.

'I'd rather be behind the scenes making these things, though,' said Teddy pointing at the ceramic plates and trays on which he printed images of Stanley and, of course, penguins. 'But on a day like this, it's all hands on deck.'

I was extremely happy for Teddy and Sybella. Like so many other local people, they had shaken themselves loose from a history of menial second-class citizenship. In the colony of old, they had had to know their place and stick to it. They may well have been the first generation of their families to own their own business.

'Excuse me, Graham,' said Teddy, noticing two corpulent Americans browsing through his ceramic plates and baseball hats. 'Looks like we've got some business.'

I wished them a successful day and said goodbye. My visit to The Pod had been an unexpected and heartening experience; real flesh and blood evidence of progress being enjoyed.

Around the corner from The Pod was the Tourist Board's information centre and shop. By no means were all of the visitors ashore yet, and I thought I would see if it was possible to meet Paul Trowell, the manager of the Tourist Board. I asked one of the women who staffed the office if he was in, and whether he might be able to see me for a chat. She disappeared upstairs and came down a minute later saying the kettle was on and Paul would be pleased to see me.

Paul Trowell smiled, extended a hand and gestured towards a chair. He is an outgoing New Zealander appointed on contract, and had another year or so to go before he moved on to another job, probably in another part of the world. He measured his success in the number of visitors and the scale of their spending, and those figures that he was able to rattle off to me were impressive. 'Last year, tourism accounted for about 4.2 per cent of GDP,' he said. 'The industry is worth around £6.85 million annually.'

This would be a drop in the ocean in any other market, but it's big money for the Falklands, and growth is happening in spite of the Argentines doing whatever they can to halt it. The global cruise industry is a rolling juggernaut, with such great financial power that narrow-view politics hardly impact on it. Furthermore, the world's severe economic strife has not reversed growth, although it may have slowed.

'We've have had about 7 per cent growth in tourism per annum over the last four years,' said Paul, with his tight New Zealand diction. 'And we are forecasting about 16 per cent growth this season. That's 47,000 visitors, most of whom are cruise clients.'

It is not all cruise-based, however. The Tourist Board is expecting some 8,000 land-based tourists during the 2011/12 season, many of whom will be using the imperilled weekly Lan Chile link.

So what of that particular weak link in the chain? It seemed that everywhere I went, I was meeting people who believed Argentina would persuade the Chileans to cut the service, or would simply deny Lan permission to fly through Argentine air space, and most thought that would happen around March or April 2012. 'It worries us almost every day,' said the New Zealander. 'But you shouldn't worry about something you can't control.'

I narrowed my eyes to indicate scepticism, and pressed him on the point. 'There is a great old saying: "Don't let the bastards get you down." So yes, we just get on with it. What will be will be. We are putting in place strategies to work around the problem and we're working hard to create new air links and keep the doors open.'

I assumed he was referring to those plans to develop an air link with Florida, which the Legislative Assembly Members Dick Sawle and Jan Cheek had told me about. 'Yes,' said Paul. 'We are well down the road to establishing something there. It's about nine hours' flying time, but we would need a refuelling stop somewhere. A passenger exchange for the smaller cruise ships will form the backbone of the service. All I can say is that there is huge interest in the expedition cruise market.'

I could not get over my sense of awe about this plan to forge a link with the US rather than beg and bargain a concession from Argentina and its neighbours. It even crossed my mind that it might be bluff; a message to the Argentines saying that no matter how tight you make the noose around us, we will always get out of it. But I was becoming certain that the effort was genuine. It was, after all, entirely consistent with the pugnacious and square-jawed attitude. Every time the Argentines did something to them, Islanders just worked around it. This never-say-die attitude had worked in fishing and oil. And now it was being applied to tourism also.

The cruise industry is the cornerstone of tourism here, and clearly much of Paul's time was being spent maintaining good relations with the operators and trying to satisfy their needs. 'We have to think about the wants and needs of the cruise companies,' he said. It struck me that a good deal had been done already. The town was looking good, dedicated tourist shops had opened, there was a good landing stage for launches that ensured visitors did not get their feet wet, and there were coaches and taxis taking the visitors wherever they wanted to go. But Paul spoke of the need to repair or replace the old timber town jetty and to develop better facilities in the outer harbour, where the bigger ships had to anchor and remain at the mercy of winds and waves. Stanley Harbour had been fine in the 1840s, when the town was founded, but now it was too shallow for many ships, and the cruise industry was building ever-bigger ones.

I asked if the new deep-water port that the government was considering, mainly for the fishing industry, would also be good for the big cruise vessels. He thought they needed no more than a breakwater for shelter, but spending was necessary. 'If you don't start to reinvest their landing fees, they are going to wonder why they are paying them,' Paul pointed out. 'We have the opportunity to be the new Galapagos, that is how we are positioning ourselves, but we are perceived to be an expensive destination, so we have to give them value for money.'

Could the cruise ship business grow indefinitely, or would it soon reach a ceiling? 'I think there is limit to what we can take here in Stanley. The biggest ship that visits carries between 2,000 and 3,000 passengers. There's been a lot of hoo-hah about that one, with some people saying it is too large, but we've surveyed the passengers, and they registered a high rate of satisfaction. I say bring it on. They spend a lot of money here, and at the same time we're making friends and promoting the Islands.'

Government money is being invested in tourism, said Paul, listing the Stanley seafront development, boat berthing facilities and perhaps a new port. But there are opportunities for private investment too. He echoed the words of Jan Cheek and Dick Sawle who were worried about hotel capacity. He hoped that some of the stress will be taken off the Malvina fairly soon, perhaps by its own extension, but regardless of this, he said there will be demand for new, quality hotels.

Tourism here was no stranger to private involvement, even if it was mostly small in scale. The mobile coffee shop that I had seen parked nearby was doing a brisk trade among the red anoraks. And the farms that hosted coachloads of day visitors must have wondered why they ever bothered keeping sheep. And, most obviously, almost everyone with a serviceable four-wheel-drive vehicle was running a taxi or guided tours service. 'The drivers are doing very well,' Paul said. 'Demand is higher than supply and they can make very good money. It's certainly an exciting time for tourism.'

Among the Tourist Board's plans for 2012 were a Tourism Awards scheme, which would recognize quality of service, and the first hotel accreditation system, which would help visitors to know what to expect at the establishments putting them up. Stanley guesthouses, self-catering cottages, the few small wildlife lodges and, of course, the Malvina, would all be included in the scheme. Regardless of how comfortable, warm and friendly Falklands hostelries are, I could not see any being awarded four or five stars. But that wasn't the idea. 'We'll establish our own criteria,' said Paul. 'We might base it on penguins; four penguins, or three penguins, and so on.' He smiled. 'It'll be unique.'

I asked him what business he would invest in if he decided to remain in the Islands after completing his contract with the Tourist Board. He did not hesitate. 'Accommodation for land-based tourists. I'd be building a niche hotel somewhere. It's all about location, of course, but a small high-end luxury lodge out of town surrounded by beautiful wildlife would be great. There are lodges in Patagonia that charge up to $2,000 a night. We would, however, have to get around the problem of the six or seven months of the year when there is no business.'

I thought that any lodge that charged $2,000 per room, per night, for six months of the year could probably afford to close for the winter, or drop its tariff by 95 per cent to offer troops a few days away from their camp. I would be more worried by the precarious nature of the air link with Chile. If Cristina Kirchner pulled the trigger on that target that was in her cross hairs – then those rich 'high-end' tourists were not going to come. At least not until the Florida link was a reality, and, notwithstanding the upbeat attitudes, I had serious doubts about that.

'You shouldn't worry about something you can't control,' Paul had said earlier. That motto appeared to be serving him very well. There was no sign at all that the 'bastards' were getting him down. I thanked him for his time, said I was looking forward to being able to afford a night or two at his top-end lodge, and left.

Outside, the old Routemaster double-decker was being coaxed into life. After thirty years or more of running around London and climbing nothing more challenging that the slopes of Notting Hill, its old engine was having to cope with Stanley's very steep slopes. The bus coughed some noxious diesel smoke and the driver – no doubt another Islander blessing the god of tourism – crunched the gearbox.

The bus chugged off up Philomel Hill. Forty or so tourists, all heavily wrapped up in red anoraks and woolly hats despite the fair weather, applauded and settled down to enjoy their scenic trip to Gypsy Cove. They probably did not know that it was early in the breeding season, and the little Magellanic penguins would still be cosily tucked away in their underground nests incubating eggs. But I did not feel too sorry for them. On a day like this, the sheer rugged majesty of the Falklands coastline would be a wonderful spectacle. And I was pretty sure that, whether or not they saw any of the real things, they would be buying plenty of toy penguins from either Alison and Anna's Harbour View Gift Shop or from Teddy and Sybella's multi-coloured Pod.

CHAPTER 13

Manning the Ramparts

I had been making a point of ringing Media Operations at Mount Pleasant regularly to see if they had received any suggestion from London that I could be given so much as the time of day at the base. I had left a decent few days between each call, but so far nothing had been offered. What was more, I was starting to believe that nothing would be. On each occasion that I called, I sounded a little more pathetic and desperate. I thought the ignominy of the amateur dramatics would be fleeting and the possible prize considerable, so I laid it on heavily.

I had also asked my friendly members of the Legislative Assembly, Jan Cheek and Dick Sawle, to call Captain Christine Wilson and advise her that they thought I should be hosted in some way. 'After all,' one of the Assembly Members kindly pointed out, 'they speak to foreign journalists, so why shouldn't they talk to one of ours?'

I liked that logic, but, although I know they called Media Ops, it did not seem to make any difference. During my last conversation with the friendly but unhelpful captain, she had shared with me that someone at Ministry of Defence in London had been 'doing a lot of chest poking' with the Brigadier. But still no green light had flashed. However, I could take it for granted that an interview with the Commander British Forces was not going to happen. If I received any hospitality, it would take the form of a tour of the base.

I felt she was embarrassed, which was probably why she pointed out that there was a lot of 'open source' information available about the Falklands defences – intelligence-speak for trawling the Internet and reading the local rags. That I knew, and I certainly would be making use of it. Furthermore, I would be talking to people outside the Ministry of Defence and the military who knew about the defences. But nothing could fully replace seeing the things with one's own eyes and talking to the people who scan the horizon with radars and binoculars. I thanked Christine 'so much', said that 'anything she could do would be just marvellous,' and reminded her of my mobile phone number.

Nothing appeared to be making any difference. I had received another email from the Brigadier, which was interesting and sympathetic in tone, but negative. He wrote:

I am afraid that this is taking longer than I had hoped. The question of what media (in the broadest sense) we can do over FI issues is a hot topic at present. The question is with the policy people at a high level and we will get back to you as soon as we can. I would caution that the subject matter you propose has raised some concerns.

Having worked in the Ministry of Defence, I knew the dynamics that would be at work. Emails would be travelling spasmodically between the Directorate of Media and Communications and 'policy' desks in the Ministry of Defence and the Foreign Office. The latter would be urging extreme caution about saying anything at all and probably suggesting that no assistance should be given to the media. They would be backed up by the Ministry of Defence civil servants. I surmised that they feared any support to writers and broadcasters would just give Buenos Aires the opportunity to claim that the 'colonial pirates' were bragging about their 'occupation'.

I knew that Falkland Islanders would not share this desire for caution. They had longer memories than the recent graduates who sat at the policy desks in Whitehall, and they knew how any slightly ambiguous postures or messages would be interpreted by Buenos Aires as a sign of weakness. Timidity (combined with poor intelligence) was a major contribution to the invasion of 1982. At least so Islanders believe.

As I had learned from my conversations with the Governor, members of the Legislative Assembly, entrepreneurs and with rank and file Islanders, the Argentines could not do much more to make life difficult, and the nature of Falkland Islanders was such that they would get on with pursuing their ambitions regardless. So the Argentines might as well be reminded, rudely if necessary, that the military assets in the Falklands were constantly on alert, and more than capable of defending the place, whether against a full-scale attack, proxy activity using nationalist firebrands, or aggressive policing of the blockade. Whether such an assessment of defensive capability would be *entirely* true was debatable, but it would be a good message to send anyway.

I felt fairly sure that some military elements within the Ministry of Defence would share this view, and they were probably frustrated by civil service caution. They might also see it as useful to convey the message within the UK, as critics had been publicly stating that the recent strategic defence review had weakened the forces to such an extent that the country would never again be able to organize another Falklands task force. This was misleading – probably deliberately so – as the standing defences of the Falklands were now a hundred times stronger than they were in 1982. The Argentines would have great difficulty getting a toehold on the Islands in the first place, so a rescuing task force should not be required. But using the example of the Falklands was a good way of undermining the government's plans to pare down the forces.

However, none of this would cut any ice with the policy people, even as the thirtieth anniversary of 1982 approached. Better, they would think, to keep a low profile and avoid provoking Buenos Aires. This timidity had only developed recently. In December 2008, HMS *Endurance*, the Navy's ice-reinforced Antarctic patrol ship, was almost lost off southern Chile, when she suffered near catastrophic flooding. She was towed to the Falklands and thence recovered to the UK, where it soon became clear that she would not be repaired quickly, if at all. There was speculation that she might not be replaced. *Endurance* was of negligible value as a warship and although she assisted the British Antarctic

Fragile friendship: Argentine President Cristina Fernández de Kirchner with her reluctant ally, President José Mujica of Uruguay

Why Argentina still hurts: Their military cemetery at Goose Green
(Graham Bound)

Bound for Europe: Falklands fish being unloaded from a trawler of Fortuna Ltd
(Graham Bound)

Off duty challenge: Governor Haywood fishes for sea trout

Carrying the flag for a
new generation: Cadets
on parade
(Graham Bound)

Ceremonial: Governor Nigel
Haywood (left) marks
Remembrance Sunday with
Commander British Forces
Brigadier Bill Aldridge
(Graham Bound)

Rig that found a fortune:
Ocean Guardian moving into
place north of the Falklands
(FIG)

Jam jar full of promise:
The first Falklands oil
to be extracted
(Graham Bound)

Services to the oil industry: Neil McKay (left) and Lewis Clifton of Byron McKay Ltd invested £8 million
(Graham Bound)

Dwarfed by ambition: Byron McKay's principals standing by silos at their depot
(Graham Bound)

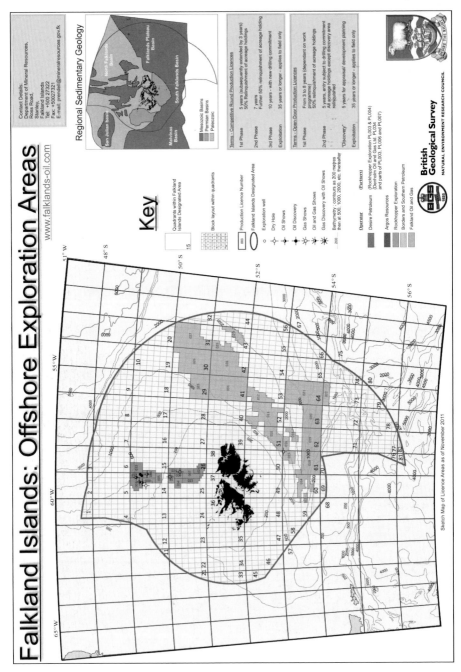

Falkland Islands: Offshore Exploration Areas

www.falklands-oil.com

Centre of a sea of wealth: Falklands economic zone with prospective oil fields (FIG)

Legislators standing fast:
Jan Cheek (left) and Dick
Sawle
(Office of the Legislative
Assembly)

Mapping a wealthy
future: Phyl Rendell,
Director of Mineral
Resources
(FIG)

Welcome to Planet Penguin: Magnificent, and possibly vulnerable, king penguins at Volunteer Point
(Graham Bound)

Long way from Piccadilly: A British icon trundles through Stanley laden with tourists
(Graham Bound)

Penguin News: Lisa Watson, pictured at her parents' farm, is the editor of the local newspaper
(Graham Bound)

Memories of thirty years ago: Neil Watson holds a rusting Argentine helmet at Long Island Farm
(Graham Bound)

Sustaining: VC10 refuels another RAF aircraft, prolonging patrols over the Falklands
(MOD)

Ubiquitous C130J Hercules: Tactical transport and patrol aircraft
(MOD)

Front-line defence:
A potent Typhoon
interceptor
accelerates into the
sky
(MOD)

Vigilance: Soldiers patrol the perimeter of Mount Pleasant base
(MOD)

Air-to-air: Rapier missiles were deployed in 1982 and still defend Mount Pleasant
(MOD)

Self-defence: Part-time soldiers of the Falkland Islands Defence Force (FIDF) on exercise
(Graham Bound)

Mobility: FIDF soldiers can deploy rapidly with a variety of vehicles
(MOD)

Command: Major Peter Biggs would, if necessary, deploy the local militia in support of the regular forces
(Graham Bound)

Testing deterrence: Missiles are unleashed from a Type 23 frigate
(MOD)

Latest deterrent: Astute Class submarines are entering service
(MOD)

Guard ship: HMS *Clyde* was purpose-built for the Falklands and is expected to serve there for years to come
(MOD)

Ice patrol: HMS *Protector* packs little punch but is a major symbol
(MOD)

Most powerful surface ships: Type 45 destroyer at speed
(MOD)

Survey, the BAS had its own vessels. But not only was she replaced with an expensive new vessel, that new ship was named HMS *Protector*. This was a signal implying commitment to defend the area. Bearing that name, she was the kind of symbol Argentina would understand.

There had been a previous *Protector* in the 1950s and 1960s, a more heavily-armed Second World War veteran, so Islanders were also pleased with this salute to a more warlike predecessor.

Another expression of commitment was evident in the outcome of the strategic defence review. The defence establishment of the Falklands appeared to have been ring-fenced. The RAF and Navy Harrier aircraft force was disbanded, destroyers and frigates were sold or scrapped and, crucially, the aircraft carrier force was depleted to just one ship (which would, in time, also be mothballed). But no major element of the forces in the Falklands was reduced in strength; indeed, they may have been enhanced. The RAF Tornado interceptors, which had maintained tight control over the skies over the Falklands for more than a decade, were replaced by a flight of the ultra-modern Eurofighter Typhoon FGR4 interceptors.

Strategic airlift capability, which would be essential to reinforcing the Islands in times of tension, was enhanced with the procurement of more Boeing C17 aircraft. These massive planes can carry hundreds of troops, vehicles, artillery and even Apache attack helicopters.

Troop levels in the islands may have varied a little under the review, but broadly remained the same. The training value of the wide-open Falklands spaces was useful for troops who would, in all likelihood, eventually deploy to Afghanistan. Those who were particularly concerned about the defence of the Falklands expelled large sighs of relief.

But back to my own little war with the forces at Mount Pleasant. I was clearly not winning, and it was time, therefore, to use those open and unofficial sources and recruit the assistance of a few experts on the outside who were able to give objective views of British vs Argentine capability.

It has always been true that if the Argentines suddenly threw all of their military assets at the Falkland Islands, regardless of recent improvements to the defences, the defenders would have a very tough time. Fortunately for the Commander British Forces, whose main role is to deter such behaviour, the 300-mile stretch of unfriendly sea that separates the Islands from the continent gives his fortress a magnificent moat. It would take many days, if not weeks, to mobilize a seagoing invasion fleet, during which time intelligence assets, both electronic and human, would have detected the activity. The Islands would be rapidly reinforced by air and, more slowly, by sea (assuming the Foreign Office did not argue successfully that such a move would be a dangerous provocation). For this fundamental plan to work, the runways at Mount Pleasant air base, plus fuel and ammunition supplies, would need to be protected at all costs.

Argentine planners would, of course, be well aware of this and they would seek to scotch reinforcement plans by using their thirty-six Fightinghawk bombers (greatly updated versions of the Skyhawks that were operated with some success in 1982) to destroy Mount Pleasant's runways, and fuel and ammunition depots.

First, though, they would attempt to bomb the three mountaintop radar sites, which are believed to be sufficiently powerful that they can detect aggressive aircraft within minutes of taking off from Patagonian air bases.

Then they would try to deliver destruction on the Rapier anti-aircraft missile sites around Mount Pleasant. Finally, they would bomb the runways and the fuel and the ammunition depots.

With the reinforcement capability neutered or at least seriously frustrated, the way would be open for an invasion. Once achieved, the Argentines would be very difficult to dislodge, and in that case, the doomsayers who predicted that in the wake of the Strategic Defence and Security Review, Britain would be unable to organize another Falklands task force, would be proven right.

Ideally, the Typhoon force, 1435 Flight, would be augmented in the days leading up to an attack. If, however, the RAF was pressed into using only the four Typhoons before reinforcements arrived, they might evoke the spirit of Malta, where appropriately enough, 1435 Flight had served during the Second World War. The current Flight pays homage to the defiant Gladiator biplanes that defended Malta at the height of the Italian siege by naming their aircraft *Faith, Hope* and *Charity*. There were only three Gladiators, but the fourth Typhoon has been named *Desperation*. In those first days after the South Atlantic current cold war turned white hot, the Typhoons – whether few or many – would be desperate indeed.

While the Typhoons deterred and fought if necessary, huge C17s, Airbus A400M tanker/transports, Lockheed Tristar and smaller C130 Hercules transports would – all going well – be shuttling up and down the South Atlantic, using Ascension Island as a staging post, bringing reinforcements to support the three main pillars of Fortress Falklands, which are:

Air defences, including Typhoons interceptors and air-to-air refuelling VC10 and Hercules C130

Sea defences up to 150 miles around the Islands, including destroyers and/or frigates, Royal Fleet Auxiliary tankers and support ships

Land defences of Mount Pleasant base and rapid deployment capability, including additional infantry, artillery and transport helicopters and attack helicopters

The next section will look at each of these in detail.

Military convention would normally require that the Royal Navy's capability is described first. But that would not be appropriate here. Of all the combat units in the Falklands, it is the aircraft, the aircrew and the ground teams of the RAF that would be absolutely pivotal as tension increased leading to conflict in the Falklands.

Royal Air Force: Defending the Right

Typhoon interceptors
The RAF's 1435 Flight exists only to defend the Falklands, and (as

already described) is equipped with four Eurofighter Typhoon FGR4 interceptors. The flight was brought out of suspended animation in 1988. Its aircraft exhibit the Maltese Cross, but the flight's motto, 'Defending the Right', is a nod in the direction of the motto that appears beneath the Falklands coat of arms: 'Desire the Right'.

In the latest chapter of its stop-start life, 1435 Flight was initially equipped with McDonnell Douglas Phantoms, a powerful interceptor and ground attack aircraft originally designed for aircraft carrier operations, which dated from the late 1950s. The jets operated from RAF Stanley, which had been urgently extended in the aftermath of the war to provide an air base that did not rely on the short take-off and landing Harriers. Nevertheless, at Stanley, the Phantoms had to deploy hooks to engage with rotary hydraulic arrestor gear as if on an aircraft carrier. The Phantoms were approaching the end of their operational lives when they deployed to the Falklands, and in 1992 they were replaced by four Panavia Tornado F3 jets.

The Tornados were modern, capable and, as they flew low over the Falklands moors and crags, notably very noisy. Not that Islanders ever complained: the sound of twin jets, preferably with afterburners ignited, was, as many an Islander would say, 'the sound of freedom'. They served until September 2009, when the F3 variant was retired from service across the RAF. To the huge relief of Islanders and the serving Commander British Forces South Atlantic Islands (his duties extend to South Georgia and the South Sandwich Islands), it was announced that air defence variants of the Eurofighter, now renamed Typhoon, were to be the new *Faith, Hope, Charity* and *Desperation*.

The Typhoon is a remarkable aircraft. It was conceived in the 1970s as a weapon to take on the Russians if necessary, but the development and procurement programme was horribly delayed and even more horribly expensive: a conservative estimate is that it cost the British Government £37 billion. However, by the time the first Typhoons entered RAF service, the Cold War was history.

The Typhoon is a highly agile, supersonic aircraft, and its performance is so inherently unstable that a pilot would not be able to fly it without the integral computer-aided fly-by-wire systems. As it is, however, the combination of pilot and computer make it among the two or three best combat aircraft in the world. Using the latest radar and targeting systems, the pilot can simultaneously handle multiple threats at long range, whether they are air defence missiles or other aircraft. (For good reasons, the Ministry of Defence does not reveal much about this capability.)

The single crewman or woman uses voice controls for many of the aircraft's functions. Combined with video screen 'glass cockpit' and a single control column incorporating throttles, defensive controls and weapons deployment, the Typhoon is a surprisingly simple aircraft to fly and fight.

Weight is kept down through use of carbon fibre composites and light alloys. With re-heat or afterburners on, the twin turbo-fan engines can propel it to twice the speed of sound and a ceiling of 65,000 feet.

All of this was of such interest to the Argentines that when the Typhoons were introduced, they passed a diplomatic complaint to London claiming that the capability was a dangerous escalation of the military presence. It was ignored.

Standard armament consists of AIM-120B and AIM-132 air-to-air missiles. The AIM-120B can be launched from a distance of 20 to 30 nautical miles, well beyond visual range, and using its own inertial navigation system, updated by data from the launching aircraft, homes in on an enemy until a radar takes over and guides it to impact. It's slightly less sophisticated cousin, AIM-132, is described by the RAF as a 'fire and forget' heat-seeking missile, which is ideal when in close contact with an enemy. It can, however, be launched beyond visual range.

However, it is a missile that is yet to be deployed to the Falklands, the brand new ramjet-powered Meteor, that will raise Argentine eyebrows to the extreme. This ultra-modern and capable missile is designed to be fitted to Typhoons, and has a 'stealthy' launch system, meaning a pilot unfortunate enough to be targeted would find it extremely difficult to detect the threat, and therefore evade it, until the last seconds. This missile will be in use soon, and the Falklands defenders will, almost certainly, be able to draw on it if necessary.

Hercules and VC10 transport/tankers

Typhoons are on standby around the clock, 365-days a year, and barely a day goes by that they are not launched on a routine training mission, a patrol or to investigate a 'blip' that might be approaching the Islands. Every time a fighter lifts off and accelerates into the clouds, a Vickers VC10 tanker, designated C1K, will follow it, ensuring that, should the volatile South Atlantic weather systems close down the air base, the Typhoon could be refueled, repeatedly if necessary, while it diverts to one of the very few semi-friendly countries on the South American coast, or loiters until the weather clears.

The sole VC10 C1K stationed in the Islands, flown by men and women of 1312 Flight, would also have an important tactical role if hostilities broke out. With the support of the VC10, Typhoons would be able to remain on combat control for hours at a time, rather than returning to base to top up on fuel.

1312 Flight also operates the only C130 Hercules based at Mount Pleasant. This aircraft also has an air-to-air refueling capability, but its unique role is maritime patrol, extending as far as South Georgia and the South Sandwich Islands. The aircraft does not, however, police the Falklands fisheries zone; that task is allocated to the Britton Norman Islander aircraft of the Falkland Islands Government Air Service.

A rarely used but vital C130 role is that of emergency medical evacuation. If a patient's injuries are so serious that he or she cannot await medevac on the twice-weekly Falklands-UK airbridge, then the Hercules will carry the patient to Chile or to Uruguay.

Both C130s and VC10s are remarkable aircraft in their way. C130s are ubiquitous in the air forces of the world. They are the most successful tactical transports ever, and have been in production by Lockheed – latterly Lockheed Martin – for over fifty years. VC10s, now serving their final years before well-deserved retirement, entered civilian service as airliners in the early 1960s. Some of the RAF airframes started life as civilian aircraft, while others were ordered from Vickers, and delivered in 1965. They have, therefore, been proving reliable, first as troop carriers, then as tankers, for forty-six years.

Sea King Search and Rescue Helicopters

A shortage of helicopters for operations in Afghanistan led to the withdrawal of most of the rotary wing inventory from the Falklands. For almost a quarter of a century, Chinooks had been a valuable means of deploying ground troops around the archipelago. The Falklands has a proud history of association with the type. During 1982, Chinook Bravo November was the only survivor of its type and was subsequently so vital to the British effort that it almost certainly shortened the war by weeks. The last Chinook left the Falklands in October 2006.

A handful of troop-carrying Sea Kings continued in service a little longer, but these too were shipped back to the UK for more pressing operational use. This left only the bright yellow Sea King search and rescue machines of 1564 Flight. The Flight's primary purpose is to provide a rescue service for pilots who might have to eject or ditch in the sea. There have been few such accidents, but many fishermen and crews of other commercial vessels in the Southwest Atlantic had reason to thank the air sea rescue crews.

British International Helicopters Ltd

Routine helicopter support for the garrison was contracted out to a civilian operator, British International Helicopters Ltd, which operates two large Sikorsky S-61s. Every day, the pair of brightly painted machines shuttle troops and supplies to radar stations and other outposts, or carry squads of ground troops conducting routine patrols of the coastline and mountains.

Royal Navy: Guarding the Seas

In numerical terms, at least, the Navy destroyer and frigate fleets suffered considerably during the Strategic Defence and Security Review. Assuming all of the planned cuts will be carried out, the Navy will soon have just nineteen of these versatile ships. These cuts were potentially important to the Falklands because the frequently rotating frigates and destroyers form the background of the Falklands sea defences.

However, any initial alarm was probably misplaced, as, although smaller, the capability of the force is becoming more powerful. The fleet of thirteen Type 23 frigates was untouched, as were the three active Type 45 destroyers. And orders were maintained for the three Type 45s still under construction. (At the time of writing, the latest of these was undergoing trials.)

The old Type 22 frigates and Type 42 destroyers had given magnificent service, the latter as far back as the 1982 conflict. But they could carry nothing like the modern weaponry of the newer ships.

Type 45 Destroyers
At the time of writing, no Type 45 destroyer had steamed the 8,000 miles to spend four months or so as the Falklands' guard ship, but when HMS *Daring*, *Dauntless* or *Dragon* does so, it will probably be an event that again has the Argentines protesting about the escalating British presence. In truth, they will be, but they will have no more ships on routine duty off the Falklands than they have had in the past: just much better ones.

The Royal Navy promotes the Type 45s as 'the largest and most powerful destroyers ever ordered for the Navy, and the largest general-purpose ships – excluding carriers and amphibious ships – ordered since the Second World War.'

A 'stealthy' design gives the ships a futuristic look. An almost complete lack of 90-degree vertical surfaces on the hull means enemy radar will not return strong signals. The radar-slippery shape extends to the characteristic pyramid-shaped central mast that is topped by a radar dome. The ships are 152 metres long and weigh in at 7,350 tons. They have a maximum speed of 29 knots, but would normally cruise at a more economical 18 knots, giving them a range of some 7,000 nautical miles.

Type 45s carry a 114mm gun for shore bombardment, as well as the joint UK/French/Italian Principal Anti-aircraft Missile System (PAAMS), Sylver, Aster and Sea Skua short- and long-range missiles. The two radar systems can detect incoming attacks and control offensive operations out to 400km. Uniquely among modern destroyers, there is also capacity for up to forty Royal Marines Commandos and their weaponry, which would be expected to use the onboard Merlin or Lynx helicopters.

Having a single type 45 serving around the Falklands will be at least equal to, and possibly exceed, the potential strength of having an elderly Type 42 destroyer and a Type 22 frigate on station.

(In February 2012, the Ministry of Defence announced that the Type 45 destroyer HMS *Dauntless* would deploy to the Falklands from March. As expected, Argentina protested loudly about Britain supposedly further militarizing the region and raising tension. At the same time, they alleged that Britain had deployed a nuclear-armed submarine. In response to the latter allegation, the Ministry of Defence said that it never commented on submarine deployments, but made it clear they would not deploy nuclear weapons to a theatre such as the Falklands.)

Type 23 Frigates
Type 23 frigates, all named after British dukes, have been familiar sights in Falklands waters for years. The first, HMS *Norfolk*, was launched in 1987, but they are sufficiently modern to feature stealthy structures angled off the vertical and weapons systems that will remain highly respected for a decade or more yet.

The 133-metre-long ships have a similar speed to the modern destroyers. Commissioned during the latter years of the Cold War, the frigates were designed to spend long patrols towing arrays of sonar detection equipment in the North Atlantic. To aid the search for Russian submarines, and to make them less detectable to the subs that were playing a similar game, the Type 22s were equipped with quiet electric motors as well as the more normal turbines.

With the Russian threat in retreat, the ships were assigned a more general-purpose role, and fitted with Harpoon anti-ship missiles and 114mm guns. However, the Sting Ray anti-submarine torpedo system was retained. Sea Skua anti-aircraft missiles complete the ships' offensive capability. Type 22s are in line for further modernization and adaptations that underline their importance as the fleet's mainstay general-purpose ship.

Attack Submarines

It is occasionally made known that a nuclear-powered (but not nuclear-armed) attack submarine is in the Southwest Atlantic. Every few years, one surfaces and berths at Mare Harbour, the military seaport a few miles from Mount Pleasant. There is no practical need to do this, as these huge boats can cruise for months beneath the surface. But political reckoning at the Ministry of Defence in London and at Permanent Joint HQ just outside London is that one cannot be totally certain that the Argentines believe that UK submarines patrol the area. This is despite the sad fact that the Argentine cruiser *General Belgrano* was torpedoed by a British nuclear-powered boat, with the loss of 323 men.

Commitment to submarines was little effected by the Strategic Defence and Security Review. Indeed, a very large amount of money is now being spent on the new Astute Class, which will eventually number seven. Two had entered service at the time of writing.

Astute is a development from the preceding Trafalgar Class, of which six are still in service, all equipped with Spearfish torpedoes for attacking both surface vessels and other submarines. Some are also equipped with Tomahawk cruise missiles. Subs fired missiles on Afghanistan during the early stages of the campaign there. Rather intriguingly, the Royal Navy also says that Trafalgar Class boats can operate on 'covert surveillance tasks', which may mean landing special forces on hostile shores. This was a task handled in the past by conventional diesel-electric boats, but the submarine fleet is totally nuclear powered.

Although there are almost certainly lengthy periods when no submarine is within easy striking distance of the Falklands, it is equally certain that they do patrol routinely, and are rapidly despatched to the Southwest Atlantic when the threat from Argentina suddenly increases. Their beauty is twofold: the mere belief that they might be in the area multiplies the deterrent power of British forces; and they can be deployed to bolster the Falklands' defences without timid voices in Whitehall protesting about the risk of escalating a crisis.

Astute Class boats can speed along underwater at 25 knots, which would enable them to reach the Falklands from the UK in about two weeks. The Trafalgar boats are a little slower. But it is likely that at most times at least one boat is closer than 8,000 miles, and can reach the Falklands theatre more quickly.

HMS *Protector*

The Navy's latest ice patrol ship, HMS *Protector*, has little tactical value, but very considerable strategic worth. With her bright red hull, white superstructure, and boxy totally un-stealthy radar signature, the vessel's value in an actual conflict would be minimal. But her presence in the area of South Georgia, the South Sandwich Islands, the Falklands and the Antarctic Peninsula every austral summer, starting in the 2011/12 summer, makes it clear that Britain retains its interest in the area. Reviving the name *Protector* at a time of increasing tension with Argentina added piquancy to the message.

HMS *Protector*, which was built in 2001, replaced the equally red, white and unwarlike HMS *Endurance* in 2011. The Norwegian ice-reinforced ship was designed for Polar expeditions, and is equipped with large cargo holds, cranes and a helicopter flight deck. However, unlike the previous *Protector* and two *Endurances*, she does not carry her own helicopters. It is not known if she will be given a hangar and aircraft after her first deployment.

The ship was chartered by the Royal Navy for three years, and went through a minor refit. She was equipped with light weaponry and special echo-sounding equipment for survey work. *Protector* also carries all-terrain vehicles.

HMS *Clyde*

This River Class ship may serve its days out in the Southwest Atlantic. Based on several smaller vessels used for patrol work near the UK, *Clyde* was specially commissioned for offshore patrol work in the Falklands. At 1,850 tons, she is some seven times smaller than a Type 45 destroyer, but a little bigger than her sister ships. Her offensive weaponry is limited to a 30mm Oerlikon cannon and two general-purpose machine guns (although in a crisis, the latter weapons might be expected to sprout from all corners). Although *Clyde* has a flight deck capable of hosting a Merlin helicopter, she does not carry her own aircraft.

Clyde took over Falklands duties from the elderly River Class HMS *Dumbarton Castle* in November 2007. Her principal task is to patrol the Islands' coastal areas and territorial waters. She has good ocean-going capability and range, however, and will visit South Georgia if necessary. *Clyde* is chartered from the builders Vosper Thorneycroft, who also have a contract to maintain her until at least 2018.

Clyde is small in Royal Navy terms, but she is versatile. There is accommodation for eighteen soldiers or Royal Marines, a capacity that could, no doubt, be increased in a crisis. There is deck space for mine countermeasures and diving support equipment, modular medical facilities, small tracked and wheel vehicles and a landing craft. She routinely carries rigid hull inflatable boats. An onboard 25-ton crane can handle all of this equipment.

The relatively minor warship was the focus of diplomatic controversy in January 2011, when (presumably weakening to Argentine pressure) the government of Brazil denied her access to Rio de Janeiro. Uruguay had denied visiting rights to the then principal Falklands guard ship, HMS *Gloucester*, five months earlier.

Royal Fleet Auxiliary Support

The Royal Fleet Auxiliary has a long and honourable connection with the Falklands, which continues to the present. In 1982, the landing ships *Sir Galahad* and *Sir Tristram* were bombed by the Argentines at Fitzroy, with heavy loss of life, mainly among the embarked soldiers. Other RFA ships, carrying fuel and vast amounts of ammunition, survived the bombing campaign in San Carlos Water. The RFA was, arguably, the forgotten service but the Falklands raised their often heroic profile.

The ships of the RFA and the civilians who crew them remain essential to the defence of the Islands. Tankers and general support ships come and go from the theatre as required, and are invariably in attendance when destroyers and frigates go further south to Antarctic waters or to South Georgia and the South Sandwich Islands. RFA ships are armed with only light defensive weapons.

Most import for the Falklands forces is the RFA ships' ability to replenish other vessels at sea. The Wave, Rover and Leaf Class vessels, as well as the general replenishment ships, rendezvous with frigates and destroyers en route to or from the Islands, or when they are on protracted patrols, often deploying from the military base at Mare Harbour. This is skilled and potentially dangerous work. Diesel and water hoses are suspended across many metres of sea, in heavy weather if necessary, while the ships steam ahead in precise formation. Meanwhile, other supplies and mail are transferred between ships as under-slung helicopter loads. The procedures are rehearsed frequently.

The largest of the general replenishment vessels, such as the Fort Victoria and Fort Rosalie Class ships, can carry up to four Sea King helicopters, although they would not necessarily deploy to the Falklands with them.

RFA ships could be considered force multipliers. Certainly no ships defending the Falklands would go far from port without knowing they were nearby.

Army: The Feet on the Ground

If the Argentine Government decided to repeat the 1982 invasion of the Falklands, they would do so differently. In 1982, the only goal for invading troops was Port Stanley and the seat of government. A small number of lightly-armed Royal Marines and Falkland Islands Defence Force volunteers were no more than a tripwire. If attacked, this thinly camouflaged line would activate a massive response in Britain. The Argentine military junta either did not understand the concept of a military tripwire, or did not believe that the one that had been erected in the Falklands was connected to anything more than a timid civilian government. They were wrong, of course.

It would be grossly unprofessional of the Argentine ministry of defence and their military if they did not now have a better understanding of the Falklands' defensive doctrine, and did not have in place contingency plans for operations should their government require them. Any modern plan would mean taking out Mount Pleasant air base in a first withering strike by air, probably aided by special forces on the ground.

Royal Artillery

Mount Pleasant is a large target, but one that, as already described, is well defended by the RAF. But the Army also has a major role to play. The Royal Artillery's 16 Regiment maintains the latest generation Rapier mobile ground-to-air missiles at strategic points around the base. They can be relocated rapidly and the operators frequently pit themselves in exercise against RAF Typhoons. Rapier was highly successful in the 1982 conflict, despite weather limitations on the optical system of the time. Today's radar-guided Rapier is much superior.

Resident Infantry Company

Infantry regiments in the UK take it in turns to detach 'reinforced' companies for six-monthly tours of duty in the Falklands. Numbering in the region of 120 troops, the Resident Infantry Company is responsible for perimeter security at Mount Pleasant, the military port at Mare Harbour, and other smaller outposts. The infantrymen also patrol the more remote corners of the Islands, often liaising with local farmers, and exercising with the Falkland Islands Defence Force. If deploying to more remote areas, platoons or smaller sections travel either aboard the ships of the Royal Navy – most frequently HMS *Clyde* – or aboard the civilian-crewed Sikorsky aircraft of British International Helicopters Ltd. The troops remain on a high state of alert against incursions.

There have been indications that such patrolling is a wise precaution. Argentine forces or nationalists may have landed a small group on a remote point of East Falkland in 2000. An inflatable boat found by a farmer on the shore of Concordia Bay was said to contain military-style equipment and a satellite phone containing Argentine numbers, although no weapons. The boat had apparently been swamped and was half buried by sand.

The Ministry of Defence and the Foreign Office refused to comment on the incident, and when the *Penguin News* approached Whitehall requesting information about the incident under the Freedom of Information Act, they met an information brick wall. The Foreign Office eventually confirmed that a boat had been found, but refused to say anything more on the grounds that it could damage relations with another country. That country had to be Argentina, the implication being that the rubber boat trail led back there, and there appeared to be no desire to escalate the issue.

Royal Engineers and Bomb Disposal

A detachment of Royal Engineers is deployed to the Falklands with the principal role of runway repair. Using heavy earth-moving equipment, the sappers would be expected to quickly return a runway to operational status if cratered in an Argentine attack.

Royal Engineers of 33 Explosive Ordnance Disposal Group also work with RAF and Army Ordnance Corps specialists in the Joint Service Explosive Ordnance Disposal (EOD) team. Unexploded weaponry from the 1982 war is still found from time to time, and although civilian contractors are slowly clearing the extensive minefields, the EOD experts still need to maintain minefield fencing and signage and dispose of mines that may, over time, be exposed near the perimeters.

Tri-service Communications and Intelligence Units

There are units within the Falklands defence establishment that are secret. These include the RAF-run radar stations at Mount Kent near Stanley and on two remote mountains on the far west of the islands. Between them, these stations provide a 360-degree electronic image of air operations up to the coast of Argentina. They are fundamental defence assets, therefore well protected, and spoken of little.

The Joint Communications Unit Falkland Islands (JCUFI) operates in an even more shadowy zone at Mount Pleasant. Tri-service staff maintain and operate the radio communications systems around the Falklands, connecting ships, aircraft, outstations and Permanent Joint Headquarters (PJHQ) in Britain.

JCUFI also operates an electronic warfare capability, which may include a signal jamming capability, and certainly includes routine monitoring of military radio traffic in Argentina.

While relatively few personnel are involved in these activities, JCUFI and the radar sites are the essential foundation blocks of Fortress Falklands.

Permanent Joint Headquarters, Northolt

PJHQ at Northolt just outside London is the nerve centre of all British military operations. As such, it is as much a part of Falkland defences as any element located physically in the Islands. Responsibilities do not come much more onerous than those that face the approximately 600 military and civilian staff at PJHQ. They are, according to the Ministry of Defence, 'responsible for directing, deploying, sustaining and recovering UK joint forces.'

From his above-ground offices near the centre of Mount Pleasant or, in a crisis, from the underground command bunker some distance from the main base area, the Commander British Forces South Atlantic Islands must liaise with the Chief of Joint Operations and PJHQ staff assigned to the Falklands operation. Conversely, PJHQ decisions are informed by intelligence assessment and resourcing information from the Falklands.

The Headquarters, established in 1996, is a tri-service establishment at the very heart of British military operations. While such individual service commands as Fleet in Portsmouth, Land near Salisbury and Strike in High Wycombe are responsible for resourcing and managing their individual service commitments, PJHQ carry out strategic decisions made at the levels of the Defence Secretary and the Chief of the Defence Staff. PJHQ would co-ordinate the deployment, if necessary, of the tri-service units at rapid reaction status should the Falklands require urgent reinforcement.

The foregoing is a quick tour of the disparate units that make up Fortress Falklands, with one important exception: the part-time civilian Falkland Islands Defence Force (FIDF). My visit to the FIDF was yet to come. First, though, I wanted to learn what it is like to command such a garrison. For that I turned to an old friend of our family, Air Vice Marshall Gordon Moulds. Gordon flew on Nimrod intelligence-gathering aircraft during the 1982 conflict. He went on to serve as navigator aboard Falklands-based Phantoms, as Chief of Staff to the Commander British Forces South Atlantic Islands, and finally to hold that powerful position himself. He, I was sure, could give me the human angle.

CHAPTER 14

A Commander's View

In the Falklands, I encountered nothing but frustration in my attempts to speak to the military authorities. By week three of my time in Stanley, I had given up. Media Ops at Mount Pleasant had fallen silent, as had the brigadier at the Directorate of Media and Communications.

I did not blame the individuals concerned, as it was obvious to me that they were hobbled by a very tardy effort to form a response to Argentina's increasingly aggressive stance. But still it seemed unnecessary. It was ironic too, because a year or two earlier, the Ministry of Defence had been welcoming almost any press interest in the Falklands as an opportunity to burnish its reputation. But the shutters had now come down. I really blamed the ultra-cautious diplomats and defence policy civil servants.

I was prepared, however, to accept that this approach – although it was certainly not a strategy – was in response to a real and developing situation that was causing jitters in Whitehall. I knew that there was soon to be a special meeting of the National Security Council that would be chaired by the PM himself, during which the military top brass would brief him on contingency plans should the situation develop into a crisis. But that hardly seemed to justify total silence at a time when the Argentines were calling the communications shots.

While the aggressive rhetoric from across the water was being broadcast at maximum volume, it simply did not make sense to say nothing about a deterrent that existed, was credible and relied for success on potential enemies knowing about it. But there was nothing I could do about it. So I looked elsewhere for an authoritative view on the task of defending the Falklands.

One name came up immediately. Air Commodore Gordon Moulds had been Commander British Forces South Atlantic very recently, and he was a family friend. Arguably, no one had greater military experience on the Falklands over the last thirty years, and few people known to me thought about the issues in such depth. So I decided to contact Gordon, who by this time was back in Britain. I could have called him from Stanley, but somehow that option seemed inadequate, so I resolved to interview him, if possible, when I returned to Britain, but bring him into my narrative at this point.

In May 1982, the then Sergeant Moulds was an electronics operator serving on Nimrod surveillance aircraft flying highly covert missions somewhere between the Argentine coast and the Falklands. This was hostile airspace, to put it mildly. The Nimrod crews were tasked to observe the movements of submarines and warships that posed a potent threat to the British task force. They flew well within the range of Mirage and Dagger interceptors, which had already proved their mettle in action.

The Nimrod operations went well out on a very shaky limb. With the benefit of a fleet of air-to-air tankers, and operating from Ascension Island, Sergeant Moulds and his colleagues pushed their aircraft and themselves very close to the limits. The missions to Argentine seas and, even further, to the waters around South Georgia were not for the timid. That all the missions were completed without loss was probably more than the RAF had expected.

The RAF had acknowledged the danger when they fitted the spy planes with Sidewinder air-to-air missiles. The Sidewinders would have been launched only as a last desperate measure, and it never came to that. However, at least one Nimrod crew detected that fighters were homing in on them. They had sufficient time to descend to near wave height and, using the curvature of the earth to avoid enemy radar signals, they beat a prudent retreat back to Ascension Island.

That was the start of Gordon Moulds' long relationship with

Fortress Falklands. After his service in Operation Corporate, as the 1982 conflict was officially titled, he re-trained as a navigator and weapons operator on Phantom jets. In 1986, he returned to the South Atlantic, completing the first of seven tours of duty in the aircraft that then provided the Islands' air defence. His career was on a rising trajectory. In June 2004, and recently promoted to Group Captain, Gordon was again posted to the Falklands, this time securely fixed to the ground as Chief of Staff to the Commander British Forces. He remained in that post until August 2006, during which time he must have made a good impression, because, in June 2009, this time wearing the insignia of an Air Commodore, he was posted to the Falklands a tenth time, to serve eighteen months in overall command of British forces in the South Atlantic.

During this career, he accrued an MBE and a CBE. His final post before retirement was as commander of the coalition air base at Kandahar in southern Afghanistan, surely confirmation of the faith that the RAF and the Ministry of Defence had placed in him.

There are few current or former servicemen who have served so often and for so long in the Falklands. And I would say there are few who grew to love the place as much as Gordon Moulds. The very down-to-earth Scot and his wife Belinda found themselves in an environment that reminded them of their home on the west coast of Scotland, and they enjoyed the company of Islanders, who in turn responded warmly and generously to their friendship. All Commanders British Forces had been very capable men (so far no woman has occupied the position), but not all were particularly friendly. Hosting dinners and cocktail parties is part of the job description, but most Commanders British Forces packed their guest lists with fellow officers, senior Falklands civil servants, elected legislators or expatriate contract Brits. Gordon and Belinda did things differently. They got to know the ordinary Islanders, especially those who lived on the sheep farms of East Falklands. They invited them to Mount Pleasant, visited them on their farms, even lending an occasional hand with farm work. As a result, they forged strong friendships. The Moulds would endure the long drive to Stanley from Mount Pleasant just to play bridge, which was how my family had met and become friendly with them.

When I phoned Gordon to set up an interview, he had been away from the South Atlantic for longer than he would have liked, and he quickly slipped into happy nostalgia. 'Every aspect of our time there was fantastic,' he told me down the line. 'Until you got mobile phones, we were away from the modern world. We could be sitting on a beach surrounded by penguins and sea lions and with no other humans in sight. It is just *the* place, and I love it.

'The people were the most wonderful I have come across. I loved the community spirit. I loved the fact that everyone knew everyone. And the farmers worked their socks off to eke out a living. They are the salt of the earth. They will always have a bed for you and always have a meal for you.'

We met a few days after this conversation at a café in Euston Station in London. It had just been announced that the Queen's 2012 Golden Jubilee would be marked with a grand Royal tour of the UK and the Commonwealth. Understandably, neither the Queen nor the Duke of Edinburgh would be doing the long-distance trips. Their children and grandchildren would carry these out, status of the planned visitor to any territory depending on its importance. Unfortunately, the Falklands were not on the first division list, and would be visited by the much lower profile Duke of Kent. The Duke's other destination was to be Uganda.

This was a little surprising, because Prince Andrew had fought in the Islands in 1982, and a Golden Jubilee visit by him would have been appropriate, as well as sending out a strong message of British commitment. This snub rubbed a little salt in the injury inflicted by the ban on Prince William carrying out any official duties while he was flying search and rescue helicopters in the Islands during the early months of 2012. If an Islander wanted to meet the second in line to the throne, he or she would be best advised to take a trip in a small boat, and get lost. But one could imagine the official thinking; a first division Royal Family visit might have annoyed the Argentines, perhaps provoking another tsunami of vitriolic diplomacy. The Duke was, therefore, a relatively safe bet.

Shortly before Gordon and I met, the Argentines had ratcheted up the implementation of their infamous Senate Decree 256; their demand that ships bound for the Falklands obtain permission to do so from Buenos Aires. A Spanish fishing vessel licensed by the Falklands Government had been harassed by an Argentine patrol ship in waters jointly owned by Uruguay and Argentina. While the Uruguayan Government had expressed general support for Argentina's Malvinas claim, it was not at all happy about the Argentine Coast Guard throwing its weight around in shared waters. A Uruguayan Air Force aircraft was despatched to monitor the incident, and watch over the Spanish ship until it reached the open sea. The Uruguayans were angry, and the head of the Navy said its air patrol had ensured that third party vessels 'can sail to the high seas with no inconveniences and proceed with their tasks.' This was, of course, music to the ears of Falkland Islanders.

The royal squirming and the escalating harassment of shipping set a rather downbeat tone for our meeting. As we sat down to consume our lattes in Euston Station, I was conscious that Gordon's period as Commander British Forces had ended about fifteen months earlier, but we were now seeing the logical development of aggressive Argentine policies that had been in play when he was in post. Despite service in Afghanistan since leaving Mount Pleasant, he had not taken his eye off the Falklands ball, and his insight was sharp.

Gordon respects the Argentine military and understands them better than most. In particular, he believes their air force is very capable. He had operational contact with them on just one occasion, in the period of thawing relations, when Argentine and British forces co-operated in a search and rescue exercise. But apart from that, military interface was usually mute and took place when RAF fighters met aircraft from Patagonia probing Falklands defences.

There was no question of serious aggression on either side. The Argentines could legitimately transit Falklands air space if they wished to do so, which did happen from time to time, although generally the Argentines turned away at a point around 150 miles from the centre of the Islands. The Argentines were keeping the Brits on their toes, and the Brits were letting the Argentines know they had been detected. It was the kind of semi-provocative game that went on between the Russian and British air forces off the north of Britain during their Cold War (and which was recently resumed). 'Testing reaction times came into it,' said Gordon. 'That's what the Argentine military got out of it. Because although there may be no intention whatsoever [to attack the Falklands], every military does contingency planning. If Argentina's president ordered the military to act, then they would have to do it. So they prepare for any eventuality no matter how unlikely.'

Looking back to his time in the cockpit, he recalled an incident that, if not typical, did illustrate the challenges the RAF faced. 'On one very stormy night, we had to shadow an Argentine Hercules all the way around the Islands. It flew just a few miles from the coast.

'These days, though, it's much better. They'll come up to the border and respect the Falklands air space, which is why it's important that we don't go into their air space.'

Low flying was an important skill and could be practised in the Islands without fear of upsetting the locals. It was a different story in the UK, where the phones at RAF bases often rang wildly with complaints from farmers whose cattle and sheep had been stampeded or whose pheasant shoots had been disturbed. For fast jet pilots, the Islands were a delight. Said Gordon: 'There was very little air traffic to worry about and we had the freedom of the Islands. We did some excellent training. The only complaints we would get would be that there had not been *enough* noise recently. Farmers would say, "Where have you been? We haven't seen you," and demand more low flying.'

Notwithstanding the Argentine Air Force probes, the late 1980s and early 1990s were the good times for those manning the ramparts. The defensive posture could be relaxed, just a bit, as President Menem and his foreign minister, the anglophile Guido di Tella, began a process of rapprochement that took the chill off the cold war. The British Ministry of Defence started trimming its Falklands budget and cautiously scaling down the defences. This was not spoken of much, but helicopter capability was gradually reduced and the overall manpower at Mount Pleasant declined by several hundred personnel. It seemed to be a sensible readjustment. But in May 2003, Néstor Kirchner was elected to power and immediately began rolling back his predecessor's achievements.

'Kirchner changed the tone for the military,' recalled Gordon, who, as the Commander's Chief of Staff, witnessed these defence changes. 'Fishing boats that had been working legally were being arrested. From very few Argentine aircraft coming to the borders, we were suddenly seeing a lot more. Lan Chile charter flights were not permitted to go through Argentine air space. Agreements were ripped up or totally ignored. You name it: there was so much being done against the Islands. From our gradual drawdown of forces, which should have continued because of the costs that could be saved, we went to, "Whoa! We need to stop now, to pause and just look at what is happening."'

From that point, the development of today's tension, bitter diplomacy, threat and blockade can be tracked. By the time Gordon Moulds returned to the Falklands for his tenth tour of duty, this time as the most senior officer in theatre, he faced a much less relaxed environment, and had the task of remoulding the defenders into a stance that was at a high state of readiness. 'I had to be politically aware,' he told me. 'And everyone had to be aware that they were part of a real deterrent. We all had to know that our jobs were to be taken very seriously. No one thought an Argentine invasion was likely. But we *had* to train for that eventuality. We had to exercise constantly and, for example, show armed guards at the entrance to the base. There was no serious risk as long as we maintained the deterrent at a high state of readiness, but there *might* have been circumstances that could lead to a threat if we relaxed it. Further, once you reduce your forces, it would be virtually impossible to increase again without significant diplomatic and financial penalties.'

The renewed emphasis on the potency of the deterrent jarred rather with the Falkland Islands Government's efforts to portray the Islands as an attractive destination for tourists and for investors; a place where there was no real threat to the attractive, bucolic and increasingly wealthy way of life. 'For me,' said Gordon, 'the challenge was trying to balance the political view with the military requirement.'

The opinion he developed then about the importance of the Falklands' defences still applies. 'If we were not there, I believe the Falklands would come under a higher level of threat. That might not be an invasion threat, but if, for example, Kirchner was unpopular and desperate because she was about to lose power, then there *might* be a number of options at her disposal to cause the UK concern.'

It was not easy to convince the approximately 5,000 members of the three services posted to the Falklands each year (most personnel serve four months in the Islands and there are about 1,200 there at any time) that a period at the Death Star (Mount Pleasant) was more than an opportunity to get very fit in the complex's gyms, to see penguins and seals for real rather than courtesy of David Attenborough, or a chance to imbibe a great deal of alcohol very cheaply. 'We had to explain why we were doing this and the importance of it,' said Gordon. 'Every person who came into theatre received a brief from me or from the Chief of Staff. The hardest part of this was explaining that it was a Cold War-style operation. We had done the same thing with the Russians, but the UK's doctrine is focused on expeditionary warfare now, and the tenets of Cold War operations are rapidly being lost. We also had to justify our case about the importance of what we were doing back in the UK, because with Iraq and Afghanistan ongoing, there were, understandably, higher priorities for funding.'

I was beginning to appreciate the importance of the political nous that Gordon had mentioned. As if incorporating the Falklands Government's need to convey normality with the need to show some teeth was not enough, he had to argue with London and monitor events in Buenos Aires. The latter was probably the most difficult challenge, but it was clear that the Argentine mood music had changed from a wheezing nostalgic tango to something almost Wagnerian.

I asked Gordon if British forces now were ready for anything, however unlikely it might be. He thought for a moment, and then said, 'Yes, most definitely. There are only a few "surprise" options available to the Argentines, and with our advantage on the air side, which includes more than just aircraft, our early warning capability and ground response times, the runway would remain operational and prepared for the reinforcements that would inevitably be sent following any aggression.

'The main task is to keep that runway open. Of course, we would not wait for an incident; if anything was seen to be developing, we would have reinforcements coming in from the UK at very short notice. We would have appropriate assets arriving to counter the perceived threat. There is a mechanism to reinforce very quickly.'

Gordon is an RAF man to the core, but his emphasis on the importance of the air operation was not a matter of bias. 'It would be very hard for the Argentines to come by sea,' he continued. 'One could insert special forces by submarine, but that's why we had our no-notice practice callouts. Everyone at Mount Pleasant knew their defensive positions. We practised that week in, week out. If the alarm went for real, we would have troops out and everyone defending so that the airfield *would* remain open.'

I queried the capability of a single reinforced company of infantry to do all that would be needed. The resident infantry company was, he pointed out, 'extremely effective and a good size'. But there were plenty more men and women who could wield weapons if necessary and if the balloon went up, all of them would do so. 'We also have Navy and RAF staff who can be put on guard. Fortunately, the military attitude and understanding is so much better these days due to the UK's recent operations. The Falklands is perfect for developing and honing the skills that will be required by personnel deploying to Afghanistan.'

The Commander British Forces has another asset to call on in a crisis: the FIDF. The part-time civilian militia is small, and would only be able to deploy at less than company strength. But Gordon said they trained hard, were committed and highly mobile. He had integrated the force into his defence planning. 'Fifty of them are worth 100 regular British troops in the Falklands,' he said. 'They know the Islands so well. The FIDF punches way above its weight. We got them up to a level at which we were genuinely using the FIDF in our plans, and with more integration there would be so much more that could be done with them. They deployed every time we planned an exercise, and they trained us by 'attacking' the base. During the first exercise I organized, they got into the hangars and took photos. They knew where the holes in the fences were and got in. As a result we brought in new equipment and during the next and future exercises, the FIDF didn't get anywhere near the hangars. But they had identified our weakness.'

The Islanders themselves were ready to play a useful role in their own defence if the Argentines ever landed. But what about moves Buenos Aires could take that fell short of an armed assault on the Islands? Almost as we spoke, updates were coming through on the web about the Argentine harassment of Spanish fishing ships bound for the Falklands. The Spaniards, who were in partnership with Falklands companies, were ignoring orders from the Argentine Coast Guard to stop and be searched. 'They can do things like that,' said Gordon, 'and there are a number of other things they can do to make life difficult, but if they raise the heat too much, they will bring international sympathy to the Falklands.'

Angry Spanish and Uruguayan reactions to the latest harassment seemed to be bearing this out. 'And yes,' he continued, 'they could cut the air link with Chile and try to enforce their blockade by force, but they would risk world condemnation.'

He believes that, while one cannot ignore aggression of this sort, the greater threats will come from complex geopolitical relationships that evolve over the coming years and decades. As we sipped our coffees we discussed how bigger regional issues might well eclipse the narrow colonial dispute, and how big global players might take the region from a state of gentle simmer to a boiling point. That would not happen overnight, but Gordon insisted that strategists must look well beyond the blockade, the harassed fishing fleets and endangered air link to see the much more worrying issues.

I was not surprised that the United States entered our conversation at this point as a possible game changing country (Washington had recently indicated admiration for the Kirchner government and urged the old combatants to talk. Furthermore, Hillary Clinton had publicly referred to the Falklands as the Malvinas). But I was surprised when Gordon mentioned, in almost the same breath, China. Argentina is among the top three benefactors from Chinese aid and investment, and the two countries had just agreed a pact of mutual support for their claims over Taiwan and the Falklands. So far, that diplomatic support had been the only requirement of the Chinese, but there are often more practical strings attached to Chinese generosity. Recipients of Chinese help in other parts of the world had been expected to buy Chinese weapons. There was no sign of this in the current Argentine-Chinese friendship, but everyone needs to watch out for it. If Chinese goodwill and cash translates into Argentine militarization, then the alarm would need to be sounded loudly.

I did not only want to discuss the big-ticket political and defence issues. Gordon and I have many mutual friends in the Falklands; people like the McPhees of Brookfield Farm (who will feature in a later chapter). I knew that he and Belinda hoped to visit their friends again sometime, but for now I was able to bring him up to date on their news.

We finished our coffee, shook hands and Gordon disappeared into the London crowds. I hoped that the next time we met we would be in Stanley or at Brookfield Farm. I also hoped that when next we sat down over coffee we would not feel the need to discuss Argentine-British relations and the state of the threat. But that was probably a futile wish. There had never been a time in my life when the threat did not hang over the Falklands like a dark cloud, and I was beginning to think there never would be.

CHAPTER 15

The Islanders' Sharp Teeth

Thirty years ago, the defences of the Falkland Islands were almost negligible. The Argentine generals who authorized the invasion must have assumed that in the face of overwhelming odds, the few terrified defenders would immediately produce white flags. The junta was good at making poor judgements, and this was another of them. As a result, they ensured their invading special forces received a bloody nose on 2 April 1982.

Port Stanley was defended on that autumn day by about fifty Royal Marines, who were well trained and brave but equipped with very light weapons, and by the Falkland Islands Defence Force (FIDF), an even smaller force of men who were equally brave and also lightly armed but not very well trained and not used to operating in concert with the Marines.

Both forces deployed on the eve of the invasion, but while the Marines threw their few machine guns and anti-tank rocket launchers into Land Rovers and sped to the beach where they expected the Argentines to land, the Defence Force was left bravely but rather forlornly guarding key points in the town. Then, when it became apparent that the Argentines had landed on a remote beach and entered Stanley by a back door, the Marines were able to speedily double back to Government House, and protect the doughty Governor, Rex Hunt. They battled on for several hours, killing at least one Argentine officer and severely wounding an unknown number of others.

That should not be seen as a slight on the part-time soldiers of the Defence Force who carried out the limited role that had been planned for them, answering to Rex Hunt, as Commander-in-Chief, rather than to the Royal Marines' commanding officer. The invading Argentines simply avoided the key points and did not engage with the local men. Most felt this was fortunate for the Falklands. Ultimately, the Argentines were going to take the Islands, and the Marines were the professionals who formed the human tripwire that would activate a massive response from Britain. The final result less than three months later was assured through engagement with the Marines.

Islanders learned a sharp lesson from the ignominy of defeat. While they accepted that they would never be able to defend their islands alone, it became important for their own sense of pride that they were able to contribute in a real way to the defence of their homeland and, indeed, if possible, punch above their weight.

Over three decades of development, the FIDF has been transformed into a small but well-armed, well-trained and motivated infantry force. Based in Stanley, and usually at considerably less than company strength, the force regularly beats the regular forces in endurance marching and live firing competitions, and is fully incorporated into the defence plans of the Islands. As the former Commander British Forces Gordon Moulds told me, the regulars rated them and wanted their involvement, even if it meant revealing some potentially embarrassing chinks in the regular forces' armour.

The FIDF's commanding officer is Major Peter Biggs, a friend from my childhood, who although well into his fifties sets a fine example of fitness for the men – and a few women – under his command. Peter jogs miles every week, leads the mountain rescue team and recently climbed the highest peak in the southern hemisphere, Aconcagua, in the Argentine Andes.

I met him in the impressive new force HQ, consisting of drill hall, garages, parade ground, offices, armoury, magazine and command centre. The Falkland Islands Government splashed out on the complex during the times of plenty in the 1990s, when income from the squid fishery was at its highest. The HQ is a prominent network of grim-looking steel and corrugated metal buildings on the ridge above Stanley and near the Lookout Rocks, from where, in 1914, the people

146

of Stanley watched the defeat of a German naval force by a Royal Navy squadron.

As I drove through the gate, I noticed two Italian-made 105mm howitzers, captured from the Argentines in 1982, forming a symbolic guard. Peter greeted me at the main entrance. He has just two full-time colleagues, a local sergeant, Paul Watson, and a trainer on secondment from the Royal Marines but funded by the Defence Force.

Peter produced a jumble of keys from the pocket of his camouflaged combat tunic. 'What can I show you first?' He was clearly proud and as he unlocked the steel door of the armoury, I could see why. Once, back in 1982, the Defence Forces had a few dozen 7.62 calibre self-loading rifles, a handful of 1950s' vintage Sterling sub-machine guns and very little else. Now, the weapons cache that lay before me was truly impressive. I had seen heavily tooled-up combat units during reporting visits to Afghanistan and Iraq, but never had I seen a depot as deadly as this accessible to such a small force. I suspected that if the weaponry that lay before us was distributed between the FIDF troops, none would have been able to move.

I said to Peter that had the Defence Force been armed with this astonishing hardware on 2 April 1982, the outcome might have been different. 'There would certainly have been a lot more dead people,' he replied grimly. He gestured towards several long aluminium cases, and then flipped the catches on one to reveal a .5-inch sniper rifle. Costing about £4,000 each, these rifles are more powerful than any in the regular British Army. Their armour-piercing rounds can penetrate a vehicle engine block. Furthermore, such is their velocity and weight that not even the Falklands' notoriously strong winds can affect their accuracy.

We turned to a rack of dozens of somewhat futuristic rifles. Manufactured by the Austrian company Steyr, the AUG assault rifles fire the same 5.56mm rounds as the British SA80 rifle that is standard issue to British forces, but were considered far more reliable than the SA80 until the latter was re-engineered. Interestingly, Argentine special forces are also being equipped with the Steyr.

Above them were matt-black grenade launchers, enough it

appeared for every soldier. 'These are much better than the grenade launchers that we used to sling under the rifles,' Peter said. 'They're less cluttered, they're accurate, and if we have a target hiding behind a rock, we can lob one up in a parabola and hit him.'

Heckler and Koch 9mm pistols – again apparently enough for every man – sit next to Browning pistols of older vintage, and propped in one corner are mighty and heavy .50 calibre Browning heavy machine guns.

General-purpose machine guns (the famous GPMG) and a lone Second World War vintage Bren light machine gun complete the light weapons. But the jewel in the crown is a 20mm Oerlikon cannon. It is the only weapon in the armoury that has been fired in anger by the Defence Force. In the 1990s the force was asked to mount the cannon on a fisheries patrol vessel of the Falkland Islands Government in an operation to deter poachers in the Islands' territorial waters. When an unlicensed ship refused to head for Stanley and surrender to the authorities, the Defence Force first fired across the ship's bows and then raked its hull with shells. The rogue skipper immediately complied. No one was killed but word quickly went around the entire international fleet and poaching virtually ceased.

We left the armoury and walked down a short corridor to a large workshop and garage, where four skeletal and camouflaged Land Rovers were parked. The flatbeds had mountings for the force's Browning heavy machine guns and smaller mountings for general-purpose machine guns operated from the left-hand passenger seats.

The British Ministry of Defence, with its notoriously overblown and slow procurement procedures, might be interested in the process by which these weapons platforms had been acquired. All of the Land Rovers had started life as civilian models. The Defence Force had acquired them second- or third-hand and at least one of the businesslike vehicles before us now had been rolled over, suffering a crushed roof, and was acquired for peanuts. In the space of six days the force's mechanics had stripped the vehicles of all superfluous equipment, including doors and windscreens, reinforced them where necessary, and welded the weapons mounts in place.

The Royal Marines training NCO had recent experience with the far more expensive British Land Rover weapons systems in Afghanistan and trained the Islanders in their tactical use. At its most simple, the fire-spitting Land Rovers work in pairs, covering each other while they frequently move from position to position.

Along with the utility Land Rovers for carrying ammunition, rations and troops, and a fleet of balloon-wheeled quad bikes, the weapons platforms give the Defence Force remarkable mobility.

A final Land Rover, with a windowless box body, was the mobile command centre. It sprouted antennae indicating the radio transceivers within, which links to the other vehicles and even to individual soldiers through their compact personal radios and headsets. Why the need for this, I asked Peter. 'One of the first things they would do in an attack is put a 500lb bomb through this building. But we wouldn't be here.'

He gestured at the moorland and the craggy mountains that we could see through the workshop window. 'We'd be somewhere out there, because with the mobile command post we can operate perfectly well. We have pretty sharp teeth.'

Peter's pride, not only in the remarkable range of weaponry and vehicles, but in the force's very real ability to fight, and perhaps even deter, was almost palpable.

'We have a serious part to play these days,' he continued. 'Our primary role is to support the regular forces in the defence of the Islands. Believe me, if there was ever a requirement to activate the defences, then we would be part of them.'

I thought I had seen the full range of the Defence Force's kit, but I was then directed outside to see a number of flat-bottomed 'rigid raider' fast boats, each with two 120hp outboard engines attached. 'These were going to be thrown out by the Army, but we got them and the lads did them up,' Peter explained. It was an example of the versatility of the Islanders being put to excellent use. 'This gives us an inshore maritime role, and with the trailers we can deploy the boats to almost any point on East Falkland.'

The force also has a number of six-man lightweight inflatable boats, which were folded up and stored in the backs of Land Rovers. These are ideal for ferrying rivers or, as Peter put it, 'for having a quiet look around.' He gestured to the range of hills about 10 miles to the north of Stanley across Port William. 'If there was something we need to look at on the other side of Mount Low, I could have some people there in forty minutes.'

We retreated to Peter's office, where he produced a reminder of the Argentine occupation: an ancient musket of a type originating in the United States in the 1860s, but manufactured in Buenos Aires. It had clearly not been operational in 1982, but perhaps the occupiers had thought they would use it for ceremonial purposes when the fuss died down. In any case, the weapon had recently been excavated from a Stanley garden, where an Argentine had, presumably, thrown it.

Then he produced two mugs of coffee and we sat down to talk capabilities, threats and strategies. Clearly there was only one potential enemy that the Defence Force and the regular forces at Mount Pleasant had to consider, and there was no point in pussyfooting around the subject. What did he think of the current tense situation with Argentina?

'The situation is as it has been for a long time. We're getting on with life, doing our utmost to develop the place, expand and create a sustainable future. But, unfortunately, we are being impeded by Argentina. And that's a bit short-sighted on their part, I would say.'

I suggested to him that Buenos Aires' attitude could hardly be more different from that of the Menem and Di Tella administration in the 1990s, which effectively recognized that the Islanders had to be involved in deciding their own future. He agreed but pointed out that this was not an entirely bad thing. Menem and Di Tella were happy to find common ground for co-operation, but theirs was a stealthy approach to the same goal: Argentine sovereignty. At least, Peter suggested, one could now see the unvarnished nature of the threat.

That was not to say that he was enjoying the current pressure from Argentina. 'The rhetoric coming from over there is inflammatory; there is no other way of describing it. But I don't think their unveiled hostility helps them. They are trying to win some kind of diplomatic conflict at the moment, and I don't think they are doing very well.'

Peter's language was cautious, which did not surprise me. He is a local government employee who cannot speak beyond his limited remit. But, in any case, he is not someone I would ever describe as aggressive, in speech or deed. I think of him mainly as one of my older brother's best friends, doing his best as a teenager to introduce a love-dripping hippie culture to Stanley. So he was not likely to indulge in insults, taunts and accusations.

Some of the limitations the Argentines had placed on shipping to and from the Falklands were, Peter believed, contrary to international law, and while he accepted that the British Government was pursuing its own diplomacy to counter this, he was disappointed not to have seen signs of success.

I asked him about the FIDF's relationship with the professional soldiers, sailors and airmen based, for the most part, at Mount Pleasant. How do they work together? Apparently that relationship is close and warm. And at least from the Defence Force's side it is highly respectful. The part-time soldiers have been visited by instructors from the Army's UK-based Small Arms School, and they regularly participate in islands-wide tri-service exercises, though not always, because too many long exercises over areas with which they are perfectly familiar could actually demotivate the locals.

'We have such common goals that all our training and doctrine is the same,' said Peter. We have some slightly different equipment, such as the Steyr rifles and the heavy-hitting sniper rifles, but all weapons are compatible with British ammunition. There are also some differences in our uniforms, which helps to maintain the identity of the Force. Other than that, we blend in quite well. I could send a section of my guys to exercise with the regulars at Mount Pleasant, and you would hardly be able to tell the difference.

'We have a role that uses our local knowledge and manoeu-vrability and our skills in using the ground. The enemy's first tactic would be to try to get us doing what we were not prepared for, so we train over a very wide range of skills.

'In a crisis we could distribute elements of the force to work with the regular troops, or we might operate as a unit in our own right, collaborating closely, of course, with British forces. It would depend on the nature of the threat.'

In common with the British Territorial Army, men and women from a remarkable diversity of careers and backgrounds join the Defence Force. Professionals spending time in the Islands on contracts often join up while they are there, perhaps less for ideological reasons than for the opportunity to enjoy a challenging experience. Currently serving are scientists, plumbers, mechanics, and even a nurse. The level of education can be high. Many of the soldiers have degrees and post-graduate degrees.

Peter Biggs certainly appears quietly confident. His men seem to be well equipped and skilled. But if a reprise of 1982 was on the cards, would the overall Islands' defences be adequate? He answered affirmatively. 'There is a potent force here in the Islands. The level of forces is adequate for the overall defence plan. And it's a good plan.'

Did he think another military attack was possible, perhaps even likely? Peter again pondered for a few seconds before coming up with an answer that was cautious and qualified. 'I don't think so, as long as no one was given the political incentive to do such a thing. I think it's very unlikely. But signals are important, you could say that last time they misread things a bit.'

Was there, therefore, a greater level of military tension and preparedness? 'My job is to keep the FIDF ready and alert at all times. We're constantly vigilant. I know that there is no immediate threat evident at this time. Probably. But, then again, at times like this the potential for some kind of maverick or terrorism activity becomes higher. There is that possibility.'

I thanked him for his time, and promised to return in a few days to see the force mobilizing for an exercise with their stripped-down Land Rovers and enough weapons to fight a small war. I just hoped they wouldn't have to.

Even as we were speaking, Argentina was responding with rabid fury to the latest development in Fortress Falklands. The plan to deploy Prince William to the Falklands as a search and rescue helicopter pilot was, perhaps, one of Peter Biggs' signals, and it was clear that they were interpreting it in a way that suited their agenda.

Of course London had known that this would not be well received by Buenos Aires, and, in an effort to calm the Argentines, they let it be known that the Prince would not be carrying out any official functions – the kind of ceremonial activity that might involve parading flags. Furthermore, he would have left the islands by the thirtieth anniversary. This was not enough for Buenos Aires. The Uruguayan news agency MercoPress reported that 'Argentine official Sebastian Bruno Marco said Argentina could not ignore the "political content" of the mission. He said: "It is one more provocative act that shows Britain's military presence in a zone of peace where there is no armed conflict. One cannot ignore the political content of this military operation."'

The same site reported that the veteran Malvinas pundit and politician Hipólito Solari Yrigoyen had said: 'The ultra-conservative government of Prime Minister Cameron and the British Royal Family have launched a new act of aggression against the Argentine Republic. This aggression confirms that they have converted the Argentine islands into a military base, where they train troops to fight in Afghanistan.'

There are audiences in Argentina who lap up such deliberate misinterpretation of the facts. Messrs Yrigoyen and Bruno Marco were stoking the Malvinas' flames, and they would have known that perfectly well. This made no sense if they were interested in nurturing peace. To accuse the Royals of 'launching a new act of aggression' was just nuts. It would have been laughable, if it had not been so dangerous.

CHAPTER 16

Distant Rattle of Sabres

W e are permanently vigilant about the protection of the Falkland Islands and their defence, and I've spent a serious amount of time making sure that's the case. We must make sure their defences are strong, and that's exactly what we are doing.'

Those words were uttered by David Cameron to political chat show host Andrew Marr live on BBC TV in early January 2012. He was speaking with a degree of urgency and conviction that surprised me. I recognized the PM's tone and style from my time working in communications planning with the Ministry of Defence, and it appeared to me that, at last, the officials had confronted the Falklands issue and had sorted out a communications strategy. I detected that they were now seeing what should have been obvious to them months earlier: the Southwest Atlantic was a nascent crisis. The PM was picking his words very carefully from a list of 'key messages' a 'narrative' or a 'core script', which had, almost certainly, been approved by policy desks at the Foreign and Commonwealth Office and the Ministry of Defence.

His words were, however, of scant interest to British TV audiences. They were far more concerned about the dire state of their economy. That did not matter, because they were meant for Argentine consumption. In the Argentine Embassy, just off very posh Bond Street, and in Buenos Aires, they would have been picking over every word and every emphasis for nuance of meaning. For all their fear of rocking boats, the Foreign Office appeared to have remembered that confusing signals contributed to disaster in 1982, and that from time to time Buenos Aires needs to receive unambiguous signals that Britain cares.

The need for such reminders is surprising. After all, the 1,200 or so members of Her Majesty's Armed Forces are really no more than a grand statement of British commitment; the kind of signal that the Argentines really should understand. But there is a proven tendency to ignore such evidence, and that is very dangerous. How dangerous depends on the state of Argentine forces.

In the wake of the 1982 war and the disgrace of the military government, the country's armed services were unpopular and virtually emasculated by lack of investment. That probably suited Néstor and Cristina Kirchner just fine, and they did not change that when they came to power in 2003. They had opposed the junta, and did not accept the military's traditional view of itself as the sacred protector of the nation's values, which, conveniently, they were free to determine. In the past, that uncontested attitude had enabled them to take control of government, brutally persecute perceived threats, and pursue territorial ambitions when they saw fit. But Néstor Kirchner kept military spending to a trickle, and rescinded laws that protected some of the most notorious names in the military junta.

The military were tamed, and in 2006, Néstor, then President, revealed plans to develop more modern and capable forces. Those plans stalled as the government's economic health fluctuated. But, according to defence industry observers, modernization is now set to go ahead. A more upbeat future for the military has, however, not released them from tight civilian control. Trials and imprisonment of those who committed crimes against humanity in the 1970s and 1980s continued under Cristina, and she did not hesitate to purge the high command when she considered it necessary in 2011.

The commercial intelligence company, iCD Research, states that the Falklands dispute and commitment to international peacekeeping missions will both be drivers of change for the armed forces. The company says that Argentina's defence budget grew over several years, reaching $2.6 billion in 2010, and is expected to reach $5.5 billion by 2015. The analysts describe this as a 'robust' pace of development, although it pales into insignificance next to the UK's defence budget of around £45 billion, which, despite cuts, is still the fourth largest military spend in the world. But then Britain also has a hugely expensive nuclear deterrent to fund, and when this is discounted, the difference in the strength of the two countries is narrowed.

The company's analysis continues: 'The US is expected to continue to dominate the Argentine defence market until 2015 and Russia will likely enter the market through the supply of transport helicopters. Argentina is expected to procure patrol vessels, nuclear submarines, transport ships, multipurpose vehicles, helicopters, communication systems and fighter aircraft during this time.'

If this is correct, only limited comfort should be taken from the limitations of Argentine forces today. The balance of power in the Southwest Atlantic could swing another way. The military think tank The United Kingdom National Defence Association suggested as much when it produced a report written by five former defence chiefs gloomily pontificating on the effects of the 2011 Strategic Defence and Security Review. 'Our assessment is that current force levels are inadequate to hold off even a small-size invasion,' said the report. 'This is a potential disaster waiting to happen.'

There are, however, plenty of people – mainly, it should be said, on the Argentine side – who say this is nonsense. They insist that the military threat is imaginary. Dr Carlos Escudé is one such voice. He is a distinguished Argentine academic, political analyst and journalist. He was educated at Oxford and Yale, and speaks English perfectly. In the days of the Menem administration, he was an advisor to the then Foreign Minister, Guido di Tella, who pursued a refreshing policy of making friends with and influencing the Islanders. I rang Dr Escudé in Buenos Aires to discuss the threat, and whether Mrs Kirchner's current aggressive policy could be slipping into the danger zone.

He was impatient with what he clearly thought was an outdated attitude of fear and suspicion. 'We could not undertake a war against Paraguay for more the twenty-four hours, because we would run out of munitions,' he said. 'We do not have the physical means. In the 1990s, Argentina unilaterally began a process of disarming itself. It eliminated the draft, it privatized and shut down just about every arms factory in the country. It also reduced the military budget. In late 2001 and 2002, we had a terrible economic crisis, and from that time on the percentage of our budget given to the military has shrunk and shrunk. Argentina practically purchases no arms and is comfortable with this because South America, comparative to any other area of the world, has been a zone of peace, relatively speaking, for all of the independent history of our countries. And it is continuing to be a very peaceful region.

'Britain need not fear at all Argentina's military prowess,' he continued. 'The Islands can be defended with practically no military power. Argentina is like the dog that barks but cannot bite. It is absolutely toothless.'

Dr Escudé went on to assert that the military are no longer political players in Argentina, and there is no risk of them precipitating a crisis alone. That was easy to swallow. But, despite his impeccable credentials, I found it very hard to accept that British forces are maintaining an around-the-clock alert in response to ... well, *nothing*.

I knew he was right about the Menem government's virtual neutering of the forces and the domestic arms industry. But that had been a decade ago, and I could not accept that military spending continues to slide downwards. Indeed, the evidence is to the contrary. I was just about willing to accept that the Argentine military machine is not currently a serious danger. But I was not sure it would remain that way for long. And anyway, the whole Falklands issue is so unconventional, old-fashioned, and sometimes downright weird that it is not safe to assume anything.

The dispute fits no current template for armed conflict. There are no ideological differences. There is no fundamentalist religious element. It is not a struggle for wealth and resources (despite the presence of oil and fish). And it is not about manoeuvering for pole position if the race to exploit minerals in Antarctica commences. No, the Argentine Malvinas cause is entirely emotional. It is about two levels of hurt pride; the residual hurt from the loss of real estate almost 180 years ago (pain that Argentines did not even know they felt until politicians began telling them about it); and the real hurt of a recently lost war.

157

Argentines have not followed the behaviour of other countries that lost territory a long time ago in conditions that may not have been fair. Few people are actively seeking the return of land denied them, perhaps unfairly, in the nineteenth and twentieth centuries. A notable exception is China, which threatens Taiwan, but that dispute dates from 1950, a time easily remembered by many Chinese alive today.

Closer to home, Paraguay lost territory to Argentina in the nineteenth century (part of Paraguay is now Formosa Province). And the Mexicans lost Texas to American aggression. Paraguay and Mexico have lived with far greater loss of real estate than the Argentines, and yet they appear to accept that it is better to move on, and trade with their old adversaries rather than sustain endless animosity.

And then there is the current Argentine activity, which already verges on aggression. Establishing a trade and communications blockade and harassing ships en route to or from the Islands is dangerous, as misjudgement or foolishness could lead to violent escalation or inspiration to terror or guerrilla groups.

So, if Argentine forces were inexplicably committed to action, or blundered into it in 2012 or 2013, what form might such aggression take? There are four very broad scenarios.

Attempted full-scale attack
As at 2012, this is unlikely, but only if, at the very least, current defences and reinforcement capability are maintained. Invasion might become a practical option if the capability of Argentine forces was modernized through increased funding. Risk would also increase if a future British government reduced its forces, perhaps following a bilateral agreement to demilitarize the Southwest Atlantic. In such a case the Argentines might be very tempted to renege on such an agreement and invade. Even then, however, the invaders would probably want to have real allies (not just voices of sympathy).

Escalating the current economic blockade
To an extent, attempts are already being made to forcibly police the

blockade. Armed Argentine vessels have intercepted ships bound for the Islands and demanded that they stop for inspection. So far, most ships have refused to do so, and some have changed course into Uruguayan waters, while using VHF radio to remind their pursuers of the international maritime right to travel unmolested from one port to another. So far, the Argentines have not shown any inclination to apply real force, but it is conceivable that they might do so. Such action might lead to discussions in the United Nations Security Council, and, following failure there (as would be likely), to British naval and air assets squaring up to the Argentines. The result would be sporadic skirmishes that the Argentines would not win, but which could hurt the Falklands economy severely, particularly the oil industry, by scaring off investors.

Maverick military attack and terrorism
British forces might find themselves scrambling to defensive positions in response to unauthorized and small-scale attack by disgruntled members of the Argentine forces or by nationalist terrorists.

The maverick attack scenario was seen as a real risk in the aftermath of the 1982 war, when genuinely hurt pride could have driven angry men to take things into their own hands. However, military subservience to elected civilian leaders is a stronger principle in Argentina today, and, as already noted, the Argentine military machine is now much weaker. This is not a serious threat.

The risk of guerrilla action or terrorism, however, is high, especially in 2012, the thirtieth anniversary year of the Falklands War, when the dispute is being stoked by Buenos Aires, and is high in the news media. Passions will be strongly aroused.

There would be a precedent for such terrorism. In 1966, a Douglas DC4 airliner of the flag-carrier airline Aerolineas Argentinas was hijacked while flying from Rio Gallegos to Buenos Aires. The right-wing Condor Group ordered the pilots to fly to Stanley, apparently unaware that the town had no airport. Remarkably, the four-engined aircraft landed safely on the grass racetrack on the outskirts of Stanley.

The well-armed gang, the innocent passengers and a number of local hostages were surrounded by the Falkland Islands Defence Force and the few Royal Marine advisors who were then posted to the Islands, and eventually forced to surrender. London decreed that the Condor Group should be returned to Argentina rather than face trial in Stanley, and they went home as heroes, although some spent token periods in jail. Some of the hijackers went on to more serious guerrilla warfare during Argentina's 'dirty war' of the 1970s and early 1980s. In 2009, the survivors were awarded special state pensions, in honour of their escapade.

Aircraft, boats and ships following unexplained routes to the Falklands are certainly monitored by forces in the Falklands, and this threat will be reviewed throughout the thirtieth anniversary year.

It remains Argentina's capability for conventional warfare that most preoccupies the defenders of the Falklands. In the assessment of the country's military strength that follows, it is important to note that serviceability, modernity of equipment, supply of ammunition, training, morale and ability to deploy are factors every bit as important as strength on paper. I do not go into these issues in any depth here, but (to borrow Dr Escudé's phrase) it is hard to dismiss this as a picture of a 'dog that barks but cannot bite.'

Army
Since conscription was abolished (although the government retains the right to draft young citizens if inadequate numbers of volunteers are recruited), the army has slimmed to just 41,000. This is compares with the slightly less than 100,000-strong regular British Army.

Notable among army units are one specialized air-deployable brigade, three mountain infantry brigades, a battalion-strength aviation group and a battalion-sized special forces group.

Equipment
The army has 375 tanks, including domestically designed and manufactured models; 822 armoured personnel carriers and infantry fighting vehicles; 850 anti-tank weapons; 375 anti-aircraft weapons

(missiles and artillery); ninety-three self-propelled guns, and 289 towed artillery pieces. It also has fifty-eight multiple-launch rocket systems and 1,754 mortars.

Navy

The Armada Republica Argentina (ARA) suffered badly during the Falklands War, both materially, losing several important vessels, and reputationally. Its potentially powerful surface vessels failed to engage directly with the British fleet following the sinking of the cruiser ARA *General Belgrano*. Notably, however, the Argentine naval pilots performed courageously with their Exocet missile-equipped Super Étendard aircraft, severely limiting the movement of the British carrier groups. The ARA's sole carrier, the *Veinticinco de Mayo*, was barely operational in 1982, and spent most of the conflict in port. The ARA no longer has a carrier, although it sustains its air unit, and regularly exercises from carriers of friendly nations, particularly Brazil and the United States.

There appear to be no current plans to build or procure a carrier for the ARA, but the government stunned observers in 2010 when it said that it had plans to convert at least one, and possibly two, modern diesel-electric submarines to nuclear power, with the first sub being completed by 2015. Some experts have expressed doubt about the ability of Argentina to achieve such a goal, but if they did so, it would cause the Royal Navy to reconsider the deterrent value of its own submarines, which, although not permanently present, are a pillar of Falklands defence.

20,000 men and women are in naval uniform today. They crew and support forty-two ships.

Destroyers

The core of the naval surface combat force, that which is designed for blue-water operations, is made up of four destroyers. The 3,600-ton ships are all of the Almirante Brown Class; Meko 360 designs dating back to the early 1980s. They were designed to Argentine specifications and built in Germany.

These are potent ships. They have a top speed of 30 knots. Each is capable of carrying Exocet missiles, and they have torpedo tubes, surface-to-air missiles, 40mm cannon and single 5-inch guns. They also have hangars for a single light helicopter, upgraded in the case of at least one ship-to-facilities for a single Sea King helicopter. Their electronic warfare capability is considered sophisticated.

Corvettes

The ARA has nine warships that it classes as corvettes. But the designation is confusing. In European navies, six of the ships, the Espora Class, Meko German designed and built ships, would be described as frigates. They are modern vessels, the most recent of which was commissioned in 2004. With a top speed of 27 knots, the ships are well armed and form part of the high seas fleet, alongside the destroyers. They are well armed, carrying Exocet anti-ship missiles, a 76mm gun, torpedoes and anti-aircraft guns.

The remaining three corvettes are smaller ships of the Drummond Class, and are perhaps closer to the European definition of a corvette. The ships were built in the late 1970s and early 1980s and served in the 1982 war. With a top speed of 23 knots, which is relatively slow for a modern warship, the corvettes do, nevertheless, pack a punch. They carry Exocet missiles, a 100mm gun, torpedo tubes and numerous light weapons. They tend to operate close to home, patrolling territorial waters.

Amphibious warfare and command ships

Royal Navy crews might recognize the profile of the ARA's sole dedicated command and amphibious vessel. The ARA *Hercules* was converted from a British designed and built Type 42 missile destroyer, which entered service with the ARA in 1977. With her sister ship, *Santisima Trinidad* (no longer operational), *Hercules* was involved in the invasion of the Falklands. The *Hercules* is now capable of carrying 238 marine infantry and two Sea King helicopters equipped with Exocet missiles.

ARA *Hercules* operates closely with Argentina's only amphibious warfare cargo ship, the RA *Bahia San Blas*. This essentially unarmed ship, which entered service in 1978, is equipped to carry marine infantry, vehicles, landing craft and cargo.

Submarines

Argentina has three sub-surface vessels, and, as already noted, aspires to develop a nuclear-powered (although not nuclear-armed) capability, which would make part of its submarine flotilla a powerful strategic asset.

Currently in service are two TR1700 Class boats, the ARA *Santa Cruz* and the ARA *San Juan*. Of German design and build, they are among the fastest diesel-electric submarines in the world. And at 2,116 tons surfaced, they are also large by conventional standards. Delivered to Argentina in the mid-1980s, both have received mid-life overhauls and upgrades. The subs have a cruising range of thirty days and the six torpedo tubes are supported by an automatic system that can reload them in fifty seconds.

Four other submarines of this class were to have been built domestically, but work was suspended for financial reason in the mid-1980s. However, the ARA *Santa Fe* was 70 per cent built, and it is this boat that Buenos Aires is considering completing and upgrading to nuclear propulsion. One other uncompleted boat may follow.

The underwater triumvirate is completed by the sole operational Type 209, the ARA *Salta*. This is an older but still very capable boat; one of many designed and built in Germany purely for export from the 1970s. The type is probably the most extensively used submarine in the world, and is well respected. It has eight torpedo tubes and carries fourteen torpedoes. *Salta's* sister boat, the ARA *San Luis*, is not in service, but she may be modernized and reintroduced to the fleet. Both 209 boats were involved in the Falklands War. Although they did not engage with the British ships, their suspected presence in the area was a constant and limiting preoccupation.

Patrol boats and auxiliaries

In addition to the main combat vessels, the Argentine Navy operates eight coastal patrol vessels, of varying ages and capabilities. Two, the

ARA *Murature* and *King* were built in the 1940s and are only lightly armed. On the other hand, two Intrepida Class German-built fast boats from the 1970s pack Exocets and have enough range to reach the Falklands.

Supporting the combat ships are eleven supply ships and one tanker. There is also an icebreaker, the ARA *Almirante Irizar*, and two hydrographic ships.

Naval aviation

The Dassault-Breguet Super Étendard achieved almost legendary status in 1982 when Argentine naval pilots flying from land bases delivered Exocet missiles to the British task force. They sank HMS *Sheffield* and the freighter *Atlantic Conveyor*. At that time, the air arm had only a few Étendards on its books; now it has eleven (although some may not be operational).

Although the Argentines no longer have a carrier, the pilots of the ARA maintain their carrier skills through joint exercises with Brazil and the United States.

Three Grumman S-2 Tracker maritime patrol and submarine attack aircraft are also operated and exercised in a similar way.

Three veteran P3 Orion maritime patrol and anti-submarine aircraft are on the naval inventory, and were deployed to monitor the progress of an oil rig bound for the Islands' waters. These are augmented by three smaller Beechcraft Super King Air aircraft.

The Navy also operates helicopters both from its ships and from shore, most notably six anti-submarine Sea Kings.

Air Force

The Argentine Air Force acquitted itself well in the Falklands in 1982. Although many aircraft were lost, furious air attacks, sometimes in concert with naval aircraft, sank three British warships and a Royal Fleet Auxiliary ship, and damaged numerous others, some seriously. It remains respected today, to the extent that the RAF has stationed four of its most modern interceptors in the Islands, and would reinforce these rapidly if necessary.

164

Today the Argentine Air Force has 12,000 personnel and is equipped with aircraft that are largely the same or similar to those that it flew in 1982.

Interceptors
Eight Dassault Mirage IIIE aircraft protect the country's airspace, and have a range that would allow them to operate over the Falklands. The type is, however, an old design, dating back to the early 1960s.

In 1978 and 1980, Argentina augmented its Mirages with the Israeli-built variants of the Mirage 5, which also had a ground attack capability. They still operate fourteen of this type. Replacement of the Mirages and their Israeli derivatives is a priority, and the Air Force is believed to be considering purchasing much more capable and modern Mirage 2000C aircraft from France.

Ground attack
Eight Mirage 5 variants remain in this role. The backbone is, however, made up of Lockheed Martin Fightinghawks, a type based on the Skyhawk, which acquitted itself well in 1982. In an early 1990s' deal with Lockheed Martin, which worried London, thirty-six ex-US Marine Corps Skyhawks were thoroughly overhauled and upgraded with modern avionics, making a much superior aircraft, designated the Fightinghawk. The 'new' aircraft entered service in 1997, replacing the obsolete Skyhawks.

Thirty-four domestically designed and built Pucará close support aircraft are in service. The type flew from rough landing strips in the Falklands in 1982, but the turbo-prop aircraft were not designed for high intensity warfare, and did not perform well. That assessment has not changed.

Aerial refuelling
The Air Force has just two C130 Hercules tanker aircraft to support its interceptors and attack aircraft. This is a slight improvement on 1982 capability, but a greater air-to-air refuelling capability would be a priority for the Argentines if they were ever to contemplate sustained

operations over the Falklands.

Transport

The ubiquitous Lockheed C130 Hercules is the Air Force's heavy mover. It has eight of the aircraft (in addition to the two tanker C130s listed above). Also operated are a number of light transports, including the Fokker F27 (four) and F28 (six), De Havilland (Canada) Twin Otter (eight), Learjet (six) and SAAB 34 (four).

Helicopters

The Air Force operates thirty-three rotary-winged aircraft, notably two large Russian Mil Mi-17 (with more on order), and six Bell 212 Twin Huey.

Does this inventory of manpower and firepower amount to a credible military machine that, given the political will, *might* be turned against the Falklands with a reasonable chance of success? Yes. It is does not, however, amount to overwhelming power.

It is important to consider the likely political ramifications of committing these forces to action. Even if Argentina was to win in a conflict, it might be a pyrrhic victory. Were they to launch an unprovoked attack, the country would be reviled and condemned by both its neighbours, who are allies on paper only, and globally. That would be a terrible own goal for a country wishing to be taken seriously in the world. Furthermore, the lesson from history is that, regardless of passion for the Malvinas' cause, if Argentina were to lose a conflict, the incumbent government would be thrown out of office immediately.

It does not seem credible that a modern Argentine government, even that of the angry and aggressive Cristina Kirchner, would take such a chance. But this is not a normal dispute, and it would be dangerous to assume that normal rules and judgements apply.

CHAPTER 17

The Soul of the Islands

'Fancy a spot of fishing?' Robert King's phone call had woken me at an absurd hour, especially so for a Sunday. His dad, Joe, had always said that there was no such thing as a bad day in the Falklands; you just had to get up early enough to find it. Clearly Robert bought into this theory, and on the odd occasion when I had surfaced within an hour or so of sunrise, I had appreciated Joe's wisdom.

I pulled back the curtains to look out of the window, saw that it was indeed a lovely day, and decided against cursing Robert. 'Yeah, why not,' I said. 'We can have a look around the Malo and see if there's any trout there.'

Unlike most British people, Falkland Islanders do not talk about the weather incessantly, but they do curse it from time to time, especially when a door has been ripped off its hinges (as happened to me once), or a shirt carefully pegged out on the washing line has been ripped from its pegs and lifted into the jet stream. My theory – and it's as good as any – is that at this high latitude, the deep depressions keep the air rushing around the globe, and nothing gets in its way until it comes up against the stone and corrugated iron cottages of Stanley. Something does, however, seem to cause the winds to die down at night, meaning the weather is indeed at its most benign early in the morning.

The opportunity to head out of Stanley was welcome, because the words of Ken Humphrey, the friendly oilman and local rep for Rockhopper Exploration, had been on my mind since I interviewed him. He had used romantic language that might have led his hard-boiled bosses in Aberdeen to assume he was going local. 'The soul of the Falklands', was the inspired phrase that Ken had used to describe the craggy moorland, wave-lashed coasts and the tough way of life that this unforgiving environment demanded. He believed this defined the Islands. Less lyrically, Islanders call everything outside Stanley 'the camp'. This is one of a handful of words in the local vernacular that can be traced back to the gauchos who were brought in from the River Plate to farm cattle and sheep in the nineteenth century. Ken was right, and I needed to reacquaint myself with the real Falklands.

I said to my friend, 'The only thing is, Bert, I feel I should be speaking to a few more people. How would you feel if we drop by Trudi and Charles at Brookfield and the Watsons at Long Island? I can give them a ring and see if they'd be OK about that.'

'Sounds OK. It's years since I was at Long Island. I'll see you in an hour.' I thought I had a little more time than that. He had to get his stepson Jeremy up and dressed, and there was no way that Jeremy would head off into the sticks without a well-packed container of sandwiches and pop. And then Robert would have to top up his Land Rover with diesel. So I had time to have a leisurely cup of tea and then get my fishing kit in order.

I'd bought a new fly rod before leaving the UK, and I was keen to give it an airing. So far I had been spectacularly unsuccessful at this form of fishing, which in the Falklands comes with some snobby baggage. It had traditionally been the preserve of Brits who were passing through, rather than locals like us. They seemed to imply there was something spiritual about whirling a very thick line topped with a little bunch of feathers around the sky before dropping it into the mouth of a sea trout. On the other hand, Robert, Peter and the other lads of our generation had fished with brash spinners, spoons and lures, 'ironmongery', as fly fishermen disparagingly called the tackle. But we had always done very well with our hardware, often better than the fly-fisherman who had to cope with that incessant wind. Still, fly-fishing did look intriguing and as it had dropped some of its connotation of class recently, I felt it was time for me to have a go. So far, however, the charm had eluded me. So had the fish. More feather-clad hooks landed in the back of my head than landed in the river. So, as I packed the unblooded kit that day, I also tucked away a spinning rod and reel and trusty Toby spinner too. If my scalp became too torn and bloody, I would resort to this well proven piece of 'ironmongery'.

I gave the farmers a ring. I knew they'd be awake, because in summer farmers are up before most of us go to bed. What was more, it was lamb-marking season, a key period in the farming calendar when the lambs that were born a month or so earlier lose their tails and – in the case of most infant rams – some even more important bits. But it was also a Sunday, and I while I knew the farmers would be starting their work at the crack of dawn, I thought they might be wrapping it up some time after lunch. And so it proved to be. Neil and Glenda at Long Island Farm said they would be pleased to see us mid-afternoon, and Trudi and Charles said they would not be too far from home all day, so we should just give them a ring around tea time and they would put the kettle on.

Rather sooner than I had expected, I heard the diesel engine of Robert's Land Rover pull into the drive. Land Rovers are still the most common 4x4 vehicles, despite the tendency among Stanley's wealthier citizens to buy plush and expensive Japanese vehicles and Range Rovers. The day before, I had even spotted one absurdly incongruous American Humvee occupying most of the width of Ross Road. The driver rumbled along the seafront, rarely daring to take a corner, lest he run over a tourist. The relatively petite Land Rovers were still the unpretentious choice of anyone who wanted the best cross-country traction and engineering that would not be reduced to a bag of nuts and bolts after 5 miles of driving in the camp, which was what we were about to do.

I was almost as happy as young Jeremy to see the red and green roofs of Stanley receding behind us. About 5 miles down the road to Mount Pleasant, we turned north off the unsurfaced main road, onto a much narrower and poorly graded road. We climbed into the Wickham Heights. A painted finger-shaped signpost, which was far too twee in this context, confirmed that we were heading for the North Camp, which includes the little settlements of Johnson Harbour and Port

Louis. The latter was of particular interest to the Argentines, who insist it was their seat of government until 1833, when the Union flag was again hoisted.

As you drive north-west, you pass the gentle peak of Mount Kent on the left. The erect nipple of a large radar dome tops it off. Here the RAF operators constantly scan the skies, monitoring the movements of their own aircraft and looking out for incoming Argentines. The radar station is served by a blink-and-you'll-miss-it turn-off onto a string-thin track to the summit. Near this junction are the still recognizable remains of an Argentine Chinook helicopter, which was ambushed by a Harrier in 1982 and destroyed by cannon fire. I had read that the crew managed to land the aircraft in the nick of time and escape from it, which, judging by the state of the wreckage was very fortunate for them. The rusted turbine engines, some charred sheets of fuselage alloy and truncated rotor blades suggested that the Harrier pilot did his job well. Tourists liked to drop by the site and be told war stories by their guides. If there had ever been any interesting souvenirs around the wreck, they had long since been carried off by the visitors.

We were surrounded by the mountains, which because of their craggy summits are impressive beyond their mere 1,000 or so feet. The flanks of Estancia and Long Island Mountains are difficult enough to traverse on foot, let alone in a Land Rover or on a motorbike, which is what we did before the roads were built. Features that we call stone runs litter the mountains. These are peculiarly Falklands geological features; huge blankets of angular boulders, knitted closely together, that look as if they might have been tossed from the hands of a giant. Indeed, that explanation is as good as any, because no geologist has yet been able to explain how stone runs were created. There is nothing quite like them in any other part of the world.

We were out of site of any sign of habitation, and no other vehicle was visible in either direction. The mountains surrounded us. I asked Robert if he recalled an incident in the 1980s when the wife of a serviceman on a long-term posting to the Islands had become lost in the area. He did, and agreed with me that it had been a curious story.

The woman had stopped her vehicle on the main road from Mount Pleasant to Stanley and walked into the mountains, supposedly to enjoy the view. But the weather turned on her, a mist descended and she lost her way. Within a few hours, search parties had been organized, but as darkness descended, the woman was still missing. A cold night followed, and by morning the news bulletin from Falklands Radio was grave. It was feared the woman had died of exposure. But, about six hours later, she walked out of the mountains, back onto the main road, where she flagged down a Land Rover. Interviewed on the radio, she sounded absolutely fine for her eighteen hours or so in the mountains. Yes, she said, it had been very chilly, but she never felt frightened. She had sheltered among some rocks, covered herself with diddle-dee, and waited until the morning, all the time experiencing the vague and odd feeling that she was safe, and that the mountains were somehow watching over her.

The story had stuck in my mind all these years because I always felt the same way about this wilderness. I was never disorientated or felt myself to be in any danger in the camp. And there were plenty of occasions when I might have. I think Robert felt the same way. 'Do you see that old track up there on the side of the Estancia Mountain?' he said. I strained a little to pick out the black ruts that had been carved through the buff-coloured vegetation into the black peat below. 'That was one of our old motorbike tracks.' Long before today's network of so-called roads existed we had both covered this ground many times on bikes, en route to or from the Malo River. 'That was a nasty bit of track,' said Robert. 'God, it was a relief to get down to the Estancia and onto the flats.'

I agreed. 'Bob and Mally Kiddle at the Estancia were always welcoming, weren't they?'

He smiled. 'How could I forget them? The light was always on there if you broke down and had to walk in. "Come on in and sit yourselves down, boys! I'll get the kettle on."' Robert did a good impersonation of old Bob's high-pitched voice, and we both chuckled.

Ownership of this land had changed. In our youth, it all belonged to the Falkland Islands Company, and much of it was managed by shepherd families like the Kiddles who lived in isolated houses away from the main settlements. But when the heyday of the sheep farming industry was clearly over, and the expatriate farming companies began balking at the cost of employing people like Bob, the company sold their large farms in small parcels to those who wanted to get a foothold on the land. The McPhees and the Watsons, whom we were going to visit that afternoon, were some of those people. With the exception of an adventurous time in 1982 when the farmers of the North Camp had, quite heroically, left to help the advancing British Army, they had slogged on, year in and year out, eking a living from this not very fertile land.

I grumbled about the jarring roads, but progress across this landscape was ten times speedier than it had been in the old days. I had known us to take eight hours to reach the Malo, whereas today we expected to be there within an hour. But in exchange for some speed and a perhaps a little comfort, Falklands rural roads had exacted a heavy price in deaths and injuries. I personally knew three people who had died when their vehicles flipped on the scree-like surface or left the road altogether. I was not worried with Robert at the wheel, though. He expertly anticipated the ruts and the wickedly sudden turns on this ribbon of rubble. We emerged out of the mountains and onto the flat plain beyond, raising a cloud of dust as we motored past the Estancia farm where old Bob had once welcomed us. (Undoubtedly, the Heathman family who now lived there would also welcome us if necessary, but we had fish to catch.)

The Malo River was about 12 miles further on to the north-west, and there, I felt sure, I would christen that fly rod. The last mile or so was cross-country. We inched through some ditches and skirted some suspiciously green-looking damp areas, and then drove down a sheltered valley to pull up between the two corrugated iron fishing huts. We had had such enjoyable times here as youngsters. Stanley was not Ibiza when it came to entertainment, but there were plenty of raucous and somewhat drunken parties to be enjoyed. We were equally happy on this peaceful river, miles from town, where the days would be spent fishing and the evenings occupied with horseplay, the telling of tall tales, and learning how to smoke, and drink rum and whisky in the light of paraffin lamps.

Jeremy, ensconced in the back of the Land Rover with a digital toy, would not understand this. But both Robert and I felt the nostalgia. I was a little sad that almost no one spent the weekends at the huts any more. Thanks to the roads, poor though they are, it is now easy to drive to the river for a few hours' fishing and then be back in Stanley in time to watch *Coronation Street* on the telly before sleeping in a real bed.

It was still early, the wind had not got up and it was warm: ideal fishing weather. Miraculously, my flies missed my head more often than not, and they tended to land within 50 feet of the target area: good going by my standards. Robert had very wisely positioned himself a safe distance away and was unpretentiously working the water with his spinners. Jeremy, always Robert's shadow, watched eagerly. There was a loud splash and small shout of excitement from Jeremy. Robert had a nice fish on his line, probably a 3-pounder. I was pleased because at least we now knew the fish were there. He landed the trout, a good-looking silvery hen fish. And then he did the same again. And, rather unnecessarily I thought, again.

The fly rod and reel had beaten me. I quickly put my spinning gear together and lobbed a Toby in the broad direction of Robert's sweet spot. Honour was assuaged when I too got one on the hook.

Just as Joe King's wisdom had it, the fine weather had only been for the early morning. By noon, the sky was overcast and the breeze was chilly and building in strength. We carried our fish to the huts, broke into the sandwiches and chatted about the old days as we looked out over the river. It had been a good morning's fishing, thanks to the old ironmongery. Fly fishing? It was the stuff of snobs. Class warfare was resumed.

An hour or so later we were driving across the green at Brookfield Farm, avoiding the chickens and ducks that pecked and poked their way through the grass and the shrubs. We came to a stop outside the home of Trudi McPhee, her son Mark and Trudi's partner, Charles Dickson. Charles was a lot younger than me, but Trudi was more or less my age, and we had known each other most of our lives. As children, my parents would often take my brother and me to Green Patch for our holidays. Jock and June, Trudi's parents, looked after us wonderfully, and we spent those happy days 'helping' with shearing and dipping, or fishing and combing the beaches for fossils. When the large Green Patch ranch was sold, Jock and June bought part of it, and, quite literally, moved their house to their patch of land, which they called Brookfield.

Trudi was at the porch door to greet us with some robust banter. 'Oh, so you've been back for almost three weeks and you've only just got out here. Well! And you, Mr King; when did we last see you?'

'Not for a few years, but we don't see you in town that much, either.'

'You see us more now. Ever since Mum and Dad went into town to live, we've been in and out a lot more. So, have yous eaten? I've got some food here if you'd like it.'

This was just the most typical welcome. Trudi was a rough diamond and I loved her for it. We had eaten at the Malo, of course, but we said we'd love some coffee, and we pushed some cats off the kitchen chairs to sit down. Charles and Mark arrived, but could only stay a few minutes. Lamb marking had been completed, but some sheep still had to be moved, and they had work to do on their Land Rover, preparing it for cruise ship tourists the following day. Nearly all farmers within striking distance of Stanley supplement their incomes by driving tourists to and from the penguin colonies and the exhibition farm at Bluff Cove. A driver with a good vehicle could make £300 in a day.

Jock and June were both now in their late eighties, so the move to sheltered accommodation near the hospital in Stanley had been expected and planned. Their old house – the one in which they had hosted Mum, Dad and my brother and me all those years ago, and which they had taken from its foundations and dragged to Brookfield – was now empty. None of us expressed it, but I could feel the sadness. Trudi said her mum had deteriorated quite a lot recently, but they were still enjoying life. That mattered a lot to me. I had a Marks and Spencer box of chocolates for June and Jock, so I would visit them in the next day or two.

Trudi is a legend of 1982. When the counter-attacking British land forces reached the North Camp, not far from where we were now, they came to a temporary halt before the mountains that ring Stanley. Advancing further while maintaining a supply line for food, ammunition and water was an almost overwhelming problem. Trudi was the first to realize that North Camp farmers had the local knowledge and the equipment to help the Army to resume its impetus. She gathered several dozen farmers and farm hands from the area, told them to bring their best tractors, trailers and Land Rovers and make their way to the front. For the next three weeks, the locals ran a supply line from Teal Inlet, via the Estancia, to the soldiers staring down their rifles at the Argentine fortifications.

When the brigade was ordered to advance on the final ring of mountains, the locals were expected to remain behind, but very few did. Trudi herself guided a wagon train of blacked-out vehicles to the start line for the attack on foot, knowing that she could tread on an Argentine mine or come under artillery fire. When the battle commenced, she helped evacuate severely injured British troops. After the conflict, the Army honoured Trudi and several other locals who had been there. To many people, me among them, Trudi and her farming community were heroes.

I asked her how she felt about the latest chapter of the conflict; the bellicose Argentine policy and the attempt to blockade the Islands. Perhaps more than most Islanders, she had very good reason to fear that all of this aggression could only end in one way: another war. In the past I had seen her weep when remembering the dead and the injured, and I was sure she still felt the pain of that trauma.

'I hate them,' she said. 'But I can't go through another war. This time, if we make any concession to them I'll be leaving. We didn't go through all of that, and all of those boys did not die so that we could hand even a *bit* of the Islands over to them.'

I said that I did not think it would come to that again. But she, like many others in the Falklands, was not so sure. She had a view of the dispute, which disregards the bluster, as well as the patronizing reassurances of officials to get to the real level of threat. Some of us can be reassured by talk of 'bi-lateral relationships' or 'diplomatic initiatives' and so on, but for the likes of Trudi this is a black and white matter. 'The trouble is, Gray, that I don't trust the politicians any more,' she said. 'They haven't got the guts, and if we give them a chance they'll still sell us out.'

I nodded. She might be right, but I tried to bring her around to the immediate issue of communications with South America. The links were not merely threatened, they were under attack. 'What worries me,' I said, 'is that they may isolate us. How are the Falklands going to survive without an air link to Chile and with every port in South America banning our ships?'

Trudi fixed me in her gaze. 'Let them do it. Really! Let them do it. We've always survived. We've never asked for trouble, but we've coped with isolation in the past. As long as we have a link with Britain, even if it's just a ship, then that will be good enough. But I'm damned if I'm going to give in to pressure.'

The conversation moved on to more pleasant things. Wool prices were doing well and – so far at least – the blockade had not stopped the cruise ships visiting. Trudi, Charles and Mark would spend twenty or thirty days that summer shuttling visitors around the camp, and the money from this would supplement their income very nicely.

Robert, Jeremy and I said our farewells and I said that I would call by June and Jock's little house in Stanley to say hello. I wanted to do that because the old couple were among the rapidly diminishing community of old folk who had contributed to my childhood happiness.

'Don't leave it so long next time,' shouted Trudi as Robert started the Land Rover and bumped off down the track.

Long Island Farm was just twenty-five minutes' drive away. The 19,000-acre farm – small compared to most Falklands ranches – is on the mainland, but its name is derived from the nearby island, which is accessible on foot at low tide and offers good grazing and shelter for animals.

The long, pristine white sand beach that forms the western end of Berkeley Sound and the eastern boundary of the farm is linked to an odd and murky story of treasure and even piracy. The details are so scant that they are nearly non-existent, but about 200 years ago, a pirate skipper is said to have buried his booty somewhere above the beach's high tide mark. A map, or part of one, may still exist, and there have been at least two attempts to find the treasure. My Uncle John was involved in the second (failed) excavation during the 1960s, and he was teased about it for the rest of his life. But there were rumours that earlier treasure hunters did find something. It was known that a team was digging on the beach, and they denied having found anything. But one night a schooner was seen sailing east down Berkeley Sound and off to the north, and people wondered if the unknown boat had spirited the treasure away. At least one of the searchers was said to have lived out the rest of his days in luxury in South Africa. Perhaps there is something to those Argentine allegations of piracy after all.

The Watsons' main business is raising 2,500 sheep, but they love horses; the more fleet of foot the better. Neil had been a highly successful jockey at the race meetings held around the camp and in Stanley. I recalled cheering ecstatically as he, dressed in his characteristic burgundy, yellow and green silks, left the competition standing as he thundered down the Stanley racecourse aboard a graceful mount that he had either bred himself or been loaned. These days he left the racing to his children, among whom is Lisa, the editor of *Penguin News*, and to his grandchildren, one of whom competed at the Stanley races for the first time in 2011.

When we arrived at the pretty farmhouse just a few hundred yards from the treasure beach, the Watsons were about to head off for a final gather of the day. Neil did not look anything like as fit as he had been when I saw him last, about four years earlier. He'd damaged a leg in an accident, and these days he did not heal as quickly as he used to. Robert offered to drive Glenda and a family friend, who was helping on the farm, halfway up Long Island Mountain, from where they would walk back driving a hundred or so sheep ahead of them. They left Neil and me alone, sitting on either side of the warm peat-fired Rayburn stove.

177

He had been restricted to riding a Japanese quad bike for some time. But keeping him cheerful was the thought of those improving wool prices. Within the space of a year, the family's farming income had doubled to over £22,000. This was not enough to fund an extravagant life, but the kids had grown up and left home years ago, so he and Glenda had less need to count the pennies. They had paid off their mortgage long ago, and they were also enjoying some additional income from the tourism industry. In excess of 1,000 cruise ship passengers had been shown around the farm every season for the last few years, and although in 2011 they had lost some business to competition from other farms, they still hoped to make £10,000.

I asked Neil about his love of horses and racing. 'I learned to ride in Stanley before I got out of short trousers,' He said. 'I used to take my old horse out onto the common and give him a few gallops, although I was only supposed to trot him around. I was racing at twelve or thirteen, and the first Governor's Cup I won was on a Chilean horse in the early 1960s. Once I made a bit of a name for myself I had horse owners on the farms asking me to ride theirs.'

Our conversation took a leisurely route to the late 1970s, when the old-established and predominantly expatriate British farming companies could see the end of the good times approaching. They sub-divided their vast ranches and offered them to locally born people. As far as I knew, Neil had grown up in Stanley, like me, so the prospect of running a small farm in an area that was not very fertile might not have been natural. 'The truth was that I was fed up with a white collar job in Stanley, so we went for it,' he explained. 'But we came to farming with our eyes open. We knew it was going to be hard work. I couldn't shear a sheep, but I'd been milking cows, riding horses and working sheepdogs since I was a kid, when I spent every summer holiday at Port Howard Farm. My Uncle Sid taught me how to gather sheep, carry wool and so on. So I knew the camp pretty well, and of course I'd go fishing at the Malo. Glenda had grown up in the camp, which helped.'

I asked him if he expected to return to riding. 'I hope to get back to it by this time next year.' I was sure that he did, but at the same time I suspected he would not be too sad if his children, grandchildren and their friends did all the riding at Long Island. 'We still have horses – eleven at the moment,' he said. 'Most of them are Lisa's, though. We have a yearling now off one of her mares, called Darcy, who did pretty well at the Stanley races. So I reckon this little one might do well too.'

It was clear to me that thirty years of farming had brought him happiness, though not wealth. I asked him what he would do when he retired. His oldest son, Paul, was interested in taking over the farm. Lisa would have her horses grazing in the paddocks near the house or on the island, so she would be a frequent visitor when *Penguin News* duties allowed. And Glenda and Neil's youngest son, Ben, was working in Britain but was likely to return to the Falklands eventually.

'Paul wants to build a house here, and that won't be a problem as we're not short of land or water, and peat if he needs it. I'll retire here, right where I'm sitting. I'm a contented man, you know, Graham.'

I knew very well that Neil had always been outspokenly opposed to any kind of conversation with the Argentines. In 1982, his contact with them had been particularly unpleasant, which must have fuelled his bitterness. Following the invasion, he and Glenda hid Royal Marines who were on the run from the Argentines. Eventually, the Marines were captured, but Neil had hidden their weapons on the beach, and later he and other men in the area recovered the rifles and joined Trudi and other farmers supporting the troops on the front.

So I was surprised at how sanguine he now appeared about the increased Argentine hostility. I supposed that the Watsons were financially well-insulated against anything Buenos Aires could do, as were quite a few Islanders. The wool was shipped directly to the UK, and the cruise liners that delivered his visitors seemed happy to ignore Argentine pressure, presumably because the Islands' tourism 'product' was so good.

The most that could be said was that Neil was uncomfortable about the current climate. 'President Kirchner does have every South American government on her side,' he acknowledged. 'And they will all say that negotiations should commence. So they're a bit worrying, but I don't think there will be an invasion, and this coalition government in the UK seems to be united over the Islands and our right to steer our own course. So no, I'm not thinking of withering away and selling the farm. No way!

'They will probably cut off the Lan Chile flights. But we'll still be able to fly straight up the Atlantic to Ascension and the UK. And we may be able to have a shipping link with South Africa. A lot of people here would miss the Chilean wine, though. I like a red *Gato Negro*. But I guess I'd get used to South African reds and whites. Needs must!'

The Watsons came to the Falklands in the 1840s, at about the same time as my ancestors, the Biggs family. Those old-timers established that profound link between settlers and the land, the 'soul' that Ken Humphrey and I had discussed. It was still clearly evident in Neil and Glenda today, and, for that matter, in Lisa too.

The soul had survived a vicious conflict, and decades of cold war and isolation. It would not be destroyed by the latest Argentine offensive. Of that I was certain. But of course Ken Humphrey was talking about the threat posed to it by oil exploration and wealth. I shared his concern about the threat from that quarter.

Robert returned from his trip up the mountain and Neil said that he should probably get his quad bike fired up and go off to meet Glenda. So we all motored off up the track, and at a muddy junction, Neil looked back over his shoulder, gave a cheery wave, and took the left turn. I felt envious of Neil and Glenda. They had worked hard for it and weathered some hard times, but they were exactly where they wanted to be and I doubted whether anyone, even an Argentine president, would be able to move them.

CHAPTER 18

Cost, Benefit and Sacrifice

In the days of British neglect before 1982, the Islanders were poor. Most profit from farming was efficiently syphoned off to the UK, and the majority of Islanders who did not emigrate in search of better lives, struggled to make ends meet through poorly paid work, the punishing labour of excavating peat for fuel, incessantly maintaining tin, stone and timber homes, growing their own vegetables and butchering their own meat. If they were fortunate, they held decent posts in local government and qualified for occasional paid holidays overseas; if not, then they might live their lives without seeing the outside world.

It would be glib and based on only the flimsiest of evidence to say that Islanders were happier then. But they were certainly not miserable, and there are Islanders today who swear that community cohesion and neighbourliness were stronger. However, I could think of no one who would willingly go back to the days before Britain gave Islanders greater democracy and encouraged them to exploit their resources. The opportunities for much better education, to earn more, pay less tax and spend newly available credit were enthusiastically embraced. And this affluence was making an obvious difference to life here.

Expensive new four-wheel drive vehicles, rather than the rusty old Land Rovers of my youth, negotiate the narrow roads. Old metal and stone cottages are so passé when it is possible to buy modern kit houses. And many people follow the summer, travelling to the northern hemisphere when the frost arrives. Most Islanders heat their homes with expensive oil, rather than cheap peat, and they eat vegetables imported from South America.

They are said to be the most 'wired' people on earth, with broadband Internet services reaching almost everyone. Most obviously, Islanders now do few of the menial jobs; immigrants from Chile and the other, less well-known British island territory, St Helena, fill those roles.

At the same time, I thought I had noticed an emerging desire to at least dip one's toes back in the older, slower and harder way of life. My mother had told me she had noticed that during the height of the summer, Stanley tended to be quieter (and even now, no town in the world is much quieter than Stanley), as many families left to enjoy the solitude of old farmhouses now being rented out as holiday homes, or even the redundant old shepherds' houses they had bought or leased as second homes.

Most kitchen gardens in Stanley had been neglected for years, but – perhaps driven to some extent by fear that the Argentines were going to make it impossible to import fresh food – some Islanders were rediscovering the pleasure of growing one's own. The annual horticultural and home produce show was actually cancelled one year recently due to lack of interest, but the show is now again taking place. Even horse riding seemed to be enjoying a renaissance. Stanley's Christmas races were attracting great support, after a decade or two when they seemed poorly attended.

This movement did not, however, seem significant enough to reverse the trend to ever more obvious materialism. Apart from the conservationist Ian Strange, I did not meet any local person who worried about the impact of really extreme wealth that might arrive within a decade if oil exploration gives way to exploitation, which seemed very likely. By the end of the next decade, the Islands' wealth may be truly fabulous. The greatest challenge faced by the Falklands might be spending the money.

I wanted to know if my finger-in-the-wind sociology was anything like accurate. In particular, did the Falklands Government share my nagging worries? I arranged to meet some senior officials at the

Government Secretariat. Interestingly, all were British-born function-aries serving contracts of various lengths. The Treasury, and a 'policy unit' to be found in the two-story concrete office block, dominated them.

Most of my friends and relations had worked in this building at some stage. My parents had met while working as clerks there back in the early 1950s. The building had not changed much since then. Two massive cannons pointing north over the harbour flanked the main entrance; the kind of guns that London sent out to the colonies in case natives turned restless or a neighbour became covetous.

I knocked on the door of the Treasury, and Margaret Butler, secretary to Keith Padgett, the Financial Secretary, welcomed me. I noted that the inside of the offices had not changed much from the days when Dad worked there, except, of course, there were computer screens instead of typewriters.

Keith had been working in the Treasury for the best part of a decade. He had worked in local government in the UK, and he enjoyed the contrast between the Islands and the UK. He spent much of his free time in the camp, restoring and enjoying an old shepherd's house. Even he, as an outsider, could appreciate those old Falklands values.

Keith was quietly affable but exhibited a constant sober expression. And from time to time he looked a little stressed and worried; surprising because I knew that his department had just received an unexpected windfall income of £19.5 million, which would keep the budget very nicely in the black. So why the gloom? I wondered. Aren't the Falklands really pretty rich?

'Well yes,' said Keith. 'You would have to conclude that we are pretty well-off. And certainly for a public sector organization, the Falkland Islands Government has far bigger balances that anywhere else I have worked. For example, we have about £200 million in long-term investments, from which we might earn £6 million to £8 million a year. We have a £40 million budget, and, of course, we have just had that windfall of £19.5 million. But what most people miss when they see all of this is that our finances are very fragile.'

Apart from the risk posed by the Argentine blockade, things had looked pretty robust to me. But Keith pointed out that there were so many economic variables outside the government's control. Fish stocks came and went, income from investments fluctuated with the international markets and, yes, oil exploration had delivered much more money in the form of taxation than anyone had dared hope. But for the next few years any oil development would be a stop-start process. There might be another year of good tax revenue from the exploration companies and the local support businesses, like Lewis and Neil's amazing Byron McKay Ltd. But if revenue had not been better than expected last year, the Falklands Government would by now have slipped about £1 million into the red.

All these ifs and buts, I thought. The fact was that the Falklands Government, and therefore, the people, had done very nicely, thank you, wherever the money came from and however unexpected it had been. I respected his caution, but it did smack of the pessimism typical of treasurers and financial planners everywhere.

More credible was Keith's assessment that wealth varied hugely across the community. The average income per capita was very high, but this median was heavily influenced by a handful of very large earners, mainly those local businessmen and women who were involved in fishing and oil. Further down the income scale were the farmers who had, in the last few years, seen wool prices soar, and who had benefited from a new abattoir that paid good money for their mutton and lamb. Then there were the smaller entrepreneurs involved in tourism, retail or just providing services to the high rollers. However, civil servants – and the government was still the main employer – earned less than their opposite numbers in the UK. There were plenty of people earning around £20,000 annually and, worryingly, a growing number of pensioners surviving on just £10,000 to £12,000 a year.

The tax structure is generous, with a maximum of just 26 per cent for income and corporate tax (compared to the UK's maximum 50 per cent income tax). However, this benign fiscal regime benefits mainly the wealthy people and the companies. Tax, I was told, had been structured this way to encourage investment.

Firmly on the negative side was the cost of living. Almost everything is imported, and as the Argentine blockade tightens, the supply line becomes longer, more convoluted and expensive. 'I do wonder how some manage to live with our cost of living,' said Keith. 'I just don't know how pensioners manage to do it.'

I had no way of telling, but perhaps the less well-off were keeping up with their wealthier neighbours by drawing on credit. Anticipating good times in the wake of the 1982 conflict, and knowing the community would need the essential capitalist utilities, the government encouraged the Standard Chartered Bank to open a local branch. With the bank came overdrafts, loans, realistic mortgages and even credit cards. Was at least some of the Falklands' wealth just generous credit? That was a question that no one seemed able to answer.

I mentioned to Keith that whenever I returned to the Falklands I saw more signs of conspicuous consumption. 'I do too,' Keith answered. 'When I came here ten years ago, the vast majority of cars were old Land Rovers. You now see lots of new Mitsubishi Shoguns and Land Rover Discoveries. There is one brand new Range Rover on the roads and three or four recent models. But not many people go that far because the electronic nature of those vehicles makes them difficult to maintain here.'

It was practicality rather than lack of money, then, that limited posh motoring. He continued: 'I can already see some polarization in terms of wealth, mainly from fishing. I can see individuals – and I'm not naming anyone in particular – who are more concerned with their own wealth than the well-being of the community. There are some parallels with Middle Eastern states. The people working behind the tills in the West Store, for example, tend to be from St Helena or Chile. They are not very often Falkland Islanders.'

Luxury cars and immigrant labour. It was a potent mix of imagery. Despite the relative wealth, however, there was still an expectation that the public exchequer would continue to fund ever better education and medical care. It seemed to perplex Keith a little. 'To my mind we are not used to paying for very much here,' he said. 'We did start moving into a bit of means testing, in other words, asking for contributions from people for their education and healthcare. But the new council did not like that approach.'

In ten years' time, Keith Padget or his successor may not care a damn about the cost of education and medical care. If oil does begin to flow, the current wealth of the Falklands would be dwarfed by the new wealth. I asked him if he and his colleagues tried to look forward to such a time and plan for it, even while they were grappling with the 'fragile' finances of today.

'We have never included any government income estimates for oil exploitation,' he answered, 'because I wouldn't want people to go spending money in advance.'

'I can understand that,' I said. 'But you must do some blue sky thinking?'

'Yes, because we obviously need to have contingency plans. The amount of wealth that would come to us in terms of royalties from a *real* discovery would just be mind-blowing for a community of this size. You would certainly be talking about billions of pounds a year. For a community the size of ours, that's just staggering money.'

I suggested that such suddenly acquired wealth could be just as much of a problem as not having enough. 'Absolutely.' He said. 'In terms of priorities, what would we do? Well, there would certainly be a lot of infrastructure that we could sort out, but that could be done fairly easily, even if we had to bring in people to do it. Then we could easily cover defence costs, which I've been told are about £75 million a year. In terms of oil money, that's not very much. Beyond that? Well, we would certainly be looking at some kind of sovereign wealth fund. Then you would be talking about no income tax for many years into the future.'

I echoed the oil man Ken Humphrey's suggestion that there might be cash handouts for all Falkland Islanders. 'Would everyone get a cheque in the post every six months?' Keith sounded a sharp intake of breath and then laughed. 'Not if the Treasury can help it. But that does happen in some countries. You only have to look at some Middle Eastern states. The indigenous people don't do anything any more; they just bring people in to do everything for them.'

At no stage did Keith Padgett say as much, but I felt that he would rather be accepting taxation, struggling to balance a budget, and distribute limited benefits equitably, than posting out fat cheques to everyone on the electoral roll. He certainly did not seem to share the attitude of the British Labour Party leadership's Svengali, Peter Mandelson, who had felt 'intensely relaxed about people getting filthy rich.'

I moved the conversation on to other shared interests. We both enjoyed mingling with the spectacular wildlife of the Islands. I said that I had heard he got out of town as often as he could and spent time in an isolated farmhouse that he had leased with a few friends. His face relaxed and he smiled. 'Oh yes. I take a great interest in the traditional way of life. Without the camp, this place is not the Falklands, is it? You could shift Stanley and put it anywhere.' It was that 'soul' again, and I was pleased that he had identified it.

Keith suggested that I meet two more senior officials who were paid to take a keen interest in today's economic and social challenges, and those of a possible Klondike period ten years down the line. They were the recently appointed Head of Policy, Jamie Fotheringham, and the Director of Education, Health and Social Services, David Jenkins. I thanked Keith for the tip, wished him luck with his financial management and left.

I climbed the Secretariat staircase to the Policy Unit, and knocked on Jamie's door. He invited me to take a seat and listened patiently as I explained why I wanted to have his opinions. He had been in the Falklands for just a few weeks and, judging by the teetering pile of papers on his desk, he was still reading his way into the job. Perhaps he welcomed the chance for a chat.

Jamie is a lanky young Scot. He was wearing the kind of threads that are uniform in London, where he had previously worked as an economic consultant, but perhaps a little out of place in Stanley. I suspected he would soon look as sartorially relaxed as Keith Padgett. He explained that his main priority is to work up an economic development strategy, covering every conceivable area of activity. He listed tourism, rural diversification, fishing and, of course, oil. I stopped him there to pick up on the challenge of an oil-drenched future where Keith Padgett and I had left off.

He was optimistic that the Islands are giving good and early thought to the challenges they face. 'As far as the specific issues of oil are concerned, we need to be sorting those out within the next twelve to eighteen months,' he said. 'If there is going to be development of oil, how are we going to deal with it and how are we going to manage the wealth? That is not a given, of course. The general view, and I think it is absolutely right, is that the income we have already had from oil is a bonus and further income cannot be assumed. Therefore, we need to press on with all other development options.'

That was the standard health warning. I asked him what he had learned so far about the Islands' preparedness for a future, which, oil or not, would be challenging. He said he was concerned about what might be a lack of ambition among younger Islanders. There were plenty of jobs for them to walk into if they decided to leave school at sixteen and perhaps too many chose to do just that. It was true that more young Islanders were graduating from colleges and universities in the UK than ever before. But the question in his mind was whether they were bringing back to the Falklands the kind of knowledge and skills that would be needed.

I suspected that this highly qualified young man had become aware of hostility felt by some Islanders (indeed, many whom I knew) to the strategy of appointing mainly contracted British staff to be 'super-heads' in strategic areas like policy, finance, medical, education, police and immigration. The policy did not specifically discriminate against local people, but the qualifications and levels of experience required were so high that Falklands-born people could fill few of the posts. There was significant resentment that outsiders were coming in to run the government, as they had done in the old colonial times, and it had become very much more difficult for local people to reach the upper echelons of the civil service. I would not blame him if he felt a little hurt by the anger.

'It concerns me,' continued Jamie, 'that no one seems particularly keen to do anything a bit "outside the box". It's a big issue, because I've heard local criticism of the people coming in to do jobs, and yet none of the people studying overseas at the moment are studying anything remotely related to economic development and so on.

'If the ambition is to avoid reliance on contractors, one has to ask, what are you actually doing to make sure you have those kind of skills in the community? With the greatest of respect, how many more beauty therapists does the place need? A lot of people are doing those kinds of courses. I think there is a need to be more targeted.'

He also homed in on the issue of immigration. The Falklands needs more than the 3,000 people it has now if it is to develop a decent economy that can feed on itself and grow. But immigration policy had proven to be a sticky issue, and any strategy was going to find progress hard. 'This is the big social decision that members of the community need to make,' said the economist. 'Do we want to trundle along at this sort of level, do we want to have some steady growth, or do we want to have a slow decline and hope that oil is going to pay off and we are all going to be rich?'

I thought Jamie Fotheringham had his work cut out. Not only was he an outsider, he was tasked to look at fundamental important economic and social issues, and he would have to drive local people towards strategic decisions. That process might not be a lot of fun. I hoped he was not too sensitive.

My final stop on the economic and social trail was at the office of David Jenkins. He was another recently appointed 'super-head' from the UK. Previously, David had worked for thirty-six years in the Army, where he was heavily involved in military education, although he started his career as a nurse in the Medical Corps. He had spent some time running a major hospital and had worked at the Permanent Joint Headquarters, which has responsibility for military operations in the Falklands. David seemed well suited to his diverse portfolio.

Like Jamie Fotheringham, he seemed to be aware of the divisive perception that Islanders were no longer running their own government, and that local civil servants had made way for the

189

externally contracted officers. Much as I wanted to talk about the social impact of change, both existent and anticipated, he wanted to talk about the government management system and hierarchy before anything else. I felt it was important to listen to him.

'Part of the job,'said David, 'is relying on middle managers, and Falkland Islanders have not been best positioned in the past to take on management responsibilities to the degree that I am used to.' He said it was currently necessary to have contracted staff in education, health and social welfare, although he had ambitions to train local people and have them take over the senior jobs.

I was tempted to point out that Islanders had occupied some of the most senior government position in the past, including that of Financial Secretary and Chief of Police. My father had been near the top of the civil service in the 1960s and 1970s and received an MBE for his services. So I was inclined to feel that if highly-paid Brits were suddenly needed, it was as much about perception, and possibly bias, as it was about real necessity.

But this was not David Jenkins' fault, and I was sure he was dedicated to his tasks. He pointed out that UK consultants had been brought in to devise and conduct a leadership programme for young Islander civil servants, and he felt the outlook for them was good. 'They are definitely the leaders of the future. The outlook for them is fairly rosy.'

This man's portfolio was unenviable. I could barely keep up with him as he listed the challenges of education: planning tertiary education around the Islands' needs; the lack of competition among students; the need for Islanders to spend time overseas acquiring experience in their fields, and so on.

Health and social welfare seemed to be even more complex and difficult issues. The government cannot afford the specialists and the equipment that would make it possible to give everyone the standard of free treatment that they increasingly expect. An MRI scanner alone would cost £1 million to buy and £200,000 a year to maintain, and a not insignificant amount to staff. Doctors were another problem. So far it had proved possible to recruit the four general practitioner physicians that the King Edward Memorial Hospital needed, but it was becoming increasingly difficult to find GPs who had obstetric skills, which simply had to be present in such an isolated community. To cope with other medical disciplines, it had a policy to bring specialists to the Falklands for a few weeks each year, but the consultants were increasingly reluctant to travel to the Islands for the money on offer.

A ray of hope was afforded by broadband Internet, through which the local GPs could consult with a team of specialists and technicians in Aberdeen as they examined challenging patients or even carried out surgery. The Aberdeen staff had pioneered 'telemedicine' with isolated communities in the Scottish Highlands and Islands. The Falklands were about 8,000 miles further away, but this made no difference.

Still, the number of patients being sent to major hospitals overseas, either in Chile or Britain, was growing – as was the cost: by about 11 per cent every year. The bill for the previous year had been over £1 million. Telemedicine and the careful recruitment of doctors might bring this cost down in the future, but for now it was soaking up about 2.5 per cent of the total government budget. But providing good medical care for citizens was a moral imperative, and David insisted that decisions to send patients overseas for treatment is based entirely on clinical need, rather than cost.

I asked about the most common and serious medical conditions, expecting him to immediately mention alcoholism. Like most small and isolated communities, the Falklands had suffered from excessive drinking. When I was a child, the few pubs in Stanley were crude and very functional. Drunkenness was obvious. The serious boozers could be placed on the 'black list' for a prescribed period, enabling them to dry out. It was a criminal offence to supply such proscribed individuals with liquor.

But, according to David, drinking is not the problem it once was. Without historical figures, he could not tell if alcoholism had begun to reduce at any particular point, but current evidence suggested it was only a little higher than the rate in Britain. The UK has a bad record, of course, but it still surprised me. Perhaps this was a good spin-off from increased affluence. Perhaps there was less need to drown one's sorrows.

The real health problem in the Falklands is obesity. I had suspected as much just from walking around Stanley, and if David had not raised the issue, I would have done so. What he had to say was simply shocking. There is 44 per cent obesity here, compared to 22 per cent in Britain. Eight per cent of Islanders are morbidly obese; meaning their general health is at serious risk because of their weight. The incidence of diabetes, orthopaedic problems and cardiac disease is consequently high.

I recalled that in the past it was generally older people who were overweight, but my impression now was that much younger people were piling on the fat. When I was growing up, most people ate abundantly and well. Plentiful vegetables grown in kitchen gardens made up for an occasional lack of fruit. Something had gone wrong over recent decades.

'I have enough data now to say that this is a fairly substantial clinical problem,' said David. 'And it is absolutely a way-of-life issue. Everybody has to own this problem. The solution is education for kids and parents, and perhaps a government subsidy for fresh fruit.'

I asked him if this remarkable increase in obesity might be due to increased wealth. Less wealthy people, as Islanders used to be, tend not to live on processed and frozen food. But, if the price is right and money is no problem, the temptation to live on pizza, burgers and ice cream can be irresistible.

'It is more complex than that,' said David. 'There is a general acceptance that it is OK to be overweight. I think it's also down to lack of physical activity, which I can't understand because there is so much potential for outdoors activity, be it running, hillwalking or whatever. But I see people driving 100 yards down the road. I worked in Africa for a while and kids would quite happily walk 4 or 5 miles each way to school. Here, people are reluctant to walk 200 yards down the road. That is a cultural expectation.'

I was still focussing on wealth, and said: 'If they didn't have quite a lot of money they wouldn't have posh vehicles in which to drive that

200 yards, would they? So is it not about either the availability of real money or the availability of credit?'

'That may be an element, but I think it's more subtle than that. I see people on low incomes who still choose to drive everywhere.'

Could he also confirm my suspicion that obesity was moving towards younger age groups? 'I have not got the evidence for it, but I am as confident as I can be that that is so. Some children are going to have substantial problems even in their twenties.'

On the other side of the door, I could hear the Director of Health, Education and Social Services' secretary asking people to wait 'just five minutes and David will be with you.' I was taking up too much of this man's time. And he had some serious work to do. I was genuinely grateful to him for talking to me so candidly. Much of what he had said would have found no place in the government's official press releases and PR publications, but it was fascinating.

I found David's confirmation of my suspicions about obesity – indeed, his revelation that the problem was much more serious than I had anticipated – to be upsetting. I tried to work out why, and decided that it was because even when living harder lives under a neglectful colonial power, we had all that we needed to be happy.

That 'soul', of which I had thought so much since meeting the oilman Ken Humphrey, was present in the wilds of the camp. But I concluded that it also had something to do with the simplicity of the lives that we once led. Only when we began to have a surplus of both time and money did Islanders begin to develop greater appetites for food and for material possessions, and I was finding it hard to see what benefits that change had brought. Furthermore, if the community could change this much over three decades thanks to relatively modest economic growth, what would it be like three decades hence if the oil billions have arrived?

I pondered my favourite quotation from Oscar Wilde: 'Nowadays, people know the price of everything and the value of nothing.' It is doubtful that Wilde worried much, if at all, about the corrosive effects of wealth and materialism, but he accurately observed how money can skew values. I thought it had done so in the Falklands, but perhaps not utterly and irreversibly.

I hoped that the strategists like David Jenkins, Jamie Fotheringham and Keith Padgett would do their jobs well and that the young locals on that development programme who might one day take over from the contracted Brits would rediscover the 'soul' of the Islands.

CHAPTER 19

Squid Inc

When Keith Padgett, the Financial Secretary, had been telling me about the very considerable wealth that was accruing to a small sector of local society, he was referring specifically to those in the fishing industry. Personal wealth from oil might well come eventually, but the bold Falkland Islanders who plunged into the deep water of the fishing industry some three decades ago are the really big earners of today.

As both Keith and I possessed that curious British queasiness about discussing personal incomes, we skirted the issue of who precisely had reaped the most benefit, but we both knew we were alluding to a handful of businessmen and women in the Falklands who are not just well off; they are rich. They may be *very* rich. From his access to income tax data, Keith might have been able to put a fairly precise figure on the typical incomes that these few people enjoy, but I did not ask him, and he did not offer the information.

I knew, however, that one of these successful fishing entrepreneurs, very probably *the* most successful, was Stuart Wallace, my first cousin and friend. Stuart had been remarkably kind when I arrived in Stanley, and lent me a Land Rover to use. Even better, he and his wife Lillian fed me well. From my extensive experience of Falklands cooks, I can say with certainty that Lillian is one of the very best.

Another certainty is that there are people in Stanley who are envious of the money Stuart has made from his company, Fortuna. But I am not one of them. It actually gave me real pleasure to see an Islander reaping the benefits of the economy of his own land. While

Stuart may have initially seen the availability of fishing licences as an easy opportunity to make money with minimal personal investment, this had not been his ultimate goal. He muscled his way up the ladder of an industry about which he initially knew nothing, taking risks and making proportionate profits. He even had a distribution subsidiary in Holland.

What mattered to me, however, was that Stuart had been in the vanguard of a movement to usurp the expatriate colonial era companies from the superior and dominant position they had enjoyed since the nineteenth century. Such companies had consistently siphoned off their profits to shareholders in Britain, rarely reinvested in the Falklands, and fostered a class system that kept families like Stuart's and mine firmly in society's second division.

It was in 1987 that the economic and social status quo was rocked. Having lost 355 lives in a war that might have been avoided, London felt it had to justify the sacrifice by making the Islands economically viable. It was relatively easy to create a large maritime economic zone in the fish-rich seas around the Islands and create legislation enabling the Falklands Government to sell licences to companies wanting to exploit it. They probably did not anticipate Islanders themselves grasping this opportunity to make some serious money, but they did.

No, I admired Stuart and some of the other entrepreneurs, and was even grateful to them. However, I shared Keith Padgett's dislike of the conspicuous consumption that was evident in some parts of the fishing sector. Range Rovers and rich people's toys seemed to jar with the essential simplicity of the Falklands. Happily, though, Stuart did not spend his money on such things. He travelled quite often for both business and pleasure, but as far as I knew, he did not have a home or a Mercedes Benz overseas. He had a very nice but not particularly large Scandinavian-made prefabricated house in Stanley with a good view across the harbour. And he drove a two- or three-year-old Land Rover Discovery, which is a fairly high-end 4x4 car, but no pimped-up Bentley. He was modest and had really not changed at all from the days of our childhood or his early adulthood, when he worked as a telex operator for the British Antarctic Survey and then as an administrator for Cable and Wireless.

Stuart had started off in business with John Cheek, a Cable and Wireless colleague. At first the partners merely represented foreign companies, using their preferential local status to buy squid jigging licences, which they made available to the foreigners at a good profit. They could have sat back and enjoyed the ringing of their cash till, doing little and risking nothing. Indeed, some local companies were very happy to continue doing that. Instead, John and Stuart thought big. They began forming joint ventures with their European clients and buying equity in ships.

Today, Fortuna owns 50 per cent of five large ocean-going factory trawlers, and, with another Falklands company, a slightly smaller share of a sixth ship. Their Spanish partners operate and crew the vessels, but that does not reduce the risk to Fortuna. If they have a bad season, the company's balance sheet takes a tumble. Indeed, that has happened from time to time.

John died several years ago, and Stuart bought his share of the company from his widow Jan (who I interviewed for chapter ten). One of the Fortuna ships now bears John's name.

Our families had grown up together. My mother and Stuart's were remarkably close sisters. And his brother Jimmy, who was just a few months older than me, was my best childhood friend. Fishing, motorbikes and girls dominated our lives (he always got the pick of the latter). Jimmy was clever and funny, and could have been every bit as successful in business as his older brother. He too worked in telecommunications, and he spent a few years making good money in Saudi Arabia, where he was employed to maintain the military communications network. But Jimmy's downfall was alcohol. As soon as he was eighteen, he had become a denizen of the Stanley pubs, which were then Spartan facilities that facilitated the consumption of as much liquor as possible during the tightly prescribed licensing hours. As I had learned from David Jenkins, drinking seems to be less of a problem in the Falklands these days, but back then it was a habit pursued on an almost industrial scale.

Drinking was less easy in Saudi Arabia, but Jimmy even managed it there. He and his western drinking friends were arrested a few times for their crimes, but Jimmy at least was released very quickly when the military radio network began to break down. When he returned to the Falklands, he bought his own pub. He would go on the wagon for short periods, but always fall off. His life became increasingly chaotic until it cost him his wife and the two sons he adored. And then it cost him his life. In 1995, aged just thirty-eight, he suffered an alcohol-induced fit and died. I was in Britain at the time, and I vividly remember hearing the news from a girlfriend who had been contacted by my mother. I sat on my bed and said, 'Poor Jimmy. He didn't deserve to die like that.' And then I shed some tears for him.

But back to the present. Jimmy's brother, the chairman and now sole owner of Fortuna Ltd, welcomed me when I dropped by his office one day with my tape recorder. Fraser, the third of Aunt Alice's sons, also worked for the company, and after offering me some good coffee, he left Stuart and me to talk.

He was in good form, although it had been a poor season for catches of Loligo squid, which are important to Fortuna and its partners. Loligo is much valued in calamari-loving southern Europe. But just 35,000 tons of this species had been caught in Falklands waters in 2011; down considerably from the 50,000-ton norm.

Very conveniently, Loligo spends its entire short life in Falklands waters, meaning it can be monitored and conserved. Other species were also continuing to do well, especially rock cod, a fish of newly discovered international value. Then there were two types of relatively low value hake, as well as hoki and toothfish. Both of the latter are increasingly popular in Europe.

Notably, however, it had been a bumper year for a second, smaller species of squid, Illex argentinus. This is a migratory stock that travels through the high seas, then into Argentine waters, before arriving in the Falklands economic zone. Fortuna does not target Illex, but the oriental squid jiggers do, and between them they pay the Falkland Islands Government up to £8 million a year for the privilege. 2011 had seen a catch of some 85,000 tons, the best in about four years.

I had always found it difficult to understand the administration of the fishing industry, and recently my confusion had been compounded by the replacement of the annual licence system with a long-term 'fishing rights' system. I needed Stuart to explain. 'The key to the new system,' he said, 'is individual transferable quotas, or ITQs. This system is replacing annual licensing around the world, because it maintains governments' ability to control stocks, while giving fishing companies greater long-term security.

'In the Falklands we may be allocated the right to fish for particular species for up to twenty-five years. We pay for that annually, when the catch quota is also established. This quota and the government fee might vary year to year, depending on assessments of stocks. The important thing for us is that ITQs are assets that are secure and tradable. The market decides their value, but here in the Islands one ITQ can change hands for hundreds of thousands of pounds. Fortuna can now go along to a bank and use the ITQ as collateral on a loan. And when the scientists determine that the fishing effort for a particular species needs to be reduced, we are likely to agree with them, because we have a vested interest in fish being around for the life of our ITQ.'

The only Falklands species exempted from the ITQ system is Illex argentinus squid, which is caught mainly by foreign-owned licensed jiggers. Other local companies have arrangements of convenience with the oriental squid jigging outfits, but have little or no shares in the ships. (Arguably, it is the perfect business: good income for no investment and no risk.) Because the Illex stocks are so migratory and vulnerable to uncontrolled fishing on the high seas and in Argentine waters, it is almost impossible to manage stock.

The Illex fishery worries the Falkland Islands Government. There is now a real fear that the Argentine Government will wage a 'fish war', hurting the Falklands by deliberately over-fishing Illex in their economic zone before it reaches the Falklands.

They may have done this before, using a finfish called southern blue whiting, stocks of which straddled territorial waters. Once, blue whiting was so common that catches strained the trawlers' nets. But Argentina did not control their fishery and the stock is now virtually wiped out. This may have been appallingly bad management, but it is equally possible that it was killed off deliberately to damage the Falklands.

Both Stuart and I could remember halcyon days when Britain, Argentina and the Falklands actually co-operated. Under President Menem, a South Atlantic Fisheries Commission had been set up to pool scientific and commercial knowledge. There were even joint Argentine-British scientific research cruises. The Kirchners killed that spirit off, and the Southwest Atlantic became one of the few oceanic areas of the world without a regional management association. 'Ripping up the agreement was desperately irresponsible,' Stuart said. 'I have trouble seeing why anyone should want to damage their world over this relatively small dispute. There are ways that reasonable people could find to rectify this.

'I think generally people have written off the possibility of any co-operation over fishing with Argentina,' he continued. 'They are just not interested. Their scientists who have tried to work with ours have actually been sacked. It's obnoxious behaviour. They threaten our partners, which is not helpful in terms of getting capital and expertise. They even harass ships going to or from Montevideo, which the ships must do because we have virtually no infrastructure in the Falklands.

'But for all their thuggery, the impact on us has not been great. It's a shame and it's a pity that they won't co-operate, but actual economic impact on us is, I would say, marginal.'

I said that Fortuna, originally with John but latterly under Stuart's sole guidance, had done remarkable things, and he should be proud. In his modest way, he obviously was. 'It's been a hell of a learning curve over twenty-five years, you know. But this industry has kept the Falklands functioning, and you have to wonder what the place would be without the kind of money it brings in.

'I often think we haven't done enough. But we have more large freezer factory ships flying the Falklands flag than Britain does. And when you look at other new world fishing nations, New Zealand, for example, they have not progressed much more than we have. Their companies have only about forty-five ships – a little over twice as many as us – and nineteen of them are foreign chartered.'

I suggested that the future will be challenging, and not only politically. Stuart agreed. 'The Falklands' industry needs to think about fleet renewal, because most of our ships are twenty years old or more, and their technology is getting out of date. But the economics of renewing the fleet are quite worrying. We would have to buy new ones, but you can only do that if you can build the financial reserves. Or borrow from a bank, but, of course, you have to repay that with interest.'

More positively, Stuart was clearly looking forward to the success of Fortuna's subsidiary fish distribution outfit in Holland. His son, James, was running this. 'This operation opened our eyes,' said Stuart. 'We are getting key information about the end users of our products. It's fascinating. If we'd had a local market we would have had this kind of information fifteen years ago. Now we are advertising in *Penguin News* to buy other companies' fish that we can sell through Holland.'

We moved on to the general political situation. 'You know,' said my cousin, 'I'm fifty-seven now and there is a limit to how much I am prepared to worry about it. I just think that after forty years of my life, can't we move on, for God's sake? But I do find myself watching and listening. I grew up at a time when you couldn't trust the British Foreign Office or the British Government at all. I have no doubt that colours my view of the future, but I keep a terribly beady eye on anything that comes out of London, looking for nuance or any sign of change in anything.'

I said: 'The Governor told me that there is a lot of diplomacy going on, it's just that the UK doesn't crow about it. Do you accept that?'

Stuart sighed. 'You see, I think the Foreign Office has form. I accept that I am probably far too cynical about it, but I just *am*. And reassurances from people like the Governor don't quite cut it with me. It's all very well to say that diplomacy is working, but look at the situation: we are isolated from South America.

'A visit from the Foreign Secretary would make me feel better. And next time the Argentine Foreign Minister goes to the UN to talk about the dispute, I'd like to see the British Foreign Secretary there too, showing that the issue is also at the top of his agenda.'

I always felt a little awkward when asking if my compatriots feared a slide to another armed conflict. Simply by staying in the Islands and getting on with their lives, people were showing that they felt safe. But still, I put the question to Stuart, and he had an interesting answer.

'Do I think they are about to invade? No. Do I think that Mrs Kirchner and her government have created an environment in which some crazy could do something? Yes, I do. You can't pump that sort of heated propaganda into young people and then be sure that something will not happen. They are teaching their children to hate. I think the environment has changed so that anything is possible.

'The Argentines are not saying, "We have a mature political disagreement, but we will work it through." They're saying, "We hate the gringos, and in particular those Islanders."

'We are coming up for a bad time. But what we don't do is panic. You cannot live here and panic about that sort of thing. We have to get on with our lives.'

We sat there in silence briefly. Stuart broke it. 'Talking about getting on with life, what are you doing for dinner?'

Ah, the promise of Lillian's cooking again, I thought. 'Any chance of some blue whiting?'

'We'll have to talk to the Argentines about that. But we've got some squid.'

'That,' I said, 'would suit me fine."

CHAPTER 20

The Noose Tightens

For all the bombastic talk and threats that had been coming out of Buenos Aires, and all the defiant responses from Port Stanley, nothing had happened during my time in the Islands to make the noose around the Falklands any more painful. By early December, I actually felt that the term 'blockade' was beginning to lose some of its dramatic impact. That was due, at least in part, to the stoicism of Islanders. They were starting to get used to it, and did not behave like or resemble a people under economic siege.

Almost everyone I met had told me they would get by, whatever the constraints imposed on them, and they seemed to be doing so. Granted, the very little fresh fruit that managed to get through on the weekly aircraft from Chile was horribly expensive, as indeed were almost all imported foodstuffs, but there was no sign of scurvy yet, and the Development Corporation, a quasi-government agency, was working on a grants and loans scheme to encourage the commercial growth of local produce. It did not appeal to me greatly, but it seemed the future of the healthy Falklands diet was probably vitamin-packed rhubarb instead of oranges. I wasn't sure if parsnips would substitute for bananas, but every option was being considered.

Real trouble was, however, looming 1,000 miles away on the eastern banks of the River Plate. The leaders of the Mercosur countries – Argentina, Brazil, Paraguay and Uruguay – had been meeting in Montevideo, and their end-of-summit communiqué contained a bombshell. Mrs Kirchner, who had assumed the group's rotating leadership, had outflanked Brits and Islanders by convincing all of the countries in the bloc to exclude ships flying the flag of the Falklands from their ports.

Mercosur is a free trade pact aimed at abolishing tariffs, customs controls and the like, and has no requirement for shared foreign or defence policy. So whether Argentina could legitimately use the organization to apply political pressure on Britain and the Islands was, at best, a moot point. But the Argentines did not see any such impediment.

Until that point, Uruguay, Brazil and Chile (although the latter is only an associate member of Mercosur) had made half-hearted and vague policy statements about the degree to which Falklands and British ships en route for the Islands would be welcome in their ports. The Falklands-owned scheduled surface link with Chile and Uruguay had been forced to cease. Fear of what might happen had scared off some shipping and fishing companies, but many vessels from the hugely valuable fishing industry still made extensive use of Montevideo's services. Now, however, the bans seemed to be formalized into a definitively hostile position. On the face of it, the Islands' fleet was now cut off from all of its near neighbours. The noose had tightened very significantly.

Only twenty ships are flagged in the Falklands, meaning they are registered in Port Stanley and enjoy some financial benefits for calling the port home. Two of these vessels, the RRS *Ernest Shackleton* and the RRS *James Clarke Ross*, belong to the British Antarctic Survey, and they had been using South American ports less frequently over recent years anyway, favouring Stanley as a hub for their austral summer operations in the ice. However, of the remaining eighteen ships, most were deep-water freezer trawlers owned in part by Falklands fishing companies. Although nominally Falklands vessels, they were operated and crewed by Spanish partner companies. Montevideo, the most modern port in the region, was important for these big trawlers. The Spanish operators used 'Monty' (as Falkland Islanders have always affectionately called the city) for essential maintenance, dry-docking, victualling, crew transfers, and to transfer cargos. Out of season, some trawlers would even be laid up there. All of this was now to be a thing of the past.

It appeared to be a coup for Mrs Kirchner's Department of Foreign Affairs. To achieve it they had (not so subtly) changed their Malvinas narrative to appeal to the entire region. The *'Piratas Ingleses'* language was good for inspiring nationalist mobs (who these days tend to pump vitriolic and often obscene messages into Twitter, rather than shouting their messages in street protests), but it was not sophisticated enough for South American leaders, for most of whom Britain was a perfectly civilized trading partner.

The new message had its first outing courtesy of Minister of Foreign Relations Hector Timerman, when he addressed a meeting of colleagues from Latin America and Spain. He described British plundering as a 'colonial dagger in America'.

Mrs Kirchner followed this in Montevideo by stating that the Malvinas was an issue about which everyone should be concerned, because Britain was using its illegal occupation to exploit regional resources. When they had exhausted Argentine fish and oil, Uruguay and Brazil had better beware. 'I want to thank the immense solidarity for Malvinas,' the President said. 'This support is in self-defence because they are taking away the mineral and oil resources and when they'll need more they are going to look for them anywhere. [Britain] does not respect any of the resolutions of the international organizations.'

It is doubtful that anyone really accepted this message at face value, but the old imperialist references may have chimed with the left-wing governments of Brazil and Uruguay and, further afield, in Hugo Chávez's Venezuela, which is a close Mercosur associate. In reality, probably none of them cared at all who owned the Falklands. But it would have been hard not to go along with Mrs Kirchner's passion.

Paraguay's signing up to such regional action was, by the way, just amusing. Falklands ships have never chugged hundreds of miles up the river Paraguay to exchange loads of squid or wool for *yerba maté*, the bitter herbal tea beloved of gauchos. But Uruguay was different. Montevideo had always been important to the Islands. Falkland Islanders felt a fondness for the little country nestled rather unenviably between Argentina and Brazil, and for many decades until the 1970s,

Monty had been one end of the passenger shipping service that was Stanley's only link with the outside world.

I went to school in the city, as did my mother and brother, and we have family friends there. So do many other Islanders. Up until the early 1970s, when the shipping link was broken for perfidious British political reasons (and that is another story), seriously ill Islanders were taken by ship to the British Hospital in Montevideo. Even today, patients needing urgent treatment not available in Stanley are sometimes flown there aboard RAF medical evacuation flights. Relations with Uruguay have traditionally been very warm.

I had to wonder if Argentina itself did not fear it had gone just a little too far with their latest move, because almost simultaneously with the Mercosur announcement, there was a message from Buenos Aires that hinted at concession. It was announced that Argentina would re-install an ambassador at its embassy in London during 2012. The withdrawal of the senior diplomat several years earlier had been a tangible expression of Argentine anger and a snub to Britain. So rescinding the move might be significant. Did Argentina want to be in a better position to commence positive diplomatic exchanges with London when its blockade forced a resumption of talks? Or was it an emollient gesture born out of fear that Britain might have been pushed too far and could even harden its position?

If they held the latter view, they were right to do so. In Britain, media alarm bells were ringing. Newspapers were spinning the story into a possibly imminent return to the hot war of 1982. Middle-market tabloids produced bold graphics showing just how Britain's forces would shape up in a fight with those of Argentina (surprisingly well, was the assessment, even of the right-wing *Daily Mail*, which had been highly critical of recent defence cuts).

More significantly, there were calls for a show of British strength in the Falklands, as the softly, softly approach typical of the Foreign Office did not appear to have made much of an impression on Mrs Kirchner. Among those voices was that of the former First Sea Lord and Chief of the Naval Staff, Admiral Lord West, who after retirement had been an advisor on security to the then Prime Minister Gordon

Brown. He said it was time to conduct a highly visible reinforcement exercise in the Falklands and to send a nuclear hunter killer submarine to the area. More subtle signals, he implied, did not seem to make any impact.

Allan West had a personal interest: in 1982 he was captain of the frigate HMS *Ardent*, which was bombed and sunk by Argentine aircraft, with the loss of twenty-two crewmen. Speaking to the *Daily Mail*, he said: 'They are becoming more and more aggressive. I find that worrying. Far from trying to settle in a grown-up way and having better and better relations with the Falkland Islanders, they are upping the ante and becoming confrontational.'

The Admiral would have been well aware that Argentine military capability was limited, and that a full-scale attack was unlikely, but military action had seemed an almost absurd idea in the months leading up to April 1982, and he clearly thought no chances should be taken nearly thirty years on. When the submarine arrived, it should 'stick its mast up, making it clear that it is there,' he said.

There was no official response to Lord West's demands for action, at least not publically, but the Ministry of Defence had been revising its Falklands plans, and the Prime Minister was to be briefed about them at a meeting of the National Security Council, the Prime Minister's crisis committee.

There were strong rumours that a submarine had indeed been despatched to the South Atlantic, partly as a signal (assuming the Argentines could pick it up) and partly as a precaution, just in case blunders, pique and misunderstandings did tip the region over into a shooting match. Unless the sub did 'stick its mast up,' or, even better, surface near Stanley, no one would know for sure that it was there, but it was possible that its existence had been leaked through defence attachés in South America.

The Foreign Office was forced to ramp up its diplomacy. It began by issuing a statement that stopped just short of a reminder that force would be met with greater force. It was strong stuff by the standards of genteel Whitehall. The communiqué said: 'We are very concerned by the latest Argentine attempt to isolate the Falkland Islands people and damage their livelihoods, for which there is no justification. No one should doubt our determination to protect the Falkland Islanders' right to determine their own political future.'

The Uruguayan Ambassador was called to the Foreign Office to explain his president's actions. No doubt the talks were very civil and tea and custard creams were offered. British diplomats in Montevideo took similar initiatives, endeavouring to establish the extent to which the Uruguayans had been boxed into their policy by Mrs Kirchner, and whether they could be persuaded to wriggle out of it.

It helped the British effort that the Uruguayan opposition parties and probably most ordinary Uruguayans were very angry about this kow-towing to Buenos Aires. There is very little love for Argentina there, and the opposition parties were angry at what they saw as craven submission to their big neighbour's demands. It was the kind of support that Argentina did not give Uruguay. 'We can't have pressures exerted over our government that hamper the interests of Uruguay,' said Senator and former President Luis Alberto Lacalle. 'This attitude seriously damages our national interests.' He added that Montevideo's role in the fishing industry around the Falklands has an annual turnover of up to £300 million.

A prominent representative of the shipping and port services industry, Mario Baubeta, said the move would impact on jobs in Montevideo. 'These announcements,' he said, 'only help to scare away the fishing vessels that use Montevideo as an operations hub for the South Atlantic and Antarctica. It is obvious that if vessels are banned from operating in Montevideo and others are exposed to continuous harassment, they will just move to Brazil, with losses for Uruguay.'

The British diplomats must have had a rather awkward meeting with officials in Montevideo. But excellent coffee and the alfajores, a local confection that puts British biscuits to shame, may have helped to break the ice. London's people needed to establish whether Falklands ships could get through to Montevideo simply by stowing their Blue Ensign 'defaced' with the Falklands coat of arms, and hoisting the UK Merchant Navy's 'red duster', which they were legally able to do. Furthermore, were British ships registered in the UK and heading to or from Stanley able to enter the port? And what about ships of the Grey Funnel Line? If Her Majesty's Antarctic patrol ship and her destroyers and frigates were banned, it would be severely embarrassing at the very least. President Mujica had indicated that their warships would not be allowed to berth, but was this really so?

Adding gravity to Uruguay's dilemma was the reaction of Spain. It was hard to believe that the Mercosur countries had not realized that by penalizing what were effectively Spanish fishing ships, they were also going to upset a powerful lobby in Spain, and consequently the government in Madrid. Perhaps they thought it a price worth paying. In any case, the President of the Association of Marine Fishing Officers in Vigo, Spain's main fishing port, promptly asked the Madrid government to intervene on the industry's behalf. He described the port blockage as 'blackmail', stating that Argentina had no right to make fishermen victims of their sovereignty claim over the Falklands.

The Spanish Ambassador in Montevideo, Aurora Díaz-Rato, duly criticized the Argentine authorities' initiative as an 'error'. Referring to an earlier incident in which a Spanish trawler had to steer into Uruguayan waters to avoid interception by the Argentine Coast Gguard, the Ambassador added that Argentina has no right to impede the free navigation of Spanish vessels in international waters.

The Uruguayan government began to sway in the face of this diplomatic offensive. Port officials said that all British ships, whether registered in the Falklands or not, would be able to enter Montevideo if they flew the Red Ensign, the standard Merchant Navy flag. That was the kind of wriggle room that Britain had hoped existed. It would have to be tested, but it was, for the time being at least, a victory.

For a change, UK Foreign Office diplomacy and Ministry of Defence action seemed to be in concert and effective. The Prime Minster would go on to hammer home his criticism of the Argentines by stating in Parliament that it was their attitudes, rather than London's, that smacked of colonialism.

President Mujica also climbed down from his position of banning all British warships, and HMS *Protector*, the Royal Navy's new ice-reinforced Antarctic patrol ship, was allowed to enter Montevideo. The

Uruguayan naval and port authorities shrugged off suggestions that this showed sympathy to the Brits. They stated (surely in the full knowledge that it was not true) that HMS *Protector* was really a scientific research ship rather than a warship. It was difficult, however, to explain away the well-armed Royal Marines who guarded the ship conspicuously around the clock. However, many Uruguayans would have been delighted that *Protector* was in port, and that their country had pushed back against the Argentines.

Sadly for Mrs Kirchner, but fortuitously in a grim way for Islanders and the Foreign Office, the President was winding down her activities in preparation for an operation to inspect and, if necessary, remove her thyroid gland. Cancer was a possibility, but her prognosis was said to be excellent and the President would spend no more than a few weeks recovering. Typically, she was not inclined to devolve power to her ministers, so Buenos Aires was not well positioned to respond to Britain's actions. (In the event, Mrs Kirchner did not have cancer, and she returned to work invigorated.)

It was starting to look as if Mrs Kirchner's attempt to harness regional solidarity was less than successful. But the Argentines would undoubtedly be back with more pressure to put on their neighbours, particularly Uruguay.

Furthermore the boldness of the Mercosur seaports incident suggested that Buenos Aires would not balk at pressurizing Chile to cease its air link with the Islands. If Chile conceded, they might disguise the move as a commercial decision, which would be much harder for British diplomacy to counter.

Sure enough, within a few days of the Mercosur summit, the Buenos Aires aviation authorities had refused Lan Chile's request for landing and take-off slots at the Jorge Newberry Metropolitan Airport in Buenos Aires. Existing congestion at the airport *may* have been the reason, as the authorities claimed, but it looked like a message to Chile: Lan and the government in Santiago might like to consider which was more important to them; a single weekly Falklands service of minimal economic value, or the growth of traffic between the two major capital cities. Observers felt the issue would be properly addressed and the fate of the air link decided when Mrs Kirchner met her opposite number, Sebastián Piñera, during an official visit to Santiago that was scheduled for early in 2012.

I turned to Gavin Short, who serves as a member of the Falklands Legislative Assembly, for a local's take on the situation and an assessment of how Mrs Kirchner's latest activity might have moved the dispute's centre of gravity. When we spoke, the Uruguayan position on port access had not yet shown much sign of weakening. Gavin and I were friends from way back, and we had worked together spinning records and reading the news and government announcements at the local radio station in the 1980s. We enjoyed some memorable times together, and I knew he had a good sense of humour. It struck me that he needed it.

'As far as diplomacy goes, she is rather like a pit bull with toothache, isn't she?' he said. That was funny, not just because Mrs Kirchner's diplomacy was indeed bullying and bare-fanged, but because her anger and bitterness were constantly evident in personal attitude and body language. If she deployed feminine guile backed up by her exotic looks, she might come over better.

'I have a lot of sympathy with Uruguay,' continued Gavin. 'Argentina can and probably is exerting terrible pressure on them. Montevideo has things that it wants to do that are dependent on Argentine co-operation and I wonder if the Uruguayan president's initial statement, which even took their own port authorities and diplomatic service by surprise, might have been made in order to try and get something that Uruguay needs. The real worry I have is that the Uruguayans will cave in and that will make the Argentines bolder in actually trying to stop vessels.'

As Gavin suggested, the Uruguayan Government was between a very sharp rock and a very hard place. Bernard Jones, a journalist colleague writing for the news agency MercoPress in Montevideo, offered me an explanation for Uruguay's difficult position. 'Mr Mujica said, "We have nothing against England, but we have a lot in favour of our neighbours," and that helps to explain what has happened in the last few weeks. His foreign policy priorities are establishing and maintaining the best possible relations within the region and particularly with Argentina and Brazil, the country's main trade partners.

'With Argentina, this means overcoming the rough period of his predecessor, Tabaré Vázquez, who had the worst of possible relations with the Argentine ruling couple, Néstor and Cristina Kirchner, because of differences over the construction of a pulp mill on the shared and jointly managed river Uruguay and the dredging of one of the two River Plate access channels.'

I asked Bernard if, despite President Mujica's partial climb-down over the ports ban, his policies could continue to be moulded by Argentina. 'Yes,' he said, 'until he can achieve some of his objectives.'

By the sound of this, there was no room for complacency. I returned to Gavin Short for his view on the current Falklands' position. 'I'm starting to have some understanding of the Cuban mentality, Graham,' he said. 'We are almost in the same position – having to find ever more inventive ways around the blockade. But we do and will continue to do so. I would rather go hungry than surrender one inch of my country to the buggers.

'I suspect we will eventually see South America closed off to us, which, while being a bit sad, isn't going to stop us. They've left it too late, because our economy is too strong for their tactics to have the devastating effect that they wish.'

Regarding Mrs Kirchner's specific threat to the Lan Chile link, Gavin said: 'We suspect she will be left with no alternative, especially as she sees her other measures and actions having absolutely no effect on the good ship Falklands. But if Lan goes, then I suspect – no, I will demand – that we start taking practical action. So I will be pressing for a ban on Argentine passport holders entering here.'

Anyone involved in this dispute, on any of the three sides, must have remarkable stamina and self-belief. If one initiative to force Britain into talks fails, or if one option to loosen the noose ceases to exist, then others are immediately sought. The dispute has escalated to the point that the pace is frantic and pressurized.

Argentina inflicted another major blow on the Islands shortly before the Mercosur/Montevideo affair, but this is relatively little known because Buenos Aires did not trumpet it. No wonder: this was such a blatantly reckless move that no reasonable country, no matter how pro-Argentine, could support it. Stuart Wallace had told me he feared Buenos Aires would deliberately over-fish the valuable Illex argentinus squid stock, therefore denying income to the Islands. That was precisely what they began to do. Fishery authorities in Buenos Aires brought forward the squid fishing season in the seas they controlled by two months, meaning the species would be targeted in the middle of its breeding season as it moved towards the Falklands. Normally, the Illex squid were left alone to breed and grow until 1 February. A few years of heavy fishing in December and January might wipe them out for ever.

Perhaps for the first time, a country was waging eco-warfare; attacking a neighbour by destroying a commercially valuable and sustainable species. When Mrs Kirchner said that her country would restrict its Malvinas policy to peaceful measures, no one could have expected this. To most reasonable people, an economic blockade and an attack on natural resources would appear to be pure aggression.

For how much longer could this continue, I wondered. Probably for longer than Mrs Kirchner anticipated, because, as far as I could see, the spirit in the Islands was strong. 'Happy days, Graham,' Gavin Short said to me with a grin. 'It must be boring to live in a country that hasn't got a neighbour who is trying to throttle you.'

CHAPTER 21

A Question of Destiny

I left the Falklands again shortly before Christmas. I was looking forward to seeing my family, my friends and my animals back in London, and I could almost smell the aroma of the fresh coffee I would soon be savouring while I read the day's paper in my favourite Portobello café. But I was sad to be leaving. The Falklands were, and would always be, home. I told many people that I would be back soon.

In fact, I had done something much more fundamental than just promising to return. I had bought a patch of land at Teal Inlet large enough to build on. Teal Inlet is a neat little farming settlement to the north-west of Stanley, about an hour's drive along one of those rubble-strewn Falklands roads. It is quite close to Trudi and Charles at Brookfield Farm and Neil and Glenda at Long Island, whom Robert and I visited that day when we set off to catch trout. I was not sure how my wife, Nadia, would take this news, but she had often said that it would be lovely to have a little place out in the country and far from anywhere. Well, that box had been ticked.

Just as it had done when I arrived, the aroma of the camp wafted through the door of the Boeing 767 as I sat there waiting for the cabin crew to check their last oil man, soldier or tourist on board and then go through their peculiar little safety rituals. The great slab of the plane's door slipped into place and, almost immediately, the air conditioning system and the chemical air fresheners from the toilets overwhelmed any lingering scent of diddle-dee, white grass and gorse.

I found myself sitting next to a youthful man in tracksuit trousers and an ill-matched rugby shirt. I assumed he was a serviceman heading home after a four-month tour of duty. But he introduced himself as a barrister who had been in the Islands for just a few weeks, defending an elderly man who had been charged with, and eventually convicted of, some deeply unpleasant sexual offences dating back to the 1970s. Thirty-five years ago, the police and legal authorities had ignored the tearful testimony of several young girls. But recently, in the modern Falklands, more enlightened men and women had re-examined the allegations, sought out evidence from witnesses who now lived in other parts of the world, and acted on it.

The convicted man would now do a decade or more in jail. In the past, those guilty of crimes requiring more than about a year at Her Majesty's pleasure would be sent to the UK. But recently, Stanley had rebuilt its Victorian-era cellblock, and it now met European humanitarian standards. So Stanley's septuagenarian sex offender would stay in the Islands.

It may not be wise to make judgements based on just one incident, but I felt this preparedness to confront the darker issues of a small and once introverted community, and then handle the consequences, was an example of positive change. It was a nasty subject, but a good thought on which to end my fact-finding visit.

My neighbour produced a compressed pillow from a voluminous carry-on bag and allowed it to expand into a huge, soft marshmallow of comfort. 'I know,' he said, acknowledging my look of surprise. 'But I can't travel without it.'

Where were you back in 1982? I thought. I'd have fought you for this pillow on that damned old RAF Hercules. And then I realized: he had not been born then.

Back in the UK, there were a few more people I needed to talk to. Until that point, I had, as it were, been peering through a microscope, and it had been difficult to get a broader picture. Now I wanted to see how the situation in and around my islands looked to those half a world away who panned telescopes across the region. I knew a man who could help. Back in the mid-1990s, I had shared my own views with an academic called Klaus Dodds. He had produced several learned papers and books about the geopolitical issues of the region. I found Klaus's email address and sent him a note asking if he was still following affairs in that part of the world, and whether he could share his knowledge with me. The answers were 'yes' and 'yes'.

I drove to Richmond on the outskirts of West London, and we met in a café near the Underground station. Klaus was now Dr Dodds and a professor at nearby Royal Holloway, part of the University of London. He was as affable and helpful as I remembered him to be. His views were fresh and thought-provoking. The Falklands, he suggested, are now part of a bigger regional issue for both Argentina and Britain. Traditional emotions about the Islands still apply and are genuine enough, but the old posturing, pouting and spouting are by no means the whole story.

When the Kirchners came to power in 2001, they had two big foreign policy ideas. One was to throw out the Menem government's policy of cuddly co-operation with Britain over the Malvinas, even if it made economic sense for Argentina to co-operate. Argentina would deny itself the potential fruits of co-operation and ramp up the pressure on Britain and the Falklands to talk about the only issue that really mattered: sovereignty. There was, said Klaus, a rationale. 'If they did not apply real pressure, diplomatically and more directly through impeded communications, then there was a danger that British sovereignty of the Islands would simply be consolidated further.'

The second big idea was to drag Argentina back from its Falklands War humiliation and the near apocalyptic fiscal and economic collapse at the turn of the decade. The Kirchners wanted to restore the country's dignity by making it a regional leader. Happily for them, the two goals could be made to complement each other. Even if the aggressive policy towards the Islands did not yield concessions from the UK, Argentina could be made to look as if it was bravely tackling big, bad latter-day imperialists on behalf of its neighbour states. That could start to look like regional leadership. Indeed, recent events had born this out. At that meeting of the Mercosur leaders in Montevideo, Mrs Kirchner told her colleagues that Britain was thumbing its nose at the whole region, and when it had finished stripping the resources around Argentina's territory, the Brits would move on to other countries' backyards. The Malvinas was, she proclaimed, therefore a regional issue, justifying other countries to gather around Argentina. They did that, albeit reluctantly and without as much effect as had been hoped for.

Britain also has a wider and longer-term agenda for the area, but it is less obvious, said Klaus. It does, however, amount to something bigger and more important than simply guaranteeing the freedom of British kith and kin. 'In terms of the geopolitical picture,' he said, 'the Falklands are always going to bound up with a broader conversation about the Antarctic.'

Delegates to a recent United Nations conference considering ownership of continental shelves and their consequent economic value were shaken when the Argentines arrived with maps of their maritime territory that included a huge slice of Antarctica. 'This,' said Klaus, 'was considered deeply provocative.' Other countries attending the conference had dormant claims to Antarctic territory, but none had included these in their continental shelf calculations, believing that the Antarctic Treaty, which has been a surprising success story since its introduction, placed a moratorium on such claims and a ban on economic exploitation. Here, though, were the Argentines apparently posturing for a commanding position if and when the treaty breaks down.

Decades ago, this would have been seen as laughable nationalism. But there is now open speculation about Antarctica's mineral resources, particularly hydrocarbons. And the Antarctic Treaty, which only bans mining and drilling until 2048, is not fixed in perpetuity. It can be amended by agreement of the members, and, arguably, it could disintegrate if some member countries militantly disagreed with its terms.

'There are a lot of stresses and strains,' pointed out Klaus, 'including profound issues over illegal fishing, the growing presence of "biological prospecting" (for example, commercially valuable research into the way some fish survive in almost freezing waters). And there is growing tourism. At the moment there is just about enough self-restraint by all the parties, but will that last?'

If the treaty were to fail in the coming years, there would be a rush to the south, almost certainly with Argentina in the lead. Klaus is sure Britain is concerned about this, and is itself positioning for a stronger presence. They are doing this not just by maintaining the territorial claim, but by consolidating friendships with other nations in the area, particularly Chile and nations further afield that also watch the Antarctic with interest.

If this theory seems far-fetched, look north to the Arctic, where even peaceful Canada is now aggressively territorial about its northern coastline, and where the Russians have planted flags on the seabed.

Klaus's views on the challenge of defending the Falklands were also fascinating. He agreed that much current activity was designed to show the world that Britain is serious about the Islands. However, there is a risk that while the symbolism is strong, the reality of the garrison might not match up to a real military threat. In other words, Britain might not prevail in a re-run of 1982.

Through off-the-record conversations with military planners and defence analysts, Klaus had gained the distinct impression that those charged with defending the Falklands were genuinely concerned that exploitation of oil in the area might become a 'tipping point'. They wanted to know that if another crisis was coming, the Islands' current defences would be strong enough to deter Argentine military action. They were also keen to discuss such issues as Antarctic riches and the strength of the Treaty.

'All of their questions,' said Klaus, 'were predicated on the notion that threats of various descriptions were likely to materialize in the next ten to twenty-five years. There is, I believe, a heartfelt anxiety that we do not want to be exposed again, and we do not want to be humiliated. They also know that rational analysis sits uneasily with this highly emotive and highly charged issue.'

I cast my mind back to the conversation I had with Carlos Escudé, the Argentine academic and journalist who also watched the dispute from a distance over a long time. He had not touched on the role of Antarctica in the dispute, but then our telephone conversation had been rather short. However, he did make it clear that he thought the Kirchner government was taking the long view, and was anticipating important shifts in the geopolitical tectonic plates. One seismic shift was of particular interest to them: the decline of Britain and the rise of Brazil.

Dr Escudé believes that Mrs Kirchner and her team are planning a decade or more ahead, although they are not likely to admit that publically, as to do so would invite dangerous criticism from an electorate who always expect a quicker fix. But Mrs Kirchner firmly believes that geopolitics will do the job.

Carlos Escudé agrees. 'If Britain continues its present decline,' he said, 'and Brazil continues its ascendant path, sooner or later Britain will have to surrender the Falkland Islands. We have recently heard that Brazil is now above Britain in terms of gross domestic product, and if this continues and Brazil continues to support Argentina, then sooner or later, in say twenty, thirty or forty years, Britain will have to do what it did with Hong Kong: hand back the Falklands.'

It seemed to me that there were some important 'ifs' in this argument, but I could follow his logic. To supporters of the Falklands' status quo, it is a chilling thesis, and that British weakness may already be evident. Diplomats appeared to have successfully countered Mrs Kirchner's recent effort to persuade her neighbours to bar Falklands-flagged ships from their ports (although time would tell), but only by finding them a technical way to wriggle out of the commitment. It was a damned close-run thing, and Britain's lack of easy influence had been laid bare.

Klaus Dodds said something very interesting to me about the Falklands' relationship with the mother country. For three decades, the Islanders had been taking steps away from colonial administration; small and cautious ones at first, but bigger and bolder ones as time went by. After so many generations of colonial exploitation, the British Government had opened the door to financial independence (thanks to fishing), to unfettered self-government, to a great sense of pride – and perhaps to a degree of hubris that did not help them to win and retain friends.

These days, Islanders still see themselves as loyal subjects of the Queen, but they are equally fond of their wealth and autonomy. But

Klaus wondered aloud if there might be an inherent danger in that drift away from London's embrace. If Islanders look less like ordinary Brits and more like rich but distant relations, it would be harder to maintain public support in the UK, and easier for a future British government to abdicate its defence responsibilities by forging some kind of political arrangement with Argentina.

'The Islanders want to have their cake and eat it,' said Klaus. 'They want to tell the FCO, "respect us, we are virtually independent." But every time that things get tough, it's, "Ah! We're really glad you are around."'

He believes that Islanders will become more vulnerable as the southern cone countries close ranks behind Argentina. It may be better to sacrifice some autonomy for a relationship with Britain that is so close that they might be considered part of the UK, in the same way that former French colonies are now part of France. 'I think that if I was a Falkland Islander I would want to be formally integrated into the UK. Big time,' said Klaus.

I wanted to pursue this line of discussion with people inside the British political establishment. Andrew Rosindell was perfect. He is a Conservative Member of Parliament, whom I have known for many years. We first met when he was a travel journalist visiting the Falklands in the mid-1980s. I had hosted him for a few days and showed him the natural charms of the Islands. We had kept in sporadic contact since. Andrew is a great enthusiast for the Falklands and for the people, and he has taken this to Parliament, where he chairs the Overseas Territories Group, sits on the Foreign Affairs Committee, and never fails to exploit any chance to raise his pet subject in the chamber.

As a right-winger, he is not someone with whom I would normally take tea, but we have common interests in the Southwest Atlantic. And anyway, he is not particularly evangelical about his politics. So we get on well. We met at Portcullis House, the dark and vaguely gothic building a stone's throw from the Houses of Parliament, where most MPs have their offices. Andrew has Falklands souvenirs on show in his small corner of the building, and a large Union Flag rug. Not wanting to risk offending him as he was welcoming me, I gingerly stepped over the rug, and sat by a window looking out onto Big Ben.

We chatted about the Islands and mutual friends over tea for a while, and when another Tory MP knocked on the door, Andrew invited him to join us. This was Daniel Kawczynski, a youngish man of Polish descent who was both affable and aware of Dependent Territories issues.

I asked both men if they believed the Falklands are still safe in the care of Britain. They gave the stock politician's affirmative but bland answer. However, as our conversation developed, it became clear that they had important concerns.

'Look,' said Andrew. 'What happened in 1982 was so significant, and is so deep in the thoughts of British people, that they cannot accept that Britain would not again stand by the Falkland Islands, whichever government is in power. The issue, however, is to ensure that we have adequate defences on the Islands. I don't think there is likely to be a direct threat, but you can never rule it out.'

I asked if he believed those defences would be up to the challenge. 'I have been assured personally by ministers that the Falkland Islands are adequately defended,' he replied. That, I thought, was not quite a straightforward and convincing 'yes'. Perhaps that was because he, like Klaus Dodds, sees the challenge as more complex and fluid than ever.

But he was reassuring about the degree of commitment that the present government has to the Falklands, even if the issue is eclipsed in importance by such grave issues as the Middle East, Afghanistan, Pakistan and Iran.

'William Hague [the Foreign Secretary] is very pro the Falklands and very committed to the Overseas Territories generally,' said Andrew. 'That goes for Henry Bellingham, the minister for the Overseas Territories, too. They have been very supportive and they're more determined to deal with the issue of how the UK treats its former colonies than any other foreign minister or junior minister I've known.'

'Quite right,' added Daniel Kawczynski. 'Strategically, these pinpricks on the map of the world are of value to the UK. They are the equivalent of permanent aircraft carriers stationed around the world. They are unsustainable by themselves, but wanting to remain British, so we must support them.'

I told the MPs about Klaus Dodds' view that the Falklands would benefit from returning to the bosom of the mother country, because increasing autonomy was making them vulnerable to future British neglect and to Argentine hegemony. I did not expect the two MPs to agree so wholeheartedly. Both said that the Islands – indeed all of the Overseas Territories – have a status that is too 'grey' for most Britons and foreigners to understand. Their ill-defined status does not encourage anyone to think of the territories as truly British. Falkland Islanders, St Helenians, Montserratians and other remote populations should be able to elect representatives to Parliament, and their homelands should be shown on maps as parts of Britain. The French do it and the Argentines do it, so Britain should follow suit.

'We wouldn't want to interfere with the daily running of their homelands,' cautioned Andrew. 'But a large number of decisions about them are made here in London, and yet no one in these territories is voting for the government here. We need to bridge that gap. I would quite like to see Islanders having their own Member of Parliament, but I wouldn't want to do anything that the Falklands or any other territory would feel uncomfortable with. Some of the biggest opponents to this are actually in the Territories, as they fear that Britain would be taking over their rights. If we can overcome that, unification would be much safer for them.'

In the meantime, he said, the relationships between the territories and London should be strengthened by annual conferences in London, during which representatives would be able to talk directly to the Prime Minister and the Foreign Secretary.

A government consultative white paper due for publication in 2012 will address the Overseas Territories' constitutional status, and an institution likely to flow from it will be a parliamentary committee, which would examine issues affecting all the territories. Currently, the government of the Falklands liaises only with officials at the Foreign Office in London. The new committee would bring Parliament into the relationship, introducing checks and balances that would militate against subversive manoeuvring by the Foreign Office. This, stressed Andrew, would be an important new relationship, and it would inevitably develop new advocates for the Islands.

But of course the Falklands' relationship with Britain is only one part of a complicated equation. What of those relationships beyond the control of London; Argentina's dangerous liaisons with the United States, Brazil and Uruguay? Those would be hard – perhaps impossible – to control. This observation elicited an only cautiously optimistic response from the two MPs.

'The Americans are not helpful to us at the moment,' said Andrew. 'They are, I believe, playing a double game. They understand where we are coming from, but the Falklands are not important to them. Their influence in Latin America, and with Argentina in particular, is much more important.

'I went to the State Department in Washington early in 2011 with the Foreign Affairs Committee and they were very hostile over the Falklands; not supportive at all. Their view was that we should negotiate with the Argentines. I said to one of Hillary Clinton's directors, "So you are saying to me that we should negotiate over the sovereignty of one of Her Majesty's territories?" They were quite embarrassed when I put it so bluntly.'

Daniel agreed about the dangerous ambivalence of Hillary Clinton's State Department, but he was sanguine about the risk that Brazil might throw its massive weight behind Argentina. 'Our trade with Brazil is growing exponentially,' he said. 'I don't think Brazil would want to jeopardize its relationship with the UK and the billions of pounds of trade that we share, over a small territory off the coast of Argentina. I just can't see it. We are modest people and don't tend to wave the flag from the rooftops, but foreigners do see us in a very important light.'

He may have been right. Perhaps Britain does still have global influence, out of all proportion to its size. But I still felt that, in reality, the Falklands were at the mercy of other countries: Argentina and its increasing band of friends.

Daniel quoted the Prime Minister, who had, at some stage, repeated Mark Twain's stirring words, 'It's not the size of the dog in the fight, it's the size of the fight in the dog.' Daniel loved the quote. 'I think that encapsulates everything about Britain,' he said. 'We are a tiny island but we punch above our weight.'

He was not talking specifically about military capability, of course, although that was part of it. I had heard this said so many times, but it did not sound as convincing and inspirational as it once did.

I thought of Carlos Escudé, who had told me over the phone from Buenos Aires that he had once believed that Argentina would never recover the Islands. Now, however, he happily admitted that Argentina's regional policy was working.

'The world, Mr Bound, is changing,' he said. 'The Falkland Islands are South American, and there is no way they can escape their South American destiny.'

Inadvertently, the Argentine intellectual had sounded like a pastiche James Bond villain, but I had not found his words in the least amusing.

Index

INDEX